CRIME
PAYS

Also by Michael Welham

The Crabb Enigma (with Jacqui Welham)
Frogman Spy (with Jacqui Welham)
Combat Frogmen
Kampfschwimmer – Geschichte Austung Einsatze
Naval Elite Units
Operation Spetsnaz
Exploring the Deep
Corporate Killing, A Managers' Guide to Legal Compliance
Corporate Manslaughter and Corporate Homicide,
A Managers Guide to Legal Compliance

CRIME
PAYS

REFLECTIONS FROM THE FRONT LINE OF CRIMINAL JUSTICE

MIKE WELHAM

Matador
9 Priory Business Park, Wistow Road
Kibworth Beauchamp
Leicester LE8 0RX, UK
Tel: (+44) 116 279 2299
Fax: (+44) 116 279 2277
Email: books@troubador.co.uk
Web: www.troubador.co.uk/matador

ISBN 978 1780880 013

British Library Cataloguing in Publication Data.
A catalogue record for this book is available from the British Library.

Typeset in 12pt Perpetua by Troubador Publishing Ltd, Leicester, UK
Printed and bound in the UK by TJ International, Padstow, Cornwall

Matador is an imprint of Troubador Publishing Ltd

Thanks

Those who put pen to paper often receive assistance which is invaluable. I am no different and particularly thank the following for their contributions.

Ashwyn Smythe who stepped into the breach with a red pen. That said, the final cut is mine alone.

Nicky, Church Minister JP, who shared many of my views and opinions, for her invaluable contribution.

Jacqui, who has endured years of my muttering about the growing flood of injustice in our society.

The magistrates with whom I sat, who gave up their valuable time in an attempt to bring reality to justice.

Contents

Author's Note

The views and opinions expressed within this book are mine unless otherwise identified. They are the result of personal experiences, independent research and reflections on the justice system. They do not reflect those of the judiciary, any government or any other organisation. Exploring the whole subject of crime, punishment and justice in our society, would require numerous volumes and so I offer just a personal glimpse into the issues that affect the majority of law-abiding citizens directly or indirectly everyday.

When I laughingly said I would write a book about my experiences with justice and would call it *Crime Pays in the UK*, most fellow magistrates did not agree with the title. They held onto the view that in their opinions, justice was meted out in the Magistrates' Courts. However, the issue is the slow tide of do-gooder injustice that has crept in. It does nothing to enhance justice and abandons the very people it is supposed to protect, the victims of crime.

In order that I could present a wider picture of my views of crime and its impact on society, I have drawn on a variety of sources including the mainstream media. They keep us informed on a daily basis whilst *Private Eye* exposes the crime and corruption in local government, central government and large organisations.

My experience of the justice system is founded on sixteen years as an enforcement officer, sixteen years as a magistrate and six years as an expert witness. This combination has placed me on both sides in the adversarial arena and in the middle making judicial decisions. Although I no longer sit on the bench, I am on the supplemental list and still use the JP title.

Michael Welham JP. 2011

www.crimepaysuk.com

Preface

'I think it would be a very
good thing instead of
having fines as a
punishment for breach of
the law to make it
imprisonment and
flogging and pillory; I
have no doubt that would
keep them to it.'

Richard Oastler: Evidence to Select
Committee 1831

I am always being asked 'what's it like sitting on the bench dealing with
all those horrible people?' Well first, let me give you a bit of background. I was a Justice of the Peace, more commonly known as a magistrate, for sixteen years and, in that time, I rose to the dizzy heights of
being a chairman. Yes, we used the term chairman as it was readily accepted by all including the ladies. It is probably the only place in the
UK where the term is used without PC people going loopy.

Why did I become a magistrate? I was naive because I actually
thought that I could make a difference, albeit a small one, to deter crime

and provide victims with a sense of justice. In fact that is probably why most magistrates join the bench. How I managed to be selected is one of life's strange quirks and I was probably well placed with the hang-em and flog-em brigade. However, I had the belief that criminals or, as I shall call them, convicts, should be punished and victims compensated. That said, one of the major advantages of magistrates is that they cover the entire spectrum of personalities from softy to toughie.

Magistrates are essentially unpaid volunteers. This means that they do not get any form of salary, but they do get a limited amount of expenses for car travel, meals etc, all carefully checked and in line with the prescriptive requirements. Some people, such as the self-employed, are entitled to claim a loss of earnings fee. It's fairly restricted, but it does allow people who are self-employed to participate in the court process. Magistrates come from a wide variety of backgrounds, ethnic origins and political beliefs. However, I don't think if you said you were a member of the British National Party that you would be selected, so there is some control over the selection process. The concept is that the Magistrates' Courts reflect the area that they serve and it's fair to say magistrates represent the general public and their views as to how justice should be administered. However, like all things, there is enormous government control over what actually does happen.

In days of old, the selection process for a magistrate was be based on who you were and who you knew. Someone would put your name forward as being the 'right type' and you were encouraged to join. I expect to a much lesser degree that still happens today, but to reflect society the net is spread wide and there are adverts in newspapers seeking candidates. The selection period, once the appropriate forms have been filled in, can be as long as two years. Then there are a number of interviews and tests of their thought processes and decision making abilities. Those who are successful are sworn in. However, there is a good deal of training before being allowed to sit. The training explains your role as a new magistrate sitting on the bench, as well as what you are expected to do and how to do it. There is the explanation of what the chairman does, what the legal advisor does and the court protocols. One important aspect is the decision making process of guilt or not, as well as determining the sentence for those who are guilty. Once the training is completed, the new magistrate begins sitting as a member of a bench of three and gains experience at the sharp end. After that every magistrate is assessed for competence every three years. I am not saying that everyone who sits on the bench is perfect, no, not even me! It would be quite worrying if they were, but the whole idea of the Magistrates' Court system is to have people with different points of view and different thought processes. When you combine these factors into the bench of three, in my experience, it provides for a good balance in the decision making process.

Sitting in court, presiding over the continuous flow of people from all sectors of society, provided me with a not generally seen vision of every day life and it was one that, quite frankly, was and is appalling. We have a welfare state that nannies people through life from cradle to grave, so why is society broken? Among my first cases as a new magistrate [1992] were riding a bike on a footpath or without lights or dropping litter. Yes! People were prosecuted for those types of offences. Now, thugs can beat somebody to death for no reason and find that there are do-gooders arguing against prison or severe punishment for such offences. The latest trend is to argue for more unpaid community work as opposed to jail. Both, generally speaking, are a total waste of time in their current form, but community work is almost always a farce.

I sat on a fair number of cases where convicts were sent to prison. I can say that I never sent anybody to prison who did not deserve to go there and there were a few who I would dearly loved to have sent down for a lot longer period than our maximum limit of six months. Throughout the years there was a good deal of change in the way we did our business and that meant additional training. Sentencing became more structured and fines more appropriate to the ability of those being fined to pay them.

However, it was not all rosy in the garden because, following the adoption of the Human Rights Act, I felt that the system was, and is today, totally abused by many with criminal intent. Political Correctness roared in and we were drawn into its clutches. The statement 'take him/her down' when sentencing to prison had to be replaced with 'please go with the officers, thank you'. You will find other examples in the book such as where I use the word 'convict'. The dictionary defines the word as: 'convict – person found guilty of an offence against the law or person serving a prison sentence'. So where it applies, convict is the term used and if convicts do not like it then they should not become or continue to be one.

When I decided to leave the bench, it was the result of trends such as the Probation Service being in court and attempting to dictate what sentences should be handed out. I could only see things getting worse and so it moved me, along with apparently many other magistrates, to resign. This was for me, a matter of great regret. However, I remembered someone once saying, 'you can't push water back up a waterfall' and that best sums up my overall view of justice in the UK today.

Remember that famous statement in September 1993 from Tony Blair, the then Prime Minister:

'Labour is the party of law and order in Britain today. Tough on crime and tough on the causes of crime.'

In fact under the rule of Tony Blair crime increased and it got even worse under Gordon Brown. There have always been criminals and there always will be. Today we have greater access to information about their activities and we see that crime in its broadest sense permeates even the corridors of power in Parliament, banks and other highly respected institutions. The police have technology to assist them such as DNA evidence and supposedly greater cooperation from other countries police forces. Customs are able to detect drugs leading to major hauls. The border authorities should be able to track movement of people and control who enters the country. The problem is that a great deal of time and money is spent investigating and preparing for court. Trials are often lost on a minor technicality. Whilst on other occasions the wrong person is in the dock when the police and prosecutors have not done a good job. Those that do pass through and receive a guilty verdict often face what are, generally, pathetic sentences. That is why criminals love the UK. Get caught, do a bit of time in relative luxury then out to carry on where they left off. In fact the chances of doing a bit of time are diminishing every day.

What is a crime is a simple and straightforward question but one that is complex to answer. Views differ greatly depending on for example, who you are, where you live, your age and your social situation. Those living in a deprived inner city estate will have a different perspective on crime than those who live in suburbia or country areas with nice houses. Crime has always been with us and criminals have always been a scourge on our society. The difference is that crimes are more widely reported through the media and have evolved to include race, religion and culture. This means that we now have those who live in the UK whose customs are the norm in their country of origin, but are criminal acts in the UK and the problem is that they want to change us.

Dictionaries do not really help but the general view is that crime is a serious offence or serious wrongdoing especially one in violation of morality. This would include acts such as murder, rape, arson, theft, use of knives and guns, mugging, assault and other violent acts. However, the definition of crime is much wider and it encompasses unjust, senseless, or disgraceful acts or conditions. For example it is a crime to squander our country's natural resources. You could therefore imply that those who form our governments may be criminals! That is quite apart from the expenses and cash for questions scandals. The possibilities extend to 'a foolish, senseless, or shameful acts', an example being it is a crime to let a beautiful garden go to ruin. Then there is something reprehensible or disgraceful such as where it's a crime to waste good food and that could well include most homes. Today we can add greed to the list and that involves society from those at the top to those at the bottom. Two items of 'number crunching' in *Private Eye* put the matter into perspective. The prison sentence of Timothy Harris, a thug from Northamptonshire, for benefit fraud that cost the taxpayers £54,000 was fifteen months. That was balanced against the one week exclusion from the House of Commons that David Laws, a former cabinet minister from Somerset, got after paying back £56,000 he wrongly claimed from taxpayers in benefits. The other item showed that 0.13% is the percentage of the general population now in prison. That is compared to 0.61% that is the percentage of members of the last House of Commons now in prison. [*Private Eye* No: 1289]

So you will see that the whole concept of crime, punishment and justice is fraught with pitfalls. It matters little if you are a hang-em and flog-em type of person or a victim, you cannot win. The one certainty is that no matter what is claimed by officialdom or criminal welfare organisations, crime is increasing and there is a much greater impact on the victims of crime. It all adds to my firmly held view that today, crime pays in the UK and there are so many situations and cases where the saying 'The lunatics have taken charge of the asylum' is appropriate. [Richard Rowland 1881-1947]

1

All Rise

Before The All Rise

On a court day, a suit comes out of the wardrobe along with a shirt and an appropriate tie. Now, in court something as mundane as a tie has to be non-descript. This means that wearing a military tie or one attached to an organisation is not acceptable as it might be seen as giving favour to a defendant who has the same or similar tie. Shoes had to be gleaming, a trait from my father who insisted that, no matter the state of your clothes, your shoes had to be clean. I also endured a military sergeant major, who had the same philosophy. Breakfast whilst watching the news, perhaps a third cup of tea. No, I remembered a situation from the past that I did not want to re-enact.

Most trials are either half day or whole day cases and there are always opportunities to have comfort breaks. I was sitting on a half-day trial when having heard all the evidence; it was down to the defence solicitor to sum up the defendant's case. Now, I had an extra cup of tea before departing home and a cup upon arriving at court but, as the morning progressed, found a growing need to go to the loo. Rather than stop the trial which was in full swing, I decided to hang on. Then the defendant's solicitor stood up and began his oratory on the life and times of his client, a serial offender. The defence solicitor knew that we knew that his client was guilty. So it should be a brief summing up and we could retire and I could go to the loo and then set about the guilty or not guilty assessment. On this day the solicitor was soon in full flow, unlike me who was hoping to be, and very soon.

We had a re-run of the trial, only this time a little embellished in favour of the defendant and against any of the compelling evidence we had heard. The solicitor looked down at his notes and I thought, 'that's it, I can get to the loo'. He looked up and began again, only this time with a different slant on the case. I was now in agony and trying without drawing attention to myself to hold on! I scribbled a note to the chairman, a very robust lady, who looked at my words and wrote, 'I am sure you are able to hang on until he has finished.' I lost track of time and my concentration was fully on one issue, my dire need to go to the loo.

Then at last the solicitor sat down. The problem was that I now had to stand up, and to do it without losing control. My colleagues leapt to their feet and I eased myself to the standing position. So far, so good. I made the door and left the courtroom. The men's room was close by and I entered, without speed, as I was incapable of moving fast. Then I reached the place of sanctity and prepared myself. Nothing! I had held on for so long that I was unable to go. I waited and waited. Nothing! Time passed and still nothing, so I decided to go to the retiring room and set about the determination of guilt or otherwise of the defendant. I made the door, then a quick hop back the place of sanctity and it was all action. Now, I couldn't stop. It was a wonderful feeling which eventually ended. I then joined my colleagues who seemed slightly amused by my predicament. The chairman smiled as she said: 'well held'.

Although the courts do not start until 10 am, I always liked to get in early. That way you get a cup of tea and a free biscuit and a chance to chat to other early birds. Actually, whilst on the point of free biscuits, it was suggested by some senior civil servants that we should pay for them. Given that we give up our time and are not paid, in our opinion, providing biscuits was a small price to pay. It was a proposal that did not go down well and so biscuits were brought back and were free. But free biscuits were not the real problem.

Being unpaid and part time, the government could not control us in the same way that they could an employee. We were, and still are, independent and the government of the day did not like that. For example when the prisons were declared to be full, a dictate was sent down 'do not send anybody to prison'. Now the fact that prisons were full was not our problem and if we had a guilty person whose sentence warranted prison, then that is where they went. That is justice being done and being seen to be done.

Not to be outdone, some senior civil servants proposed that lay magistrates, that is to say magistrates who are unpaid and not legally qualified, should be done away with. Ministers were lobbied and so it became a real possibility that we would be cast aside. Then somebody with some sense, probably an office junior in Whitehall, raised the question as to who would administer justice in the lower courts. Ah, well we could have more District Judges who are legally qualified but most importantly, full time employees and under government control. Right, that's the problem solved!

Then perhaps the office junior dared to pose a really stupid question, how much was it going to cost to pay all of these highly paid, full time District Judges? Ah! picture the room as panic spreads among the senior civil servants having to come up with a plan that they would have to take back to ministers. They look at the office junior for inspiration, who in turn becomes embarrassed and departs rapidly from the office. He or she had only gone there to take a plate of biscuits to the meeting.

Confronting ministers, the senior civil servants would extol the virtues of lay magistrates and declare that it would cost a fortune to replace them, so better leave it as is. Ministers readily agree as they were deeply involved with sorting out more important things, such as their expenses. So lay magistrates continue to this very day.

The Retiring Room

Our large retiring room was equipped with a cup of tea or coffee and biscuits. It is the place to meet up with colleagues as they arrive and have a chat. The talk would be about all manner of things, not necessarily things related to court activities. It would be a sort of mini social gathering. The important task was to see who you were sitting with in court. I spent much of my time as chairman and that meant that I sat in the middle of the three magistrates and did all the talking.

Depending which court you were in, it was critical who you had sitting with you. Now, the vast majority of magistrates were very, very good. They were sensible and could read the situation when in the courtroom and progress business. After all, we did often have to listen to a lot of drivel from defendants and witnesses and from that we had to determine the truth. However, there were some sort of semi-do-gooders and if your luck was really bad then, as chairman, you could get two of them, one either side. Now a semi-do-gooder generally cannot see the bad side of anybody. No matter what a person has done there must be some good in them and so they deserve another chance, and another and another and another. No matter the excuse: bad neighbourhood, lack of education, no parental control, depression, oppression, drink, drugs or violence, all seem to be reasons for criminal activity. However, the semi-do-gooders do realise that in some cases punishment was the only answer and of course they brought a balance to the bench.

When sentencing, two of the team may decide that the punishment warrants, say, six months in jail. However, the semi-do-gooder thinks that a conditional discharge along with some words of wisdom from the chairman to the defendant telling them that they really must try to be better behaved is more appropriate. I was told by some defence solicitors that they always tried to get their clients into a semi-do-gooder court, because the punishment would be so much less, if any at all. I also was told that I was hard but very fair and I told them that I would work on being very hard. At that same venue I was told by some of the more outspoken solicitors that I was one of the chairmen they wanted to avoid and worked on getting their clients moved to a 'softer' court. On the very rare occasions that I had a semi-do-gooder in the team, I and the other winger spent additional time going through the evidence and the defendant's past history so as to explain our thought processes. Yes, we could go with a two to one majority but I always really wanted the whole team to agree with the decision and that is what happened.

So with a good team, a day looked much better. The challenge was to then see in what type of court would you be sitting. There might be groans from colleagues who discovered that they had a motoring court or there would be a 'wow', I've got a trial today, meaning that it could be interesting. One court would be the fast track court where you would hear a case and then sentence on the same day. I quite enjoyed those but to get through the work load you needed a good team and I must admit that during my sixteen years I was part of an awkward team on only a couple of occasions. A lot also rested on the shoulders of the legal advisor. We had good and even some excellent advisors who sat in front of us and did the general running of the court as well as providing us with legal advice where appropriate.

The 'Bench'

At about a quarter to ten we go in our bench of three, to one of the small retiring rooms where our legal advisor joins us. That's when we go into more detail about the cases that we have before us. In all the cases coming before us, we will know who the prosecutor is going to be and we will be given the names of defendants who are coming before us and the name of the solicitor who will be defending them. We will also get advice if there is any particular defendant who could cause trouble or is quite dangerous and is being brought to court to progress through the magistrates court to the Crown Court. A priority is given to those who have been remanded in custody and those who have been arrested over night and brought before the court to be dealt with as speedily as possible.

We will also be advised of any cases that are not defended by a solicitor, where the individual will be defending him or herself rather than using a solicitor. These are usually a bit of a hoot because, in most cases, the individual has no idea what to do or the processes involved. They often get carried away, not literally, but become incensed when the prosecutor gives the prosecution details with which, of course, they disagree with. At that point, the defendant often wades in with accusations and counter arguments. So we discuss prior to going into court how we are going to handle the situation.

We have to bear in mind that an individual has the right to defend him or herself, but if they are not familiar with the court procedures, they are defending themselves against a potential outcome of a fine if they are found guilty. In the more serious cases where there is the real possibility of going to prison, we would insist that the individual obtains legal advice because there is too much at stake for them with the possibility of losing their liberty.

In the courtroom we exchange nods of the head with those in the courtroom. Years ago it was a bow, but now a nod suffices. Some prefer a bow but it does not mean a bow from the waist and attempting to kiss your knees, but is merely bowing of the head and a very slight bowing of the upper body. If I am the chairman, I sit on the middle chair which, in some courts, is a bit bigger than those either side. My colleagues are called 'wingers'.

Each magistrate sitting on the bench has equal standing even though one may have been a magistrate for sixteen years and one of the wingers may have been there for only a few months. All three have an equal voice in discussions and play an equal part in the decision making process. The only thing that the 'wingers' do not do, is speak directly to the court; everything is channelled through the chairman.

As the various cases proceed you do have to concentrate, and we may at odd times be seen conversing. We also pass notes between each other; in this manner the wingers communicate with the chairman on various matters and issues as they arise. It may be that somebody is causing a nuisance at the back of the court and is unseen. A quick note draws attention and any 'yobbish' behaviour can be dealt with quickly. Another favourite is when a defence solicitor is summing up the case for the defendant and they ramble on, repeating themselves so that they end up talking drivel, so much so, that our concentration begins to fail. A note from a winger supports the chairman's intervention to ask if there is anything else relevant as the case has been well covered.

Throughout all cases, we all make copious notes of what is said by the prosecutor, defendants and witnesses because this is what we refer to when in the retiring room. Once a case has been heard, it is the time for any questions that the bench might have. I would ask each winger in turn if they have any questions, if there were, I would deliver the questions on their behalf. When all of that is done we have to decide, based on what we heard, whether a person is guilty or not guilty. If we all decide that the verdict is guilty, it has to be beyond all reasonable doubt based on the evidence of the prosecution. Of course, some defendants plead guilty upon arriving at court and so we only hear the prosecution case, then any mitigation from the defence, before we sentence.

There is one very big difference in the Magistrates' Courts and that is where an individual justice sits alone. That person used to be called a Stipendiary Magistrate, but today is called a District Judge. They are salaried officers of the court and are paid by the Crown. Apart from being qualified lawyers they sit on their own performing exactly the same function as the bench of three magistrates. However, the concept of single justice is frowned upon by most defendants, simply on the basis that if you go to the Crown Court you are in front of a judge and twelve people who make up the jury. It is the twelve people who hear the evidence and make a judgement.

In the Magistrates' Court there will be three justices who will listen to both sides of a case and then make the decisions. That is not always an easy or pleasant task. What this means is that the defendant has three minds focussed on the evidence that is presented; then, by applying the logic contained within the structured decision-making process, a verdict is reached. That's how, in the main, three people come to the same decision on the evidence they have heard. However, if you go in front of the District Judge, you have one person making the decision on a defendant's guilt or innocence. Many defendants find it a little bit disconcerting that one individual can make such an important decision which could result in somebody going to prison.

I have mixed views and concerns about the role of the District Judge. In the court where I sat, the District Judges did a good job. However, when I was an expert witness in a case before a District Judge in another court, the defendant did not, in my opinion, get a good trial. I am sure that if we had been in front of a bench of three there would have been a more positive outcome. Faced with a court appearance, I would always want to be heard by a bench of three or a judge and jury. That is in my opinion, a better option for justice.

Every court has ushers who are the people who direct the public and solicitors to the correct court and assist the clerk in the administration of the court activities. They have no legal input but are the only people to wear a black gown which is for identification. I have the utmost respect for these people as they have to deal with some of the worst parasites in the land. They put up with foul language, screaming children, some drunk or high on drugs and often with very smelly bodies. They also have to look after the victims of crime and witnesses who, for many years, had to sit among the parasites until courts had to provide a safe haven for them. It is all part and parcel of what the court ushers have to manage.

All Rise

As the words 'all rise' or 'all stand' echo round the courtroom, three of us, the magistrates forming the bench, enter through a side door. We stand and face those already in the room. A slight bow from us is met with a slight bow in return. We sit, and everybody else sits. The legal advisor asks the usher to call the first defendant of the day. It is a young male on another visit to court and so the public seating suddenly starts to fill up with his mates, who make a lot of noise in the process. Our legal advisor turns to us and explains that the case involves a defendant just old enough to attend the adult court. We wait until those in the public seats become settled then the defendant comes into court.

With his perfected John Wayne style of rolling walk he comes through the door, grinning at his adoring entourage who sit giving the thumbs up and making calls of encouragement. Entering the dock, he struts to the end closest to the bench, turning again to grin at his mates. In the dock he looks at us, sneers then turns his head to look at his support team at the back of the court. His jaw is moving at a fast pace. He is not speaking but is chewing. His mates then begin to make more noise, so I stop proceedings and whilst peering over the top of my reading glasses now perched on the end of my nose, tell them that if they are to remain in the court, then they sit down and make no noise. I told them that if they do not do what they are told, they would be removed from the court or held in contempt of court and taken to the cells. I was under the impression that no adult had ever told them to do something that had to be obeyed as they appeared unsure of the situation.

The court became very quiet and I asked the legal advisor to continue the process of obtaining the defendant's details and reading out the charge. Throughout this time the defendant's jaw had not stopped moving and I called a halt to the proceedings again. I asked the defendant what was wrong with his jaw.

'Nufink,' came the response with a grin.

'Why is your mouth moving all the time?' I enquire, already knowing the answer.

'Gum init,' he replies.

'Well' I say, trying not to snarl, 'you are not allowed to eat or chew in court and especially in the dock, so remove it'. I then remember that I have to be polite to yobs and add, 'please'. He stares at me, whilst three magistrates stare at him, as does the legal advisor, and the prosecutor and even his own solicitor.

We know that, like many before him, he wants to tell us, and me in particular, to f*** o**, but even in front of his mates he sees that discretion is the better part of valour. He opens his mouth and levers out the most enormous lump of chewing gum. He stands holding it between finger and thumb. I could see that he was going to press it on the woodwork of the dock, so I pre-empted that action and ask what he is doing.

He looks at me, 'Wat ma sposed t' do wivit,' he asks.

'Put it in your pocket,' I reply. He stares at me really unsure. I explain; 'If you have nowhere else to put it, then use your pocket.' So he puts it in a pocket in his jeans and we continue with the case.

There are no further interruptions and we deal with matters speedily. Then comes the time for the defendant to leave the dock and, in an act of pure defiance, he wants to put the gum back in his mouth and leave the court chewing it. He puts his hand in his pocket to find that gum does what it says, it gums everything up. It had stuck to his trousers and now stuck to his fingers as he struggled to get it free. As he left the courtroom he turned to face us but there was no swagger, no grinning, only a fine to be paid and of course his gum, uncontaminated by the courtroom furniture, clogging up his pocket rather than his mouth. We have started the day well!

The day did get even better because we had a case defended by one of the regular defence solicitors, a very tall attractive blonde lady who I will call Miss Cleavage and she became quite an attraction within the court. I now have a vision of the PC brigade screaming in horror because, in the retiring room, she was often the topic of conversation among both male and female magistrates. Miss Cleavage wore low cut blouses and shortish skirts and so there would be a discussion on which court she would be in and what she would be wearing.

When a prosecution case is under way, the prosecutor stands and provides us with the facts of the case and produces any supporting evidence, while the defence lawyer sits and makes notes or at least, is busy writing. In the courtroom we sat up slightly higher than others in the room, the idea being that we were able to see everybody. The thing was that you could look down at Miss Cleavage and because of the nature of the blouses she wore, cleavage was the name of the game. She would sit all prim and proper, leaning forward, making her copious notes. It was impossible for anybody on the bench to miss the view. When in court, our lady colleagues would extol the intricacies of the uplift bra while us mere men could only review the benefits. So you see magistrates are human and not bigoted! No doubt the PC brigade will now be in total melt down. Well I do hope so!

The real do-gooders will wonder whether the attention of the magistrates might be more focussed on Miss Cleavage making her notes, rather than the facts of the prosecution case being put forward. There was never a problem with this. I sat on many cases defended by Miss Cleavage and in every case, both male and female members of the team had made copious and accurate notes and knew the details of what had been said. Once the prosecution had finished delivering the facts they would sit down. Miss Cleavage would then stand up and the view changed. It was argued in some quarters that perhaps with less to look at, the male magistrates' concentration would move to the defence case.

Over the months and indeed years the blouse tended to get lower and the skirts higher. In one instance, the District Judge required her to leave the courtroom and return when she was dressed more appropriately. Perhaps the sole District Judge might have been distracted and as a mixed bench of three, we were more balanced and could spread our concentration.

There will be those who may say that Miss Cleavage was attempting to influence the bench, but she did not and whilst portraying an image she dealt with her clients, the defendants, in a firm manner. On this occasion she represented a client who was a difficult and arrogant character. When the prosecutor was presenting the prosecution case, the defendant stood up and started to shout and argue.

Before I could say anything, Miss Cleavage calmly stood, addressed us with an 'Excuse me your Worships,' and went over to the defendant standing and snarling in the dock. She leaned over the edge of the dock and beckoned with her finger. The yob stepped forward, allowing them to go nose to nose and she was clearly heard to say 'Sit down and shut up, I do the talking, do you understand?' The defendant was taken aback, nodded and sat down to remain very quiet. She then went back to her seat and with an appealing smile, she apologised to the court and the prosecutor before sitting down and continued making notes. One lady magistrate said after the case 'We got a view of cleavage and leg today,' the cleavage was while she was making notes and the leg as she leaned over to speak to the defendant her skirt raised a little bit. Her client was guilty and so justice was done. She was very firm with her clients, making sure they did as they were told and she put forward very good and sensible defence cases. It must be said that it was a sad day when Miss Cleavage no longer attended our courts.

Court Legal Advisor

Matters of law are made available to the magistrates through the legal advisor who will be a qualified solicitor or barrister. He or she sits in front of the magistrates and, in general terms, conducts the court proceedings. When the defendant comes into the courtroom they will be asked their name, address and date of birth and it is recorded on the appropriate forms. The legal advisor will then put the charge to the defendant and ask for a plea, which of course has got to be simply 'guilty' or 'not guilty'. When a case has been heard they give legal advice to the magistrates and quote case law which helps in the sentencing process. They keep a detailed record of everything that is said in court as well as the outcomes of decisions made.

Crown Prosecution Service

The prosecutor is normally a solicitor or barrister from the Crown Prosecution Service (CPS) who deals with the normal criminal case workload. There are non-CPS prosecutors who conduct private prosecutions which are taken by organisations such as local authorities, utility companies, government departments etc. The important thing is that there are no differences in the court processes. The defence lawyer can be a solicitor or barrister and has the role of representing the defendant. A barrister does not wear the wig and gown when in the magistrates court however, some do put on an act of being superior and 'better than thou' to others in the legal profession. I have had them talk down to me as if I and the team know nothing and they know everything. I can assure you that such behaviour gains nothing in front of down to earth magistrates.

The Probation Service

I attended a magistrates' training course on the topic of the Probation Service and how it fitted in with the judicial system. Everybody was gathering and sipping cups of tea or coffee. It was a mix of delegates from different courts and I got speaking to a lady attendee who asked for my thoughts on the topic of the day. I had and still do have great reservations about the Probation Service. Most of the probation officers I have encountered, seem to be very nice people who have a difficult job to do which for many of their clients, they do well. One problem for me was the pre-sentence reports which provide more information about the defendant, prior to sentencing. My comment was that I had yet to see a pre-sentence report that actually recommended custody.

I was asked why should it recommend custody. I responded that in many cases that's what people needed and it should be an official possible option. I then raised the issue of community sentences which were and are, to me, a very soft option. She defended the community service programme with vigour. Then there is this little quirk, where probation officers refer to criminals as clients. They are defendants when in the courtroom and if found guilty of an offence and convicted then they are convicts. That did not go down well. The call to take our seats came just in time because I then discovered that she was head of probation for our area. I did listen to what was said throughout the day, but still considered the community sentence a soft option and not an alternative to prison under its present guise and those being punished for a crime are convicts.

Nicki JP [you will hear more from her later] summed it up when she said: 'I'm rapidly coming to the conclusion that probation has more power than the court. Or should I say they are influencing too far, because I don't understand why we can't decide on a sentence, and have probation carry it out. I thought that's what courts were supposed to do.'

She then added: 'I've also noticed that pre-sentence reports appear to be a fixed document with the names changed as well as a few minor details. You see very little on a pre-sentence report that isn't worded exactly the same as every other pre-sentence report and it takes, how many days to get one? And I don't know why because I reckon all they do is change the names. I do believe that we should be able to make a sentence and probation should carry out the sentence, they shouldn't determine the sentence and tell us we can't do something because they don't recommend it.'

The situation is that Probation Officers are involved in the preparation of a sentencing report for an individual who has been found guilty of an offence. I found it interesting from my time in court how many magistrates used to go straight to the back page to see what Probation was recommending. So why bother to read the report because it doesn't really tell you anything? In addition to preparing reports they run the community service projects and ensure that convicts undertake any remedial programmes that are subject to court orders.

It's official, London probation chief Heather Munro tells us that convicts must be treated as customers not offenders. They should be invited to speak about their needs and asked how they feel about the treatment they receive. She tells:

'These people should not have to spend time in shabby waiting rooms or be sent to dingy offices to be interviewed. Giving criminals the same consideration a company gives its customers will steer them away from committing future crimes.'

Mrs Munro added: 'It's a bit like running a business. Any business would ask its customers how it can improve its service. It just doesn't make sense not to.'

We are told that the call for probation officers to make life more comfortable for offenders comes at a time of growing concern over the way their service deals with criminals under its supervision. It is claimed that about half of those given community punishments never finish them, and in London where Mrs Munro's service supervises 70,000 criminals a year, probation officers have a particularly poor record. The decision to refer to criminals as 'customers' follows efforts by police forces to find softer language to refer to some groups of offenders. [*Daily Mail* 13th April 2011]

Surprise, surprise, the two-year Diamond Initiative costing £11 million has failed. A report for London's Criminal Justice Partnership revealed that the scheme, piloted by the Metropolitan Police and London Probation, aimed to break the cycle of reoffending by offering offenders help with problems such as drug and alcohol misuse, housing, debt and unemployment has had no impact at all. The report showed that 156 of 368 offenders (42.4 %) on the scheme committed new crimes within a year, compared with 136 of 327 similar convicts (41.6 %) who received no special help. The report said helping people turn their backs on crime is a 'slow and uncertain process'. Yes, its been going on for hundreds of years and it did not need a spend of £11 million to work it out. [*Daily Express* 19th April 2011]

Thin Blue Line

We sat in court talking to our legal advisor whilst we awaited more cases from other courts. We were engaged in general banter when the courtroom door opened and in walked an individual who sat in the public seats. He provided a good lesson in not judging a person by their appearance. Poorly dressed, long untidy hair, unshaven and looking what might in the past have been termed a homeless tramp. Our legal advisor said she would go and find out who he was. There was a brief discussion when she returned to the bench with the man following. She told us that he was an undercover police officer working on a drugs operation. He had come to court to obtain a warrant for a large raid on a drug den. We went through the details and we provided the appropriate paper work. He then departed going back into a world where, if he was exposed, his life would be on the line. Drug dealers have their own methods of disposing of those who get in their way. It is an area of policing that the general public never see but we do owe a lot to these operators. They do not do shifts or work regular work days, they are submerged in the criminal world living with and being one of them.

Whilst living among the real criminals as one of them is one aspect, another police activity that becomes high profile is when masses of people take to the streets and it becomes disorderly. I experienced their work first hand and it began when I stood with a growing crowd of people, most of whom I did not know, on a windy former military airfield. We watched the van and coach loads of police officers arrive. Whilst they departed to a police area, the remainder of us civilians were ushered into a large hanger for our briefing. We were to be armed with blocks of wood and tasked with confronting the officers to shout and throw the blocks at them.

Outside, the police in full riot gear formed up into their tactical groups whilst we ambled along armed with our objects to be thrown. Rounding a corner we faced a dark blue line of faceless individuals in helmets and behind shields. I must admit some of us found it very difficult to shout abuse and throw objects at them. Younger members of the mass of civilians got into the spirit of the action and the riot developed. Some police officers in civilian clothes were on our side and carried petrol bombs and began lobbing them at the line of blue as it slowly moved in our direction. Some of the younger members of our group took the 'riot' to another level and it was interesting to see how people get carried along with what is happening and how a situation escalates.

The police moved forward and struck their shields with battons which adds to the threat they posed. As with any such event there are those who are at the front leading the group and without warning, the line opened in a couple of places and officers rushed forward and grabbed those identified as leaders of the riot, then to drag them back into the line which closed as they passed through. As we were moved back more police formations moved in to cut us off from escape. We were then captive to be processed in due course.

It was an interesting experience and I was pleased that it was a training exercise. We have seen that the real thing can get very aggressive. From the front line of riot control the majority of police work appears to an outsider to be one that meets the following job description:

Do you thrive on verbal and physical abuse? Do you relish being spat at, kicked or punched? Does the prospect of standing between two opposing groups bent on violence thrill you? Are you a natural carer with a desire for social work and care in the community? Are you driven to wear a uniform that make many who you meet, really hate you? Are you up to the challenge of never being right? Are you destined to be behind a pile of paper and the challenge of creative writing? If you were confronted with these elements of a job description would it grip you to apply? Well, as far as I know, no such job description exists, but in my opinion it just about sums up the requirements of a modern police officer. However, it's not all plain sailing because a reduction in funding and cuts in police numbers may have an impact but of course the police have their priorities.

Do not despair the police have so much money they don't know what to do with it. Well that was the situation with the headquarters of Northumbria Police. They spent £50,000 on a sculpture which comprises a steel and glass structure which is said to look like a ball bearing in a hula hoop. It now takes pride of place outside the new £27 million headquarters.

It's OK because to balance the books, staff were told 450 jobs had to go. As an insult to local police officers and staff, councillors have defended the cost of the artwork, saying it will give local people 'pleasure'. Northumbria Police Authority chair Councillor Mick Henry said:

'The cost is a tiny proportion of the overall building costs. The artwork will give pleasure to visitors to the local community.' There, and you thought that resources should be spent on the fight against crime. How wrong you are! [*Daily Mail* 6th February 2011]

The glamour model Jordan, real name Katie Price, who is I believe, known as a self-promoting reality TV person, was about to leave her mansion home when she realised photographers had gathered outside. Thank goodness for that, I thought there was nobody in attendance. Somebody called the police and complained about the photographers and asked if they could help out. So when Ms Price left home a patrol car joined up with her Range Rover to stop photographers following.

This action was to the detriment of other road users because it pulled in right behind Ms Price's vehicle as she joined the A3 from the M25 at Cobham in Surrey. We are fortunate enough that a video was posted on YouTube showing how the marked police car then put on its blue lights and a flashing sign in the back window lit up saying:

"Rolling Road Block. Hold Back. 50mph".

Those following were forced to slow down and crawl along behind the patrol car while Ms Price's sister, who was driving, put her foot down and shot off. Ian Whittaker a member of the public summed it up when he lodged a formal complaint with the force. He said:

'As a Surrey taxpayer I am concerned that limited police resources are being abused in this manner. This looks like star-struck Surrey police officers pandering to the ego of a minor celebrity.'

As you would expect a spokesman for Surrey Police said:

'The officer assessed the situation and decided that intervention was required for the safety of all road users and took action. We support the officer and there is no case to answer.'

In that case the officer concerned is destined for great things as he or she has all the attributes to become Chief Constable. Former Metropolitan Police commander John O'Connor put it into perspective when he said:

'For a woman who makes her living out of staging publicity this stinks. For a police force to get involved is disgraceful. The Police Complaints Commission should get involved.' And all because the lady is desperate for publicity! [*The Sun* 5th February 2011]

Getting To Court

Did you know that solving a simple domestic burglary takes more than 1,000 separate processes by the police and prosecutors. This means that to bring a suspect to court for a house break-in, it involves more than thirty people in 1,107 actions. There are no less than seventy different forms that have to be completed. In fact, just booking in a suspect at the police station involves thirty-eight steps, including twenty-one checks on their treatment and condition. It is claimed that only 98 of the 1,107 actions are actually dedicated to investigating the crime. These include interviewing the suspect and examining the scene, finding and labeling evidence.

It appears that more than half of the steps involved data entry once a case file had been passed to the Crown Prosecution Service. Every entry was duplicated on up to five computer systems, three for the police, and one each for the CPS and the courts. Each case file went back and forth between the different agencies seven times and was copied six times for each agency present at court. So although crime is increasing, there are fewer criminals being put through the legal system and the overall cost of the criminal justice system increased in five years to more than £22billion. Why? Well the answer is simple. The New Labour government in its fifteen years of power introduced fourteen items of criminal justice legislation and that has created a system that is out of control. [*Daily Mail* 3rd November 2010]

John Thornhill, chairman of the Magistrates' Association, revealed that 37,000 violent thugs got away with a caution rather than jail in a single year under Britain's 'incoherent' justice system. Mr Thornhill said:

'Yobs that could have been hauled before the courts to be properly punished just received a slap on the wrist.'

He added: 'Victims were being cheated out of an "opportunity to see justice being done", as well as compensation. The wrong cases were ending up before the courts.'

The fact is that in one year, 37,000 offenders received a simple caution for an offence that in court would have attracted at least a community order if not custody. This is a total failure of the system and supports my 'crime pays in the UK' proposition. [*Daily Mail* 30th November 2010]

Guilty Plea

The CPS loves a guilty plea. It gets the defendant into court, a quick sentence and another conviction notched up to meet the targets. The target culture came from the Blair government so they could produce figures that would claim on paper that they were dealing with crime. The reality was that crimes were being downgraded so that they could be processed without trial. So if it's a guilty plea, we will first hear the facts of the case from the Prosecutor. They will indicate the seriousness of the crime, and any other factors that we should take into account including any history of previous convictions.

Because the defendant has pleaded guilty to the charge, the defence lawyer will then put forward any mitigation. That can be straight forward or a fairytale, it varies from case to case and from solicitor to solicitor. Once we have all the information, we are then given a completed means form showing what money the defendant has coming in and going out. This is done so that if we are to impose a financial penalty we know how much disposable money is available. If the defendant has no money, then there is no point in imposing a £1,000 fine, because it will be impossible for it to be paid. If, on the other hand, the defendant is a professional footballer, earning £100,000 a week, then the fine will be substantially higher. That's the theory anyway!

If magistrates, having heard the case, consider that their powers of sentencing are not great enough then the case can be sent to the Crown Court for a judge to impose a sentence.

Did You Know?

Did you know that if a defendant pleads guilty, they will get a third off the sentence that the court gives them. So if they are fined £90 they get a discount of a third which means they have a fine to pay of £60. Even if they change their plea on the day of a trial they will still get a discount. The amount of discount is reduced because they may have incurred the costs of witnesses coming to court, even though they will not have had to give their evidence. This system is also applied to jail sentences. If magistrates gave a six month sentence, the maximum in their powers, and the convict pleaded guilty, they get a third off, which means that they have a sentence to serve of four months. Once they are banged up they only serve half the time inside. So for a crime that warrants a six months jail sentence, they actually do two months. If they do not warrant the full discount, they still get some credit, after all they have been to court and endured the court process and that means that nobody sentenced in the magistrates court actually does a six month jail term. [This controversial aspect is examined further in the section 'Vision and Reality' at the end of the book]

A Not Guilty Plea

Every person summoned to court charged with an offence has the right to plead guilty or not guilty. With many crimes the defendant has the right to have the case heard in the Crown Court, in front of a judge and jury. That is not a problem for serious cases but many petty criminals opt for the higher court when they face charges of, say, theft of two cans of beer or a chocolate bar or some other minimum cost item. The rules say that the defendant's case must be transferred so that it can be heard by a jury, with all that entails.

However, prior to actually getting into court the defendant changes the plea to that of guilty. The Crown Court judge imposes a fine on the lowest level of crime and may well just give a discharge. Remember, judges are dealing with crime of murder, manslaughter, rape and GBH etc. The very minor crime is the type of case suitable for a magistrates' court but there is apparently more likelihood of a harsher punishment than one passed by the Crown Court so the system is abused.

Louise Casey, the former government's anti-social behaviour tsar, said:
'In a time of spending cuts, we need to abandon some of the genteel traditions and niceties of the legal system. How can it be right that a jury can be made to convene to hear arguments about the theft of £20 worth of tea bags as is the case now, when a magistrate could do the job justly but costing far less?' [*Daily Telegraph* 3rd November 2010]

Once a 'not guilty' plea is made it then requires a trial. Generally trials in the magistrates' courts last a half-day or a whole day, some may take two or three days. Anything longer and it would be a serious case and sent by the magistrates to the Crown Court for trial.

Swearing In Court

When a defendant or witness enters the witness box they are asked to swear either on a religious book or to affirm that they will tell the truth. You know the sort of thing, 'I swear by almighty God to tell the truth, the whole truth and nothing but the truth...' This is done whilst holding up a bible. They do have the option to say; 'I solemnly declare and affirm that I shall tell the truth and nothing but the truth...' It is fair to say that in a multicultural country as the UK has become, the oath comes in many forms and many languages but for those requiring the services of an interpreter, it always left me feeling that I was never sure that the defendant knew that they were required to tell the truth. In the English oath, it begins with 'I swear' and that is a good start because there is generally an awful lot of swearing.

Having told the court that they intend to tell the truth, what it means in reality for the majority of defendants, is for us to watch their lips because they are going to lie in every way possible, 'so you lot (the magistrates') believe my version of events.' I looked up the meaning of 'truth' and you may wish to check your dictionary in case mine was a miss-print. Mine says, 'Truth: honesty, accuracy, integrity, true statements or account, reality, fact.' Hopefully yours says something similar. Well, there is the answer to the problem. Our dictionaries differ from those of some prosecution witnesses and many defendants and their witnesses. I can tell you that the oath and their understanding of the truth really does differ. That is because their view of telling the truth, is to say what they hope will get the desired result.

You may well ask why the courts bother with this time old tradition. Why not just get those concerned to give their version of events and let the magistrates or jurors make the judgement of who they believe? Well it used to be that the courts required people to tell the truth. It followed that if they had not told the truth, then they could be charged with perjury. The problem is that generally nobody is ever charged with the offence of lying so why bother telling the truth unless it helps the case? So we listen to those who provide information as witnesses and as the accused and make our own minds up. The reality is that we believe one version of events and do not believe the other. I am told that in Germany following a case if somebody does not tell the truth then they are charged with an offence. It does focus the mind and the mouth.

Bail Or Not To Bail

Most people will have heard the expression 'given police bail'. Well for those who don't know, it is where somebody has been arrested for committing an offence and is released on bail to return to the police station at a given date and time. Depending upon the type of offence, the police may hold the person in custody until they are able to either charge them or let them go. If charged, they enter the criminal court system to come before magistrates who will begin the judicial process. With more serious cases the prosecution may make a request for the defendant to be remanded in prison to await the trial. At that point the defence solicitor will generally make a request for bail unless it is a case where it is obvious that bail would be denied. Everybody is entitled to bail unless there are extenuating circumstances, so refusing bail can be a tricky one.

The prosecutor will put forward all the reasons why a defendant should not be given bail which can be challenged by the defendant's solicitor. The magistrates then have to balance all of the reasons and decide to bail or not to bail. If bail is not given, the defendant is kept in prison but can immediately appeal against that decision. There are options to give conditional bail which can include such things as reporting to a police station on set days and times. A passport can be surrendered to stop a defendant absconding abroad or the defendant can be tagged and a curfew imposed. A surety involving a sum of money can be sought as security which means that if the person does not conform to the bail conditions then that sum is due to the court.

The majority of time, bail is not an issue and is given without conditions which means that the defendant is released until he/she is required at court again. Failure to attend is an offence and the prosecutor will ask for a Bail Act Offence to be added to the main charge. The big problem has been that in most cases the defendant is given a very small fine or if the main sentence involves a large fine then there may be no separate penalty for the Bail Act Offence. This causes the threat of such an offence to be ineffective as a deterrent.

In Custody

We have defendants who have been arrested by the police and brought to court and are kept in the cells under the courtrooms to wait their turn in the dock. All courts have a secure dock that is enclosed (up to the ceiling) and prevents any form of escape. When a defendant is called, they are brought from the cells to the courtroom by security officers. They stop before passing through the door to allow the handcuffs to be removed. They then come into the dock. The only time that changes is when the offender is coming into an unsecured dock and for some reason, there is concern that the prisoner could turn violent or try to escape. In that situation a case is made to the magistrates that they should be handcuffed whilst in court. This means that they would, whilst in the dock, be handcuffed to one of the officers. It is extremely unusual for this to happen these days, however, there are occasions when a defendant doesn't like what's being said, so hops over the dock and departs the court in great haste. But generally, with the officers in court the process is managed and maintained. If there is somebody who potentially might do a runner, one of the officers will stand by the court door and the other one will remain in the dock with the defendant. There are no police officers in court. If there is a situation that requires the police to attend then a 999 call is made and we hope they respond.

Once the case is dealt with, the security staff take the defendant back down. If the defendant is found innocent and they are to be released, then there is no need to handcuff them. They are just led through the door and back to the cells where they can collect their belongings and leave. If they are going to be taken off to prison, they are handcuffed to a member of the security staff and with the other security person accompanying his/her colleague, escorted down to the cells. The secure dock works and I haven't heard of anybody escaping from one yet. One of the reasons for having a secure dock is that magistrates hear about 98% of all cases that come through the criminal courts. That means that all those who commit very serious crimes such as murderers and rapists generally appear before the magistrates before being sent to the Crown Court for trial. They are the ones who, at the first opportunity, would abscond. Having got them to court they need to be kept there and dealt with.

The Crown Court

The Crown Court hears what are called indictable offences, which are cases that can only be heard in the higher court. These include cases of murder, manslaughter and rape and other cases of a serious nature. There are cases where the prosecution or defendant elects to have the case heard before a judge and jury. However, a case can be sent to the Crown Court from the Magistrates' Court if it is deemed that the case may last more than a couple of days or their powers of punishment are not sufficient for the case to be heard.

The Crown Court sits with a single judge and a jury of twelve who are selected from members of the public. England and Wales retains the formal dress code of wigs and gowns, both for the judge as well as the Queen's Counsels (QCs) and barristers who prosecute and defend cases. The QCs, sometimes referred to as *silks*, are appointed by the Lord Chancellor and are the senior members of the Bar. Both sides will present their case to the jury; the prosecution has the task of providing evidence that will prove their case beyond all reasonable doubt. The defence lawyer's task is to counter that evidence to put sufficient doubt in the jury's mind as to the defendant's guilt. At the end of the prosecution and defence case, the counsel for each side will sum up, highlighting the salient points of the case that provide evidence of guilt or innocence. The judge then sums up the case to the jury with the focus on points of law, before sending them out to determine their verdict.

The jury retires to a room equipped with copies of all the evidence, including any exhibits that have been taken into court. This will also include photographs, videotapes, drawings and statements. They remain in the room until they reach a verdict on which they all agree. When they reach that point, they re-enter the court and the person appointed as foreman of the jury announces the verdict. If the jury cannot reach a unanimous verdict, a majority verdict may be accepted of, say, ten to two for a guilty verdict. With a guilty verdict the judge will hear representations from the defendants as to any mitigation before passing sentence and reports about the defendant may be called for. A judge can commit individuals to prison but has guidelines depending on the nature of the offence as to how long a sentence can be.

Here Comes The Judge

In one case a judge stunned a courtroom when he told an ASBO thug he had 'deserved a good kicking,' for punching a woman police officer's private car. Judge Anthony Scott-Gall told binge-drinking Dexter Vidal he was 'not surprised,' the WPC's two grown-up sons had confronted him in the street after he attacked their family car. Judge Scott-Gall told the court:

'I'm not surprised he was given a good kicking, it's what he deserved...'

He continued: 'If someone punched my car then I would make sure, if I had two sons, that he was given more of a good kicking.'

But the judge added: 'Possibly not having regard to the job one holds down.'

After dealing with the case, a sentencing hearing at Lewes Crown Court, the judge turned to the press box and said:

'Lest the press think the judge conducts a vigilante campaign against people that terrorise his neighbourhood and his car, he doesn't and they haven't and I have one son, not two.' [*Daily Mail* 15th October 2009]

Another judge, in a controversial move, allowed a violent thug to walk free from court despite admitting that the public think judges are 'going mad' for passing soft sentences. Luke Marshall had a criminal record for violence and punched and kicked a drunken stranger who asked him if he could buy a cigarette. Judge Bowers told Marshall:

'People think judges are going mad because the whole purpose of our job is to bring home to the public that mindless violence will not be tolerated. This was sickening at the best, and the trouble with you is that you have done it before and that concerns me seriously. But on the other hand, you are a Jekyll and Hyde character, a caring and thoughtful young man.'

Marshall had pleaded guilty to actual bodily harm which can warrant a custodial sentence. However, the judge sentenced Marshall to forty-five weeks in jail suspended for two years, gave him 240 hours unpaid work, eighteen months' supervision, ten sessions of education for employment and a six-month tagged curfew from 8pm to 5am, and ordered him to pay £500 compensation... If he had sent Marshall to prison he would probably be released after ten or eleven weeks. [*Daily Mail* 19th January 2010]

Then there is the judge who has had ten of her sentences increased on appeal, placing her top of a list of judges whose decisions have been overturned for excessive leniency. In seven of the cases that were referred for review, five of them, involving ten defendants, saw the sentences increased. One case involved a robbery and sexual assault and was described by High Court judges as 'every homeowner's nightmare: two women in the sanctuary of their home defenceless against violent men'. The judge said the offences were 'horrific' but sentenced a male to just four years. The Court of Appeal ruled the punishment was 'wholly inadequate' and 'should not have been less than ten years'. A child sex offender was jailed for six years for rape, attempted rape and indecent assault. The Appeal Court increased the sentence to eight years. Six drug dealers who had been selling heroin were given unduly lenient terms. The judge had sentenced the ringleaders to five years, but this was increased to eight. Four accomplices also had their sentences lengthened. [*The Sunday Times* 9th August, 2009]

For Mr and Mrs Average it is worrying that ten cases, most of which were serious offences, were not sentenced appropriately. However, it does show that the Appeal Court can take action, providing that cases are referred for appeal. Also not all is lost as most judges want to deal with criminals but they are barred from imposing real justice by the antics of the do-gooders.

Judge Anthony Hughes was 'dismayed' at the maximum sentence for aggravated vehicle taking because the maximum custodial sentence he could impose was just two years. He also had to take into account the thief's early guilty plea and give some credit. Dewan Choudhury, aged seventeen, took his parents' car and drove it having not passed a test and being uninsured. He was pursued by police for almost five miles and drove at speeds of up to 80mph before he eventually hit a vehicle head on, whilst on the wrong side of the road. The driver and four women passengers received terrible injuries. Having been bailed over the incident, it was only twelve hours later that he took his brother's hired car without consent to get a takeaway. He was sentenced to twenty months jail for the first incident and five months for taking the hire car. [*Daily Express* 7th February 7 2011]

Judge Julian Lambert spoke out about the sentencing guidelines that prevented him from sending a burglar to prison. He lambasted the justice system as 'soft' after he was forced to hand burglar Daniel Rogers, aged twenty-five, a community sentence. He said:

'I've never seen anything so wet in all my life — eighty hours' community work for burgling someone's house... We live in soft times.'

He was following sentencing guidelines which say he should not send him straight to prison. [*Daily Mail* 29th January 2011]

Then in another case, Judge Ian Trigger spelled out what most people think about workless Britain. He said it was no wonder foreign workers were 'flooding' into the country when his court dealt with so many 'workshy' layabouts. He was sitting in a case involving Anthony Roberts, a thirty-year-old career criminal who was arrested after bursting into a terrified family's home. Roberts has never worked, perfectly illustrating why newcomers did so well here. Judge Trigger said:

'People say there are no jobs around, but why are immigrants flooding in and why are they working hard? There are plenty of jobs, they are just dirty jobs and people do not want to do them, it is easier to stay on benefits and get up when they want.'

He added that Roberts was a workshy 'drain on our resources,' who should get off his 'backside and stop boozing'.

He then raised the matter of the rules preventing him from sending Roberts to jail and commented:

'I wonder whether if the members of the Sentencing Guidelines Council lived in the victims street the results might be slightly different.'

The case involved Miss Shuttleworth and her teenage daughter who barricaded themselves into a bedroom when Roberts forced his way in through a window. They feared for their lives but he was only convicted of criminal damage. A comment from Miss Shuttleworth summed it all up when she said:

'Yet again the victims don't count – it's just "how can we help and accommodate the perpetrator?"'

Because nothing had been stolen, charges of burglary ended up being left on file which meant Judge Trigger could only give him a twelve month community order with twelve months of supervision and a six-month alcohol treatment programme. He did ban him from Miss Shuttleworth's street for two years and ordered him to pay her £100 compensation.

The *Daily Mail* informs us that Judge Trigger has in the past been hauled over the coals by his seniors for speaking out in court. We are provided with some of his memorable observations:

2011: he blasted the "ladette" drinking culture while jailing a seventeen year old girl for blinding a mother by stamping on her head in a nightclub. 'Our towns and city centres are becoming for decent law-abiding people no-go areas,' he said. He told the attacker: 'Society is becoming increasingly fed up with the boorish and drunken antics of people such as yourself.'

2009: when sentencing a failed asylum seeker for car theft and drugs possession, he told the thirty-one year old: 'Your case illustrates all too clearly the completely lax immigration policy that exists and has existed over recent years. People like you, and there are literally hundreds and hundreds of thousands of people like you, come to these shores to avail themselves of the generous welfare benefits.'

2008: Shortly after the notorious gang murder of Garry Newlove, judge Trigger hit out at how an obsession with rights had created a society 'bedevilled by feral youth'.

Sentencing a teenager who attacked a woman with an iron bar, he said: 'It is time for parents to resume control over their offspring. It is time for parents to teach values and respect to their children, value and respect for other people and not to allow their offspring to engage in selfish and irresponsible behaviour.'

1997: He sparked criticism for his remarks to drug-addicted burglar Jamie Kirk, who had been put into care after his parents split up when he said:

'Apologists for single parents only have to look at you. Young people cannot fend for themselves without example and this should come from a mother and father together.' [*Daily Mail* 9th February 2011]

Oh dear, whatever next, a judge speaking the truth and he gets told off. Still, at least some of society believes him.

Judge John Walford told a defendant who was a jobless former alcoholic to stop 'sponging off others'. The judge had heard that a man called Clifton had been ruled too sick to complete his community service. Clifton who has never done a day's paid work in his life, was branded by the judge as 'the embodiment of the welfare dependency culture'. He had been convicted of common assault and ordered to carry out 100 hours of community service. However, he only completed forty-nine hours, having failed to turn up for two appointments. Probation workers then discovered that he was unfit to work because he is on incapacity benefit and therefore not insured. The judge added to his comments by saying:

'...It seems to me you are receiving an awful lot of benefit for doing very little and it is about time you realised that life is about rather more than sponging off others, and it seems to me to hide behind a liking for drink is not an attractive state of affairs.'

The judge initially wanted to jail Clifton, but imposed a three-month supervision order. He then warned Clifton that he could be jailed if he committed further offences. Clifton said he cared for his four children aged twelve, twins aged ten and a four-year-old because his partner was unable to work due to depression. He claimed they receive £100-a-week in incapacity benefit, but with jobseekers' allowance and child benefit their annual income is likely to be more than £18,000. The cynical among you may think that it's a good thing that he is incapacitated and she has depression, because if they were in good health who knows how many children the taxpayer would be supporting.

Emma Boon, of the Taxpayers' Alliance, said the case 'seems to defy common sense. He was well enough to assault someone, but not fit to carry out a sentence'. [*Daily Mail* 10th March 2011]

Victims Of Crime

I was always very aware that for every criminal case that I sat on, it generally involved a victim. One exception to the rule was motoring offences such as speeding where the driver of a vehicle is responsible for his or her own actions. So when, having heard a case and in discussions about a sentence to be administered, I would often indulge colleagues to consider the victim and what would they feel about our decision. I expect that was wrong on my part because quite frankly, the victim does not count. A search on the web will show that in the UK, the main support comes from an organisation called Victim Support whilst the number of organisations that offer support to convicts and former convicts are far too many to mention here. Mention human rights and it's always in defence of a convict never a victim.

Now nobody plans to become a victim or witness to a crime. It just happens and then, suddenly, a person's world is turned upside down. It is little wonder that many who have been the victim of a crime may have decided not to report it to the police. They may think that the crime was trivial compared to others or perhaps they felt the police would not, or could not, do much about the situation. Many victims are scared to tell people about what happened in case it happens again. Many fear reprisals from the perpetrators of crime, particularly if they are asked to go to court to give evidence. Victims who are injured as a result of a violent crime are of real concern because, unless a criminal pleads guilty, they will have to attend court and give evidence. It can be no easy matter giving evidence against a violent thug for, if nothing else, there is the fear of a repetition. This means that many victims and witnesses can be intimidated by a defendant's family, friends or gang members and may well decide not to cooperate with the prosecution. The proposition of police protection may be okay for big, high profile cases, but forget it in the smaller more general cases. Convicts take precedent. It was only in the later years of my sitting at court that special, separate areas were provided for victims and witnesses. Before that, they shared the public area with those charged with the offence.

I am not alone in my views and it is nice to know that the first commissioner for victims of crime in England and Wales, Louise Casey says:

'The criminal justice system treats them [victims] as a poor relation and an afterthought. Too often victims found themselves a 'sideshow' as police, prisons, lawyers and the courts focused on the offender. She said too much time was spent trying to help all crime victims, rather than focusing on those in genuine need.'

Ms Casey added: 'Victims needed clearer information on sentences.'

She had met victims who were angry with the way they had been treated, some who were confused by the courts and many could not see that criminals had been punished.

Ms Casey was clear on one point: 'Victims want people punished and they want them rehabilitated. Victims will be the first to say, I don't want this to happen to anyone else. We need to get a lot tougher on punishing people properly in the community before they even move on to where they could be locked up.'[*BBC News* home affairs correspondent, 20th July 2010]

A survey for the organisation Victim Support found that 30% of people said they would volunteer their time for animal and wildlife charities compared with just 20% who said they would give up their time to support families affected by crime. The survey found just one in five people would want to help people bereaved by murder, manslaughter or dangerous driving. However, nearly half of people said they would not want to volunteer out of fear they would not be able to offer the right support.

The National Probation Service operates the probation victim contact scheme, which provides eligible victims with information about offenders sentences at key stages. A victim liaison officer will provide information about how the Parole Board considers and makes decisions about offenders' cases. The officer will explain how views can be put to the board in a victim personal statement. There is also information as to how views can be made about restrictions which may be attached to an offender's licence which could be necessary for a family's protection. In fact such information will be of more harm than good if the victim sees how their views are ignored in favour of pandering to the convict.

A report by the Commons Public Accounts Committee was produced eight years after they had previously drawn attention to the failures of the criminal injuries compensation system. The committee had earlier drawn attention to the failings of the Criminal Injuries Compensation Authority and was appalled to see that the body's performance had deteriorated even further. A major factor is that a large proportion of people who are injured by violent criminals are left in ignorance of the compensation scheme, leading to the absurd situation that only 5% of victims apply for compensation. The tiny proportion who apply are then confronted by complex application forms.

The scheme can, if anybody manages to make an application, award compensation. The payments range from £1,000 to £250,000. The maximum figure awarded when taking into account loss of earning is £500,000.

However, a victim may get less than the tariff or nothing at all if:

1. You have a criminal record
2. You contributed to your own injury, for example by provoking an assault
3. You don't help the police to prosecute the offender.

I find the third option of this tariff the most interesting because those who have been subjected to violence and live in fear of violence, will not put themselves at added risk of further serious harm. If they will not help the prosecution it means they will not be eligible for compensation.

Following the disclosure of the report, a Ministry of Justice spokeswoman said: 'The government continues to improve the quality of the practical and emotional support victims receive, providing access to compensation, ensuring they have timely access to information and ensuring their voice is heard in the system. Since 2006 CICA have improved the access to and quality of services for victims of violent crime and a more efficient case handling process is resulting in faster decisions.' [*Daily Telegraph* 19th Nov 2008]

Please do not laugh at this point because the CICA are serious and they really will continue to try *not* to be efficient and help victims. You cannot spend money on convicts and victims and you know who is first in the pecking order. Now you can laugh. Or cry!

My wife was a volunteer with Victim Support and she found that providing support was valuable to some whilst others shunned it. The point was that they were at least offered support. But the real support that was required was seeing the perpetrator properly punished and that does not happen.

I had personal experience of this when my son, Joe, was walking home with an old school friend who was over from America visiting the UK. It was Old Year's Night and they had been out to see all the celebrations going on and were walking back to Joe's flat. They were not drunk, they were not lads that went out bingeing. They walked through a shopping precinct and were suddenly surrounded by a gang of thugs looking for trouble. They rode bikes and wielded hammers. Joe is not an aggressive type of person, but instinctively he and his friend had to defend themselves. During the altercation that ensued, one of the yobs raised his arm to strike Joe and it was very fortunate that he actually saw the arm raise, realised that there was a hammer in the hand and that the blow was now coming down towards him. He was able, just in time, to put his head back and the hammer, continuing its downward journey, caught his face and caused a small cut. Had he not seen the hammer, he may well now be dead.

This was obviously a very disturbing incident but they managed to get away safely without further injury. Because the incident occurred in a shopping precinct which was well lit and used particularly at that time of night by people walking home, it would have been covered by CCTV and so I asked Joe if the incident had been reported to the police and what was happening. He told me that they had decided it wasn't worth reporting, although, yes, he agreed it was serious and potentially the next victim would not walk away from it. His view was that, would the police have bothered? And if the thugs were identified and arrested, would the CPS have prosecuted? If they did it meant that Joe and his friend would have to go to court and give evidence. That meant that the thugs would then get to know Joe's name and possibly his address. What would have been their punishment?

In his words, there would not have been any real punishment. And quite seriously, I had to agree with him that 'yes' that was the case. However, in a very weak way of defending the system, I said that if they could identify who these people were, the police could at least give them a warning to show that their card was marked. However, if they committed any future acts of violence it may be more serious. But as Joe said, if they had his name and his address they could then go round to where he lived and finish the job properly.

Of concern to me was how many of these violent incidents happen, but are never reported? From Joe's knowledge the majority of incidents that occur are never reported, particularly by younger people, because in their view the police don't do anything and in particular the courts don't do anything to those found guilty.

Yet another report was published, this one in August 2009 by the Commons Justice Committee. It was produced following an inquiry into the activities of the Crown Prosecution Service (CPS). They confirmed that prosecutors who had to meet government targets and boost conviction rates, were charging offenders with lesser offences. This meant that violent offenders such as muggers, burglars and sex offenders were escaping prison, because the CPS wanted to guarantee a guilty verdict. Just what do they expect? Set a target and people will aim to meet it and if that means bending rules, then that's what they will do.

The committee obtained their evidence from magistrates, police and barristers who stood up to be counted and gave evidence to MPs. Police officers told the committee some prosecutors were 'risk averse' so they could hit conviction targets and the Magistrates' Association raised the prospect that it was 'plea bargaining by the back door'.

The report concluded: 'Telling a victim that their views are central to the criminal justice system, or that the prosecutor is their champion, is a damaging misrepresentation of reality... violent offenders being charged with common assault instead of actual bodily harm, muggers being charged with theft from the person instead of robbery or burglars and sex offenders being given cautions rather than facing court and possibly jail.'

Do you remember Frances Lawrence, the widow of murdered headmaster Philip Lawrence who was stabbed to death by Learco Chindamo, an Italian? Well you will not be surprised to hear that the authorities have treated Mrs Lawrence appallingly. But she was the victim so we should not expect different. When Chindamo was released from prison, the government repeatedly refused to reveal his whereabouts to Mrs Lawrence. In fact, officials asked the Lawrence family to keep updating them about where they're living. Can you believe that Mrs Lawrence and her family are being treated like common criminals? In the UK today the answer is yes. She has been and remains the victim of a do-gooder system that thrives on the freedoms of evil people instead of defending the rights of those who abide by the law as well as the victims of crime.

It was about eight years ago when Mrs Lawrence was actually telephoned by a probation worker to be told that she should apologise to Chindamo for saying that he had shown no remorse. In fact she had said no such thing. However, the probation worker accused her of deliberately obstructing the killer's rehabilitation. That probation worker was a disgrace to the criminal justice profession and should have been dismissed, but was probably promoted. [*Daily Mail* 3rd December 2010]

Chindamo has been allowed to stay in Britain after his release because deporting him to his native Italy would breach his human rights. Utter utter rot! Italy has signed the European Human Rights Charter so what is the problem? In fact, France has changed its laws to allow criminals who were not born in the country to be sent back to their country of origin. Chindamo has since been arrested for robbery and still our do-gooders pander to him so it is little wonder that he wants to stay in Britain. His home country would no doubt deal with him properly. In the case of Chindamo the rehabilitation certainly failed providing another probation failure. Have the do-gooders no shame? I believe the answer is no and that they actually revel in the injustice to victims. [*Daily Mail* 21st February 2011]

After a savage mugging by two yobs at his shop a barber nearly lost his arm and was left unable to work. He and his wife are battling to keep their home after he lost his income. As you would expect, it took months of arguments before he could even claim £151 a month disability living allowance. The charity, Victim Support were on hand to offer help, not practical or financial help, but a face-to-face chat with violent criminals in a bid to cure *his* anger. Ah, its nice to see that there is no State support system for crime victims. I expect the injured party would have to pay for the tea and biscuits!

I Am Not Alone!

When I laughingly said I would write a book about my experiences with justice and would call it *Crime Pays in the UK*, most fellow magistrates did not agree with the title. They held the view that justice was meted out in the Magistrates' Courts. Yes, to a degree it is, but it's the changes that have occurred over the years that have had an impact. One day you wake up and realise that things have changed dramatically. Some colleagues I spoke to did agree and would quote a case that they had sat on, by way of example. One who did speak out and wanted her views quoted, was Nikki a church minister and JP. [see chapter below] Then I found a gold nugget. It was Eddie Jefferson JP, who wrote an article 'Who will we let off next... rapists and murderers?' Now, I could have para-phased the content but it would have not had the same impact. I have therefore taken the liberty to quote it in full.

'The man appearing before us was an old hand and had used just about every trick in the book to avoid paying the four-figure fine he'd run up. Time and again, court appearance after court appearance, he'd prevaricated, delayed or postponed. But eventually my colleagues and I on the Huddersfield Bench had had enough. Today we were going to send him to prison. So we told him so. He looked shocked, and even the clerk of the court looked surprised, but both knew we had the legal powers to do so: even today, magistrates can still send someone to prison for six months.

'Can I have five minutes to talk to my relatives?' he asked. We said he could. Five minutes later, he sauntered towards the bench, his face bathed in a semi-triumphant smile. In his hand – finally – was a cheque. But it was only the threat of prison that persuaded him to pay up. And it had only taken three years!

My goodness, the life of a magistrate today can be a frustrating one.

I've just retired after twenty-six years as a Huddersfield JP and that's exactly the sort of case I'm not going to miss. But it's a good example of how much grass-roots justice has changed over the last quarter of a century. When I first became a JP, joining the hard-working band of unpaid volunteers who preside over the country's local courts, we had three words absolutely drummed into us, punishment, deterrence and re-education.

Now it's all about rehabilitation, human rights and endless – and I really do mean endless – excuses. 'I was depressed,' 'I had a bad childhood,' 'I had a headache,' 'I just lost my job,' 'I missed the last bus,' – in the last few years, I seemed to spend half my working life listening to these endless and often highly ingenious excuses. But what made it worse is that we're now officially required to take these sob stories into account. The simple idea that if someone does something wrong – breaks the law – they should be punished seems to have gone out of the window.

Instead, if little Johnny tells us that his dad used to smack him when he was a kid so he became a burglar, or Mrs Brown says she's menopausal so had no idea shoplifting was wrong, we're virtually required to send them home with a cup of tea and a pat on the head. There, there, we soothe, it's not your fault. 'Yes it is!' I've wanted to shout more and more over the last few years. You've broken the law, here's your punishment, now make sure you don't do it again. It's not complicated, is it? And yet that's exactly what sentencing guidelines handed down from on high make it. And please, don't even get me started on the European Court of Human Rights. We live in a topsy-turvy world where even those facing serious charges can get their bail extended... because they've got tickets for The X Factor!

Don't get me wrong. I've loved my time as a JP and still passionately believe the Magistrates' Court is the backbone of the entire British judicial system. Without it, I'm convinced our judicial system would collapse. And yet I'm equally convinced this backbone is neither anywhere near as strong as it once was or anything like as strong as it needs to be. Over the years, it's been progressively weakened by over-liberal reforms, misguided do-gooders and now the pressing need to save money.

Only this week, we heard that judges and magistrates are being told to send fewer violent thugs to prison. Now those found guilty of actual, or even grievous, bodily harm will not be going to prison at all, particularly if they are young or express remorse. Makes you wonder who we'll be letting off next? Rapists? Murderers?

Ken Clarke, the current Justice Secretary, may have come to the highly convenient, money-saving conclusion that prison sentences do not reduce crime — which I don't believe — but I'm more inclined to side with former Home Secretary Michael Howard and his famous 'prison works' speech. It addressed the problems of criminals and criminality in a way that the latest milksop, so-called 'community payback', never will. A couple of weeks loafing around in high-visibility jackets? Oh yes, I'm quite sure that will get hardened criminals back on the straight and narrow, Mr Clarke.

At the grassroots level, the judicial system is currently a mess, where something as serious as shoplifting can earn you an £80 fixed penalty fine, while dropping a cigarette butt can land you with a £1,000 fine. It's a world where the police keep telling us that crime is falling but only, I'm convinced, because they're letting repeat young offenders off with warning after warning, caution after caution. Sometimes I wonder why they don't just raise the age of criminal responsibility to twenty and solve the whole problem of youth crime overnight.

I'll cheerfully admit that I retired from the bench both frustrated and a little fed-up too. But I must quickly add that I still have absolute faith in the magisterial system in this country. No single magistrate is perfect and I'm sure I made the odd mistake or two but collectively, we perform a tremendously important service for this country, administering justice at local level. It's just that if the political interference – both from Whitehall and from Brussels – stopped, and we were left to get on with it, we could to it so much better.' [*Daily Mail* 15th October 2010]

Mr Jefferson and many like him are leaving the Magistrates' Courts and as you read through the following chapters you will see many of the points that Mr Jefferson raises are similar to those made by Nikki the Church Minister and JP. The do-gooders are growing in number and are changing the country beyond recognition. Unfortunately, it's not for the better. The glimpse of the courts structure is only the overview. It is what goes on in the courts on a daily basis where society and its values are tested. That is where the law abiding in society expect those who breach the law to be faced with trial and retribution.

* * *

However, not all magistrates leave because of the demise of the judicial system. One magistrate has been removed from office after he fell asleep on the bench, causing an assault trial to collapse. John Harrison, a former city councillor, claimed he was just resting his eyes during the first day of a trial. But after discussions with his colleagues and a court official he decided to halt the case after a day and a half. An investigation was launched after the mother of the seventeen year old defendant, who cannot be named for legal reasons, complained about the magistrate's behaviour and an application to this effect was made by the defence solicitor. He told a local newspaper:

'I was not asleep, but I rested my eyes for five minutes or so. It was just a normal reaction in the middle of the afternoon. The court was warm, the heating was on and the sun was pouring in through the window. I was still listening to the defence solicitor speaking to the defendant and I was able to take down some notes related to what was said.'

In a statement the Office for Judicial Complaints said: 'Following a complaint about Mr Harrison's conduct in a Lancaster youth court, a conduct investigation panel found that his behaviour risked bringing the magistracy into disrepute and recommended Mr Harrison be removed from judicial office. The Lord Chief Justice and the Lord Chancellor accepted the recommendation to remove Mr Harrison from the magistracy.' [*Independent* 28th September 2010]

The final point on magistrates is that The Howard League for Penal Reform wants to remove the powers of magistrates to be able to commit convicts to prison. They are behind the idea of curbing the numbers of short-term prisoners and want jail sentencing powers placed in the hands of Crown Court judges. The League criticised magistrates, saying they overused their sentencing powers. What a lot of twaddle! Magistrates powers of imprisonment should be increased not removed. The League is of the opinion that the move to curb their power would 'reduce short-term sentences', forcing them 'to work more closely with community projects and programmes'. Current community projects and programmes do not work. Get them to be effective then look at prison sentences. At least the former shadow home secretary, Ann Widdecombe, was onboard when she said the 'ludicrous' plan would undermine the justice system. [*Daily Express* 14th March 2011]

2

Trial And Retribution

The Ubiquitous Mrs. H

On the bench where I sat there were some characters who really stand out and for me; one such person was Mrs H. Now here was a lady who had been on the bench for many years and she could be described as one of the old school. She was for me, an informal mentor. I liked the way she operated, standing no nonsense from anybody, however, the way she conducted her court would probably be frowned upon today. She was fair, very direct and dealt with everybody in the correct manner, but most of all she administered justice. She would enter the courtroom carrying her handbag which, to me, seemed very large. It was very reminiscent of Margaret Thatcher and her handbags. Many of us were absolutely convinced, though of course, it was never proven, that she had a house brick in the handbag ready for any emergencies. We had a vision of a yob leaping over the dock and onto the bench, and her swinging the handbag in self defence and flooring him or her!

On one particular day there were just the two of us sitting in court. She was the chairman, I was a winger and it was a fines court so we could manage with just two. This is where defendants came to court because they had not paid any of their fines, or they had fallen behind with payments. The objective is to find out why they haven't paid or why they are unable to pay and then resolve the situation. Mrs H had recalled 'good old days' when she was a new gal on the bench. It used to be a case that all the fine defaulters were gathered together and they sat outside the fines court waiting for their time to go before the bench. The worst offender for not paying would be identified and summoned into court first. The questions began to the point.

'X, you were fined £500, you offered to pay £10 a week but as of this date, some eighteen months later, you have not paid a penny. You have been back to court on many occasions and given a sob story as to why you couldn't pay or wouldn't pay, but your buying a car comes after paying your outstanding fine.' There would be a slight pause, then, 'Tell us why we should not find wilful neglect or refusal to pay and send you to prison, today, for the appropriate number of days that equates to the level of the fine.' Another slight pause whilst the veiled threat sank in, then, addressing the legal advisor, 'How many days in prison for £500?' The legal advisor would provide the details. The members of the bench would then look at the fines defaulter. 'Well,' would exclaim the chairman, 'what have you got to say.' The defaulter would continue the sob story which had worked so well before. He or she had no money, would not sell the car to pay the fine, and so there was a stand off. The chairman consulted with the wingers and then sentenced the defaulter to x number of days in prison. Then to the words of 'take him/her down,' the defaulter was taken to the cells and then to prison.

The Usher would go back out to seek the next person to come in, muttering to the people waiting to come in, 'They're a hard nosed bunch in there today they've just sent the first one to prison for not paying the fine.' Of course, when he bought the people in they would all come offering all sorts of options about how they were going to pay, and even offering some of their money on that very day to get things under way. That speeded up the process and the message to defaulters was that prison was a real option and if you don't pay your fines then that is where you will go.

On this particular day, I sat with Mrs H as a defendant entered the court. His demeanour showed that he was an old hand in the courtroom. He was progressing in years, and it showed. He made his way to the dock as if he was going to the pub and as he walked across, I noticed that he turned and took a long look at the clock. He entered the dock and stood there shuffling about. The legal advisor asked him to give his name and address, which he did. I noticed that he then again glanced at the clock at the back of the court. The legal advisor gave us the details of his fines which had accumulated with fines for further offences, showing that he now owed the court £600 of which nothing had been paid for two years. He had been back to court on numerous occasions and given a multitude of pathetic excuses as to why he couldn't pay. To get away each time he made an offer to the court to pay some unreasonable sum which he had no intention of honouring and that gave him more time. Mrs H asked why he had not paid any of his fine.

Now he thought he was dealing with a kind, sympathetic elderly lady who would pat him on the head (oops, sorry not allowed to touch anybody, that would be assault) and send him away with another sob story delivered and a promise to pay. He advised us that if we were to remit some of his fine he could manage to pay what remained. But remitting any of his fine would not solve the problem as he had not paid anything anyway. Also, he had committed more crimes and was fined for the offences, so why should we let him off. Again he looked at the clock. Mrs H told him that his fines remained and what was he going to do about paying them. He shuffled about, thinking that this elderly lady was not going to be such a push over. Mrs H asked him if he had any money with him. He replied that he had no money but could pay a bit more than £2.50 a week. Mrs.H studied the paper work and told him that he continued to commit offences but had not paid any of his fines and that could not go on. He saw the position changing and said he would pay £3 a week. Mrs H told him that he had said he would pay two years ago, but nothing had been forthcoming. He looked dejected and stated that he would now pay. Again he glanced at the clock.

I leaned over to Mrs H and said to ask about his clock watching. She had already noticed his activity and asked him why he kept looking at the clock. He was reluctant to answer the question and became agitated but Mrs H was persistent and asked the question again. He then told us that he had a train to catch.

'Where to?' asks a surprised Mrs H.

'Scotland, ma,am,' he replied.

'Scotland,' exclaimed Mrs H, 'why do you want to go to Scotland?'

There was no answer was forthcoming. Mrs H asked again. He then mumbled that he was going on holiday. Mrs H asked if he had a ticket. This was followed by a long pause followed by a whispered 'No'.

Mrs H had neatly caught the fish and now reeled him in. She asked how he intended to purchase the ticket as he had clearly told us that he had no money. The defaulter became increasingly agitated and Mrs H asked again if he had any money on him and if did not cooperate then she would get someone from security to search him. He realised that he was in a corner and told us that he had his train fare.

'So,' said Mrs H, 'you're going on holiday and you have got your train fare. How much money have you actually got on your person?'

'Don't know ma,am,' said the defaulter.

'Well,' said Mrs H, 'it's quite simple, you put your hand in your pocket and take out the money and then count it.' She then added for good measure, 'The fines outstanding to this court come before any holiday and any payment of train fares. Do you understand that?'

The defendant, still very agitated, looked up at us and replied, 'I have to go on holiday.'

Mrs H looked at him and said, 'We have to collect outstanding fines and you have an outstanding fine.'

He now looked particularly glum. Mrs H said, 'Enough time has been wasted so show us how much money you have.'

He rummaged in his pockets and eventually pulled out a rather large bundle of bank notes and held it up. Mrs H looked at the bundle, then at me, then back to the bundle and said, 'There appears to be a considerable sum of money, so if you have that amount of money you can pay all or a good part of your fine.'

The defaulter glanced at the clock and explained that he had to go on holiday and that the money was for that. Without further delay, Mrs H asked the legal advisor how many days in prison the fine that he had outstanding equated to. A quick exchange between us confirmed my agreement at the next step. Armed with the number of days, Mrs H told the defaulter that we were sending him to prison for failing to pay his fine and asked the legal advisor to get the jailers up to the court. It suddenly dawned on him that we really meant business. Mrs H continued quite matter of factually and told him, 'We are just waiting for the jailers and as soon as they come up you will be sentenced and sent down.'

As the jailers entered the courtroom brandishing a pair of handcuffs, Mrs H looked at the man and said, 'Of course you can still pay the fine and that will avoid the need for you to go prison.'

The defaulter, being a bit stupid said, 'But I want to go on holiday.'

Mrs H said, 'You are going to prison, not on the holiday you planned for and certainly not to Scotland.'

At this point, one of the jailers stepped forward and got his handcuffs ready. Mrs H was about to pass sentence and advise him of the number of days he would serve. The defaulter realised that he had lost the game and handed over his roll of banknotes to the jailer. The money was counted out, all £600 so that his fine was paid in full. Two £10 notes remained and were given back to him so he could go on holiday. Justice had been done, the defaulter had been fined for criminal offences, the fines were outstanding, we had recovered all the money owed and we had not put a person in prison. It was all quite satisfactory. This is how you did it! Of course you may also consider how the defendant, who was on Job Seekers Allowance of about £80 a fortnight, had £620 in cash in his pocket, for a holiday. Well you must not ask because that would be an infringement of his Human Rights. However, I leave it to you to consider the possible options.

Another courtroom, another day, another case; Mrs H was in the chair and I was one of two wingers. In the dock was a young woman who had pleaded guilty to theft. She had quite a list of previous and had built up a debt of unpaid fines to the court. It was a case of yet another fine but it could be added to the fines already owed. She was on benefits and she actually claimed to spend more than she got in. It was offered that we could reduce the total fines by remitting some of the money. In other words, write off some of the fines for previous offences. Some magistrates thought that this was a way of dealing with the problem but I did not subscribe to that option and neither did Mrs H.

Defendants who are found guilty have to complete a means form so we can see what money comes in and what goes out. And more to the point, what the money is spent on. Whilst we waited for the form to be passed up, the courtroom door opened and a young woman came into the court, stood and shouted at the defendant in the dock words to the effect of, 'You gotta cum and see to your lot as there screamin and crien' all over place.' She immediately turned round and went back out of the door.

It was all over before Mrs H could say or do anything. She turned to the defendant and asked what that was all about. It transpired that the defendant had three young children and had brought them with her, to court. She left them with another woman who she knew whilst she came into the courtroom and they were probably upset. Mrs H asked why she didn't make other arrangements for the children.

'Ain't nobody else,' she replied.

'What about the children's father?' enquired Mrs H.

'Which one?' asked the woman, then added, 'They ain't no use, they only come round when they want summit.'

Mrs.H saw where the questions were going and reverted to looking at the form.

The defendant was on benefits. She had three children. Her rent and local taxes were paid, leaving her to pay for the electricity, gas and food. So from her total income after subtracting the heating, lighting and living costs it still left a reasonable sum. Then the next column provided a better insight: £x a week on cigarettes, £xx a week on mobile phone, £xxx a week on entertainment and £xxxx on shopping catalogues. Also on the form was a huge amount of money for disposable nappies. The legal advisor then added that none of the outstanding fines had been paid.

Mrs H moved into top gear. 'Right, your fines have not been paid, why not?'

'Ain't got no money,' replied the woman.

'Right' said Mrs H, 'we will have a look at that shall we. Let me first point out that fines come before luxuries.' She then spelt out situation. 'You spend £x a week on cigarettes, that's a luxury.' She paused for that to sink in, then continued, 'You spend £xx on a mobile phone and the majority of that will be a luxury because you can get people to call you and so we are really only talking about emergency use.' Mrs H paused, then said, 'You spend £xxx on entertainment, what's that?'

The young woman quickly gathered her thoughts, 'I go out once a week wiv me mates to a night club to get away from the kids.'

As quick as lightning Mrs H enquired, 'Who looks after the children?'

'A mate,' was the reply.

Mrs H responded, 'You get a mate to look after your children while you go clubbing, but you can't get a mate to look after them, whilst you come to court.'

The young woman did not reply.

Mrs H looked at the form, 'You spend £xxxx on clothing from catalogues.'

'Yep,' replied the woman.

'Have you ever tried shopping in charity or second hand shops or the really cheap high street shops?'

She replied that she didn't want second hand clothing for her or her children. Mrs H reminded her that she was on state benefits and had to do the best she could, and that if she wanted designer or expensive clothes then she should go to work to earn the money to pay for them. The woman said nothing.

Mrs H then looked at the woman and said, 'You spend a lot of money on disposable nappies. What ones do you use?' The woman replied with a brand name. 'I sometimes shop for my daughter and I know they are very good, but expensive. There are much cheaper ones available. Why don't you use them?' asked Mrs H.

The woman was about to reply but was pipped at the post by Mrs H who continued, 'When I had young children and not a lot of money I used towelling nappies that could be washed after use and reused.' The woman stood with her mouth open. 'You spend money on buying them but they will last. You need to boil them to get them clean but you have time to do that, you don't do anything and you will save money.' Mrs H continued, 'My grandmother, my mother and myself have washed nappies for our children. There is no reason why you, a young woman on state benefits, with three children should not have to wash nappies.'

Wow, what a stroke of genius. Mrs H then went back to her figures and proudly showed them to us, her wingers. So from being in the red each week the woman was in the black and could start paying her fines. Added to which was the additional fine we then imposed. The young woman who had been cocky on arrival, departed rather shocked. That said, Mrs H had probably breached the Human Rights Act on the grounds of torture, mental anguish etc, in proposing that a woman would have to wash nappies and look after her children.

Assault PC

Some cases are really unpleasant but it's all in a days work at court. A particularly nasty case was an 'Assault PC'. Initially, it had been an Actual Bodily Harm offence, but it had been downgraded to Common Assault. A lesser charge was proposed because the defendant agreed to plead guilty to that offence. This was a case that caused the three of us on the bench some concern and we asked a question that the Court indicated we shouldn't be asking. We wanted to know why the CPS, who were prosecuting the case, had downgraded it, but whilst they did not answer, we knew the real reason. Government targets! 'Assault PC' is often added onto a number of other more serious charges and occurs, for example, when individuals coming out of night clubs, having had far too much alcohol, get a bit belligerent with the police. This is followed by a half hearted blow against a police officer and they quite rightly add 'Assault PC' as an additional offence.

Whilst it is considered to be serious, the degree of assault is often quite low in the overall scheme of things. In this case it was an assault to a female police constable and it was serious. It had happened in the evening when the police were called to an incident in the city. The officer went to confront the male defendant who was drunk. He was upset about something but unbeknown to the officer he was a martial arts expert and clearly everybody was going to find out by his actions. As the constable approached the man to try and sort out the situation, he viciously attacked her delivering karate chops and punches leaving her with very nasty injuries. Because the individual had pleaded guilty, the officer would not have to give evidence, but we were provided with a series of photographs. These were taken after the event and showed the extent of the injuries to her body. The officer was in court, sitting at the back, wedged between two rather large male police officers whose looks showed that they were not in the least happy about what had happened to their colleague.

I was chairman that day and I can still picture the photographs of the bruising to the woman's body where her front, face and back were black and blue from where this thug, oh yes, I am being very polite when I use the word thug, had given her a severe beating. She ended up in hospital undergoing treatment and had been off work for many months. All we had before us was a charge of Common Assault. This offence can mean as little as somebody slapping another person on the face and leaving a little red mark or, in fact, no mark at all. The assault in this case was, in fact, Actual Bodily Harm (ABH), if not Grievous Bodily Harm (GBH), although GBH usually requires a wounding with blood flowing. There was no wounding as such in this case, just a brutal beating leaving large areas of severe bruising and a lot of pain.

We heard the details and evidence of the prosecution case which were of an unprovoked attack on a person in a position of authority, doing their job. The defendant, a thug, clearly showed he had little regard for what he had done or that he had used his knowledge and skills in martial arts in the assault. He sat impassively in the dock whilst his solicitor vigorously defended him which is what he is expected to do. It is often the manner and body language that a lawyer uses when putting over a case that reflects the degree of sympathy they have with the prosecution. In this case there was none. He said that his client had been out drinking and that there had been an altercation with others leaving him pretty angry. Consequently, when the police arrived he was infuriated they had been called and took his vengeance out on the first police officer who approached him. It happened to be the victim in this case. He really played down the fact that the defendant was a martial arts expert.

We listened patiently to what was considered pure and absolute drivel about the individual who could not control himself when out drinking. We were told what a nice chap he was, that he did not have a record of violent behaviour and was well liked by his employer. That of course means that we were expected to reduce the sentence even further. Having heard mitigation at which not one tear was shed by any of us on the bench, the solicitor had the audacity to ask for a conditional discharge for his client. Now, a conditional discharge means that we do not punish him for the offence at this time. He would have a period of time, maybe one or two years, in which he must not commit any further offences. If he did commit further offences within the time frame, he would then come back to court and be sentenced for the crime that we were listening to, as well as the new crime. Now, so many crimes never reach the courts and if he did commit another offence, the next bench may not have the detailed information and photographs as to the seriousness of the offence that we had.

When the case had been heard we went out to our small retiring room to discuss the evidence. I have never seen two colleagues so incensed as we progressed through the process of what to do with him. We studied the photographs and as a bench of three, were so disturbed by the case, we sought further advice through our legal advisor. We wanted to know what the reasons were for the case to be downgraded to such a low grade offence. Our legal advisor was very professional and could not comment on the actions of the Crown Prosecution Service. Why was it downgraded? It's quite simple, the CPS had to meet government target figures for prosecutions and convictions. Pressure could be put on police officers, so it was an easy target to get a guilty plea. They were not concerned that prison should have been a real option, a much lesser sentence which could be dealt with by way of a fine or low end community service, would mean they had another figure for their successful clear up statistics. It was yet another case of 'damn the victim', be it police officer or member of the public.

The argument was that if there had been a plea of not guilty, then there would have been a trial. With that goes the possibility that the defendant could be found not guilty. This will not reflect well on the conviction rates. A trial will cost money, therefore, the CPS will, wherever they can, get an individual to downgrade the offence so that they can get a guilty plea.

Magistrates are often put into an extremely difficult position because when an offence has been committed which deserves a custodial sentence, they often face a situation where they only have the ability to impose a fine or maybe community service. In the case above, from the moment we stepped into our small room to discuss the case, each of us had already considered that this offence was so serious that the defendant should have gone to prison. In our minds there was absolutely no doubt about it. However, we could not send the man to prison and we needed to get a report on the individual as the charge had been downgraded to common assault in order to get a guilty plea. From a potential six months custodial sentence, we were left with very limited options of a fine or a low end community sentence, the former to be based on the individual's ability to pay a fine. In this case we requested a full pre-sentence report to see whether prison could be considered or if a high end community sentence would be an option. We were not happy with this, because it meant that the case would go before different magistrates who would not have the option of looking at the photographs of the severity of this assault. However, it was found that two members of the bench could return for sentencing but this was not justice, just fudging figures for the government.

PC Assault

The defendant stood in the dock and looked a sorry sight. His face on one side was bruised blue and the other side had scratch marks. He faced charges of drunk and disorderly, Assault PC, obstructing police officers in the course of their duty and criminal damage. He had pleaded guilty. The case was one we had heard many times before, male goes out clubbing, has excess alcohol or takes drugs and loses control. A fight breaks out and the police attend. In this case, when the police arrived the defendant was in the thick of a brawl. The police moved in to break up the action but the defendant did not want to stop and so turned his attention to the police. We had heard cases before where defendants had developed some super human strength and required a number of officers to deal with them, but this was something else. Four officers struggled but could not restrain him. Two more joined in but were having problems controlling him and some officers were victims of the defendant's anger. Two more officers joined the foray. There was now eight officers, trained in restraint techniques, struggling to get control of the defendant. Finally they overpowered the defendant who was abusive and attempting to struggle. All of the officers were surprised at the power the individual had shown.

On the ground and secure was one thing, but they had to get him into the police van. There was, what could be described as, a cage within the confines of the back of the van. Once an individual was in and the door locked they could scream, shout, swear and throw themself about. There was little option, it's the way the police have to deal with a situation. Remember there were the other people who were in the fight to be dealt with as well. They, it seems, were just vocal rather than aggressive. The van was backed up close to the defendant and the cage door opened. Having been unable to get handcuffs on the defendant, it was to be a case of lift and shuffle the defendant into the van and get the door shut. That was to prove easier said than done.

Upon command they lifted the individual and as quickly as they could, moved to the van and began the process of bundling him in the back, avoiding injury to any of the officers. To achieve the plan, a sergeant and a constable climbed into the back of the van and pulled whilst the others pushed, letting go as he went further into the van. The sergeant told the constable to get out quick leaving him exposed to kicks. As he let go, the sergeant made his escape by moving over the top of the defendant as fast as he could and out of the van. In this process the defendant, laying face down, turned to carry on the fight just as the sergeant's foot caught his head. Clear of the van the doors were closed and it headed for the police station followed by the police officers who would be required to off load him and get him into a cell. The defendant could be heard shouting obscenities and hammering on the inside of the cage. They fared little better at the police station but he was booked in and placed in a cell. It was noted that his face was battered and bruised and as soon as the effects of the drug and alcohol had worn off he received medical attention. When questioned at the police station with his solicitor in attendance, he could remember nothing but admitted the charges.

With the case delivered, the defence solicitor stood and prepared to provide mitigation for his client. He opened his speech with a broadside against the police. He said that it was pure police brutality delivered against the defendant who was unable to defend himself. His face and his body bore the evidence of the aggression shown against him. He told us that he was going to make a complaint to the police complaints commission. We were then told that he met a mate who sold him some 'stuff' which he had never used before. It was very powerful and he remembers nothing until he came to in the police cell. He cooperated with the doctor and then with the police. He had been asked for the name of his mate and where he could be found but that information escaped him. Yes, he did have previous convictions for violence but he was trying to avoid trouble. He did not work but was looking for suitable employment. He had no money so could not pay a fine nor did he have a permanent address and so could not be tagged and his bad back would probably render him unfit for work. Bad back? He was fighting eight police officers. Ah, that was the drug he was given. On his means form he spent more than he received, but of course smoked, had a mobile phone and who paid for the drink and drugs? Oh, his mates treated him. Who are the mates, names please and where do they live? Oh, he can't remember. In the end we put the case off for reports from the probation service to look at his past and come up with options for a punishment. Such is life on the front line of policing when one drunken and drugged yob ties up the time of so many officers, even causing them injuries.

A Good Night Out

Ms X was called into court as the defendant in a case. An attractive young woman, just into her twenties entered the courtroom and walked to the dock. Dressed in a dark suit, her hair pulled back away from her face. She wore little or no make up and presented an image of a young business woman, set for a successful career. In fact she worked for a multinational company and was progressing with promotions. She entered the dock and faced us. Her responses to the legal advisors questions were confident and clear. It was that which made it difficult to grasp that she was before us on trial, charged with Actual Bodily Harm (ABH) and with using threatening and insulting behaviour, likely to cause alarm and distress to others. She pleaded not guilty to the charges.

The prosecutor began to give details of the incident which happened in a night club. The defendant was on a night out with others and had been drinking when a fight ensued. Two women, one of whom was in the dock, took their argument to the ladies' toilet where they began fighting each other. The doorman had to intervene to separate the two women but was himself assaulted and required emergency treatment at hospital.

The first witness was called and it was the doorman. A burly male, looking every inch the typical image of a bouncer, took his place in the witness box. He told us that he was on duty the night in question and was the only doorman. He explained that the owners had cut back on staff and one problem this caused was that if, whilst on duty, he had to go to the toilet, he had to use the ladies' toilet as it was the closest to the entrance. The mens' toilet was on the far side of the building and to go there would leave the entrance unguarded for too long. On this night he had to go to the toilet and went into the ladies' and into a cubicle. He had just entered and was relieving himself when he heard a number of women enter shouting at one another. He recalled that there was a lot of foul language and threats. Then before he had finished a fight broke out. Securing himself, he left the cubicle to find two women, pulling hair, slapping and punching each other. A third, much younger, girl kept out of the way in the corner but was upset about the fight that was before her. The doorman explained that he managed to get himself between the two women, who continued to slap and punch. But then it was him on the receiving end.

One of the women started to get hysterical and so he turned to face her and speak to her so as to calm her down. He had his back to the other woman. He explained that the next thing he remembered was the severe pain in his head and then the warm liquid running down his face and neck. It was blood. His blood. He said that he had one thought and that was to get out of the toilet so that he could get control. He pushed his way past the woman and out into the crowded club but then everything became a bit of a blur. He recalled police officers, ambulance people and then being in hospital.

The prosecutor asked the doorman if he would recognise any of the women if he saw them again. He said he would. When asked he pointed at the defendant and said that she was one of them, the one behind him when he was attacked. The prosecutor asked if he was certain. He was and had first picked her out of a police line up. He told us that she looked different. At the club she wore make up and wore trendy party clothes which made her look older. He then explained that whilst in the toilet she used a torrent of foul language which he found a bit embarrassing. Throughout his evidence miss 'prim and proper' sat passive and unflinching.

The second witness was called, a young woman of similar age to the defendant and the other woman in the altercation. She told us that they had been friends for a number of years and the fight ensued over the affections of the third, much younger girl. She explained that the doorman had stepped in to separate them and was trying to talk to her. She then told us that the next thing was the blood running down his face and neck. He pushed his way to the door and left the toilet. She saw the defendant holding a stiletto shoe in her right hand. Fearing for her own safety she then got out of the toilet. She recalled that the police were suddenly there and they must have been just outside the club when the alarm was raised.

The third witness was called and was the much younger woman, accompanied by an adult because of her age. She was still at school. The defendant sat in the dock and the other woman, having given her evidence, sat at the back of the court in the public seats. The witness could look at each in turn. However, our legal advisor spotted the situation and told the girl to look at us as we were hearing all of the evidence. The girl told us that she had been the lover of the defendant but had fallen in love with the other woman. The defendant did not like it and there had been a lot of arguments.

On the night they were at the night club she told the defendant that she wanted to be with the other woman. That developed into a serious argument and then in the toilet, a fight began. She was upset and frightened as the two women fought and did her best to keep out of the way. She told us the doorman got involved and that he was facing her new girlfriend trying to talk to her as she was very upset. The next thing she knew was that the doorman had blood running down his face and neck. He ran for the door, leaving the defendant standing with her stiletto shoe in her hand. The defendant then told them to keep their mouths shut but the young woman fled in fear. The police arrived and took the three of them to the police station.

We heard from the police and we were provided with a medical report giving details of the injuries which amounted to three head wounds done by a sharp object.

With the prosecution case concluded, the defence solicitor stood and was called over to confer with his client, the defendant. We had heard a lot of evidence and thought it appropriate to have a break to allow the defendant to speak with her solicitor. Returning to the courtroom we anticipated a change of plea to that of guilty, but no, the not guilty plea still stood. The defendant was called to the witness box. She agreed that there was an argument between the two women but that the doorman stepped in and started pushing them apart. He was a big man and she was frightened of him. She had very high stiletto shoes on and in the pushing one shoe had fallen off. She bent down and picked up the shoe and held it up as she struggled to gain her balance. She teetered on the other shoe and as she lost her balance her hand came down and she must have clumped the doorman on the head. She did not hit him deliberately. In cross examination she was referred to the hospital report which stated that there were three wounds. She of course had no idea how they got there, but did not think that they were inflicted by her.

Armed with a file of evidence, we departed the court to our retiring room to sift through the evidence and the decision making process. We returned to the courtroom and declared that she was guilty of the ABH charge. Had we not adopted the more serious offence we could have gone for an offence of Affray. Her solicitor rose to present mitigation before we passed sentence. She had no previous convictions and had never been in any sort of trouble. Her work record was exemplary with letters of reference. We were told that by being found guilty, she would be dismissed by her employer and with a criminal conviction, she would find it more difficult to obtain employment. It was accepted that the doorman had been injured and for that she apologised. The solicitor proposed a conditional discharge. We were in no doubt that the case was serious and in evaluating the punishment options, the defendant was given a high end community sentence, with a considerable number of hours carrying out unpaid work in the community. She was ordered to pay compensation to the doorman. There were no court costs as compensation took precedence. We never knew if she lost her job but it yet again shows that alcohol plays a major part in violent crimes. It did in this case, and a number of individuals were affected by it.

Ladies of the Night

It was always very concerning when young people passed through the courts, often with a long list of previous convictions, and, in many cases, for more serious offences. A young woman, just old enough for the adult court, entered the courtroom and walked across to the dock. She was before us charged with soliciting and was very young looking and not dressed for work in the red light area. The court legal advisor went through the preliminaries and read out the charge. She was unrepresented and upon advice from the duty solicitor, pleaded guilty to the charge. The prosecutor outlined the offence and read out the statements of the police officers who patrolled that area. They had observed her activities and then made the arrest. There were no previous convictions. The defendant stood and was asked by the legal advisor if she wanted to say anything to us, the magistrates, about why she was soliciting. She explained that she was studying at college and was desperately short of money. Having been unable to get any sort of part time job she turned to prostitution as a last resort. The other experienced girls were aggressive towards her as she was stealing their clients. It was a mistake and she hated doing it and would never do it again.

We decided that this was a case where, under the circumstances, we would give her a total discharge so that there would be no record and she could get on with her life and complete her studies. Back in court I explained our decision with a word of warning that if she did decide to do it again, the next court would not be sympathetic. She was free to leave the court. At that moment a mobile phone rang. It was her's and she answered it. Before I could say anything she said, 'I'm busy, but I am available in fifteen minutes at the usual place.' She switched the phone off and put it away. Then, picking up her bag began, to leave the dock. I asked who the call was from, because that was probably a business call. 'Just a friend,' she snootily replied, and left the courtroom. I think we three had just been duped.

The next 'lady of the night' was dressed for work in a micro mini skirt, a revealing top and teetering on high heeled shoes, as she made her way to the dock. A court usher followed ready to pick her up should she fall over. Observed and caught soliciting, she pleaded guilty. It was a part of the job, go to court, get a fine, earn more money, pay the fine, and continue working until the next time. She had a long list of previous convictions. On her file notes it was recorded that the fines went up each time. However, there was a limit as to how high the fines could be, as it had to be within the means of the defendant.

How much does a prostitute earn? The completed means form revealed all. She is on state benefit in the form of job seekers allowance and receives housing benefit. She has all the outgoings that people generally have for living and accommodation and so her income was the same as outgoings. Nothing new there then! I asked her solicitor how much she earned from her business. He gave a vacant look as if to say, why do you need to know that. 'I will enquire,' he responded. He then went to the dock to enquire. After a few moments of deep conversation he asked: 'My client is not quite sure what you are asking.' He paused, 'she is on benefits, job seekers allowance, as detailed on the means form.'

We three magistrates were baffled. We conversed and decided that prostitutes earn money through their trade and that's income isn't it? Well we thought so. I explained to the solicitor that it was a job for which she got paid, and would have to declare it as income to the revenue so as to pay tax. We wanted to know how much she earned, either a year, a month or even a week. He went and consulted her then said: 'She says that she always pays her fines based on her benefits.' He continued, 'It seems that her only income is what the state gives her.'

Not wanting to let the subject drop I continued: 'Your client provides her services for a fee, is that correct, after all that is why she is in court.'

'Yes sir,' he replied.

I then asked: 'How much money does she get in the course of a year for all of her services?'

He went to consult again and whilst the solicitor was obviously embarrassed, the defendant glared the look of death in our direction. I hoped she wasn't a witch or retribution may well have been coming our way. 'She does not know how much money she makes in year but insists that what she lives on is what she gets in benefits.' We were getting nowhere, so if those paying out benefits were not interested or indeed the Inland Revenue on income earned and no tax paid, then why should we bother. We were supposed to be working on a joined up government system. We came up with a fine that reflected her known income with an estimate of her unknown income. I asked when the fine would be paid and she asked for time to pay. As was customary we agreed, after all she would have to entertain a few clients to obtain the money. She departed the courtroom with a few choice words left ringing in our ears. I hoped that would be last time I saw her but alas no, I had a strange encounter later that day.

Leaving court it was the tail end of a hot, sunny day and I travelled home in my open top sports car, purchased to comfort my mid-life crisis, or so I was told. I drove along a wide street that was quiet during the day but later became a venue for 'ladies of the night' plying their trade. Ahead I saw the brake lights of a car showing that it was slowing down and noticed somebody walk into the road and approach the car. The car having slowed, did not stop, but sped away. As I got closer I could see somebody standing by the side of the road. In seconds it registered that there was something familiar about the person who I now saw was female. No, it can't be. I slowed the car down, yes it was, our defendant from earlier in the day. As I drove past she leaned forward to look at the car and waved an arm, not out of recognition, but a 'here I am' sort of wave. Driving slowly past I glared at the woman who in a fraction of a second realised who I was. The arm was still waving but now had the middle finger extended and her mouth let forth some obscenities. I had passed her and looking in the rear view mirror, saw her standing in the road, still waving, one lone finger raised above the rest. Nice to know one is appreciated...

Big Boys or Fierce Pussycats

The door leading from the cells opened and a member of the cells' security staff entered the dock. It was a time before we had the secure dock and so any defendant seeking to abscond could do so with reasonable ease. The first defendant entered followed by another member of the security staff, then came the second defendant. On first glance I thought of Desperate Dan, the comic character. This was quite a pair. They were huge, covered in tattoos which even adorned part of their faces and hands. That and their sheer size made them look really fierce. I thought that if this pair decided to do a runner, then they would go and none of the security staff were going to stop them. They came into the dock and leaned forward, hands on the top of the dock, waiting for somebody to speak. I sat with two lady magistrates, one being the chairman. Our lady legal advisor asked the first man his name which he gave, followed by a 'ma,am'. The second man did the same. She then read out the charges to them, that of assault in a public house and assault on a police officer. She then asked each in turn if they pleaded guilty or not guilty. 'Not guilty, ma,am,' they each responded. When told by the chairman to sit, they both said, 'Yes ma,am,' and sat. It was an unusual picture, two huge men surrounded by four security staff who were tiny in comparison.

The prosecutor began her case. 'The two defendants were in the Dog and Duck public house on the given date when a fight started. Witnesses will state that the two men before us started the fight and people were being injured. The police were called and a mobile unit arrived. PCs Smith and Jones (not real names) were the duty officers who stopped their patrol car outside the pub and could hear the noise of the fight. Jones, a young female officer went to see what was happening whilst Smith called for back up. The outcome was that the two men were arrested for assaulting a number of people.'

We heard from witnesses about the fight but the reason as to why there was a fight was never really made clear. If they knew, they were not saying. PC Jones was called. A young slender, medium height PC came into the courtroom, equipped with the full regalia of a modern police officer. It included radio equipment, handcuffs, CS gas spray, extendable baton and miscellaneous other items of kit. She explained to us that she went to the door of the pub and could see a fight going on. To get a better view, so as to assess the situation, she opened the door and looked in. The next thing she knew, she was drawn in and became part of the fight. The two defendants appeared to be the main problem. She drew her baton and with flick of the wrist, it extended. She ordered the men to stop fighting which was to no avail.

She told us, 'I stood, my baton held in the regulation position, and told the defendant on the left in the dock that he was under arrest.' Looking at her note book she continued, 'He did not heed my order and turned towards me. I warned him to stop and I considered at that moment in time I was going to become a victim. Following the correct procedure I struck him with my baton. That stopped him. I told him to turn round and put his hands behind his back so I could cuff him. He just grinned and moved towards me so I hit him again as hard as I could.' She paused in her evidence. 'This time the blow was effective and whilst he fell over I moved in and managed to get the cuffs on.' She again glanced at her notes. 'I turned to the other defendant who was still fighting and as I was about to shout he became aware that his mate was handcuffed and the fighting stopped. I told the other defendant that he was under arrest and to turn round and put his hands behind his back. He did but I realised that I could not cuff him as I had already used mine on the other male. Nobody else in the bar moved or said anything. Most couldn't but I held my baton in the ready position. I ordered the two defendants to leave the pub. I followed, backing out until in the street. Smith saw the situation and following a bit of a struggle managed to get the other one cuffed. It was at that point that the back up police van arrived and they were taken to the police station.'

The two defendants when called to give their version of events were as polite as polite could be. It was 'Yes ma'am, no ma'am.' They claimed they went to the pub for a drink and were attacked by a gang of locals but they didn't know why. Sitting in court listening to the description of events was made even more strange by the difference in size of the 'combatants'. It transpired that the two defendants, who incidentally were found guilty, had a respect for women instilled in them by their mother, said to be a fearsome lady. They claimed that they would never have harmed the female police office however, the male officers were fair game.

A Case of Domestic Violence

Cases of domestic violence were always fraught with problems because nobody seemed to take them seriously. Today, there are special courts dealing with such cases. One problem was that the court required the wife or partner to attend court and give evidence. In most cases, even after serious assault, the women, or in some cases a man, would not give evidence as they had kissed and made up. Or there was a real fear of further violence.

In one case a woman was determined to go through the courts following a physical assault by her former partner. We were told that the male defendant had pleaded not guilty to assaulting his former partner in front of three young children. The police had been called, he had been arrested and now faced a trial in the Magistrates' Court.

It was revealed to us that on a number of occasions he had failed to attend court and, in fact, had failed to attend a pre-trial hearing. The legal advisor told us that the injured party, plus witnesses, were at court along with the defendant's solicitor. Alas at that moment in time there was no defendant!

Whilst the legal advisor was telling us the situation, the defence lawyer entered the courtroom with a very swaggering demeanour and went up to his seat, dropping his file on the desk. With no apology for his late arrival he addressed the court, advising that his client would not be at court that day as he was unwell. He had a back problem and had to remain lying flat. Our legal advisor asked if there was a sick note. 'Yes,' declared the defence lawyer and in a manner that indicated that it was all too much for him, he passed forward the note. The legal advisor examined the note and then passed it up to us. We could identify that it was a doctor's note from a surgery that was about thirty-five miles away from where the defendant lived.

I raised the point about the distance between the doctor and the patient. He had always used that doctor was the reply. I then asked the defence lawyer whether or not the doctor had actually seen and physically examined the defendant. No, stated the defence lawyer, it had all been done via the telephone! We could not believe what we were hearing. Just to confirm, no doctor had examined the defendant. The defence lawyer shrugged his shoulders and confirmed the situation. For the court record I stated that the magistrates were not satisfied with the doctor's note and that the defendant had not been examined. The defence lawyer then went on to request another adjournment of the trial, this time for three weeks.

The prosecutor, a very efficient young woman, stood up and explained that for various reasons, there had been countless delays with this case. Her witnesses and the injured party had attended court in the past and were all at court, now ready to proceed. She wanted to continue and for us to hear the case in the absence of the defendant.

We then entered into discussions as to the merits of either proceeding or not proceeding with the case. The decision centred on the fact that whilst a medical note had been received, signed by a doctor, the defendant was not actually examined by that doctor at the time of issuing the medical note. We therefore concluded that the defendant had phoned this doctor and told him that he had a bad back, and thus was unable to attend court so could he please have a sick note! It would appear that the nice doctor duly obliged.

We found this scenario to be unacceptable and could find no real reason why the defendant could not be in court and, as the prosecution was ready, we agreed we would hear the case and proceed that day. Upon this decision being taken, the defence lawyer threw his toys out of the pram and argued quite strongly that the case should be adjourned; his client wasn't there and it wasn't fair to continue! But we said we would proceed, hear the prosecution case and then determine the next step in the due process.

The prosecutor outlined the case to us, which was that the defendant had been living with his partner and three children for a number of years, but there had been a break down in the relationship. The defendant had found himself another partner, but he would often return and harass his ex-partner, even in front of the children. In this particular case, he had gone round to the house and sat outside in his car. It was said that he had been drinking but he just sat there, eventually getting out and hammering on the door. The three children stood at the window of the house and observed the goings on. The man was shouting and being very abusive and using foul language. The injured party went to the door in the hope that she could calm him down and tell him to go away but, in front of the three children, he continued his abusive onslaught and there was actual physical violence. The young lad, aged nine, went to the defence of his mother and was violently shoved out of the way. The enraged man left the house, got in his car and drove away. The police were called and the man was arrested and charged with assault.

The prosecution called the injured party and she came into the court in a very distressed state and gave her evidence. She told us about the arrival of her ex-partner, her attempt to defuse the situation, the assaults committed on her and the nine year-old boy and the assaults committed in front of three young children who were absolutely terrified at what was happening. She had no contact, nor desired any, with the defendant. He had just arrived at the house and had created the problems. She didn't know, and wasn't interested in, where he lived, or with whom he was living. She had been a straightforward victim of a violent assault.

The defence lawyer stood in cross examination of the injured party and was very aggressive, all but calling her a liar and suggesting that these events had not taken place. He overstepped the mark on several occasions indicating that she was the one to blame. The prosecution's solicitor rightly stood up but I pre-empted her objection and warned the defence lawyer that he was stepping over the mark and we would not tolerate it. The defendant would get his say in due course. In the end a very disgruntled lawyer sat down.

Then the eldest child, a boy of nine years of age, was called to give evidence. He stated that he had seen everything that had gone on and, eventually, had gone to try and assist his mother, who was being assaulted by the defendant. He gave a very good account of himself and in our opinion was a very credible witness. However, when cross examining this young boy, the defence lawyer again adopted an extremely aggressive manner, and was warned on several occasions to be careful because he was overstepping the mark. He took offence at this and accused me of trying to influence his cross examination, which was quite incorrect. The cross examination had to be done in a fair and just manner, not aggressively, particularly when a nine year old child is giving evidence about a violent assault on his mother. With his card marked, the defence lawyer added that the boy had been told what to say and it was untrue. This did not phase the boy who stood by his evidence.

Once we had heard the prosecution case, which was a very confrontational experience for everybody, the defence lawyer stood up and argued that there was no case to answer. I have to say that the three magistrates and a legal advisor remained very controlled throughout. We stopped the trial there as part heard and would re-convene when the defendant was able to attend court. We then set about finding a date that was convenient to everybody. It meant that we three magistrates had to come back, the prosecutor had to change her work schedule, the injured party had to return, the defence lawyer had to be available and we wanted the defendant in court to go into the box and give evidence.

A date was agreed and the defence lawyer said that the trial would only proceed if his client was fit to attend. I made it very clear, and it was recorded in both the court log and the case papers, that, if the defendant was unable to attend court on that day, at that time, then we required a doctor to physically examine the defendant and produce a report stating the reason(s) for his non-attendance, and not a note from a doctor thirty-five miles away, given following a telephone consultation! I explained that even if it proved necessary to make special travel arrangements to get the defendant to court, or if he came in a wheel chair, the court had the facilities to cater for that. We wanted the defendant in court and if he was not we wanted a cast iron reason why he was unable to attend. The lawyer departed with the throw away line that he was going to report me for my conduct in court.

In due course we went back to court on the allotted day. The legal advisor had already pre-warned me that the prosecutor, the injured party and the witnesses were back at court. However, whilst the prosecutor was ready, there was no defendant and indeed no defence lawyer present. We went into the court and received the formal notification that none of the defence parties were present.

In the meantime the duty solicitor of the court had been making inquiries as to the whereabouts of the defence lawyer and was able to advise us in open court that he was actually on his feet defending a case in another court in another part of the county! He had not contacted our court and no information or documentation had been provided, but there was indeed a 'report' available from the doctor.

The report was a note and on examining it, we found that it was in fact exactly the same as the previous doctor's note we had seen! It stated that the defendant still had a bad back and was not fit to attend court. No further explanation was given. I consulted with my colleagues and then stated in open court that we wanted the defence lawyer brought to our court as soon as possible to answer questions as to the whereabouts of his client. I even went so far as to say that we wanted the police to go and collect him to ensure that he attended. I don't think that I was actually allowed to issue a warrant for his arrest, but in our view as a bench it was certainly contempt of court matter for not attending. We made it very clear to the injured party and the prosecution team that there would be a delay whilst we tracked down the defendant. He was summoned to get to our court immediately.

When he arrived, we resumed the court proceedings. He stood at his desk, fuming, flustered and very angry; he was also very aggressive towards me as the chairman and to the bench in general. I had to caution him that his attitude was unacceptable to the court at which point he quietened down.

Holding the doctor's note between finger and thumb I waved it in a disgusted manner and said: 'I'm not sure what this is, but if it is the requested medical report then it is totally unacceptable to the court and I want a full and valid explanation or we will issue a warrant for the arrest of your client right now.'

The defence lawyer said that he had requested a full report from the doctor in question and the note before us is what the doctor had sent. I asked why he didn't come to court and present it as he should have done. His response was that he had other cases in another court in the county and as the defendant was unfit he didn't feel it was necessary for him to attend. I said that it had been made very clear to him at the last hearing that he must produce a full medical report as to the status of the back injury to his client so that we could then make a proper decision. I asked again whether or not the doctor had examined the defendant. After much batting the ball about, the answer was 'no'. This was the second occasion we were in court and still no doctor had actually physically examined the defendant. I then asked the legal advisor for a warrant to be issued for the arrest of the defendant and for him to be brought to court.

We had to adjourn yet again and set new dates for the trial to continue. This time I told the defence lawyer that if the defendant did not attend court we would send the police round for him. Unless he was bed-ridden and had a detailed doctor's report which described his problem and indicated the prognosis for being fit to come back for trial, he would be brought to court in the police car, held for contempt of court and any other charge that the court could identify. I apologised to the family who had very patiently endured all of this, and we set a date when we could all return.

On the third occasion that we were actually able to sit, we were all at court, including the defence solicitor and, lo and behold, the defendant, who looked remarkably fit for a person who was, apparently, in a lot of pain, suffering from a very serious back problem!

We heard the case for the defence and to say that it was pathetic would be an understatement, but we were duty-bound to hear it. The defendant had been angry and upset and had decided to go and talk to his ex-partner. She wouldn't talk to him, and why should she? Their relationship was over and there was no rational reason for him to be there. He had pushed the boy away and again could give no rational reason for his behaviour. He had not apologised to any of the family and he had no remorse, it was clearly a serious situation. We retired to go through the process of considering the evidence we had heard. At the end of our discussions, we reached a unanimous guilty verdict and went back into court and announced our decision.

At this point the defence lawyer stood up and, on behalf of his client, delivered mitigation which was the worst performance I ever witnessed from a solicitor in court. He extolled the virtues of this good man, his credibility marred by an evil woman. He went on and on to eventually end with the statement that his client had no money so could not pay a fine and he was unable to do community service on account of his bad back! The only possible outcome would be a conditional discharge with a condition being that he did not go near his ex-partner again and that this should only be in place for a year.

We retired again from the courtroom to make our assessment and judgement on punishment. Having followed the correct procedure, we returned to the courtroom, and I announced a six month custodial sentence. I then stated that we were not giving him any reduction in his sentence. He had pleaded not guilty, he failed to attend court and he provided no credible evidence as to why he could not attend. The defendant was duly handcuffed and taken away by the jailers.

His defence lawyer was clearly not happy with the outcome. In fact he was outraged. I was told that he went to see the head clerk of the court to complain about my attitude. I wasn't bothered about that, and indeed my colleagues said that they were 101% supportive and that we should consider reporting him to the Law Society for conduct unbecoming a solicitor. I don't know what happened as far as the complaint against me was concerned, but nothing was ever said to me nor did I hear anything more about it. Normally the convict would have only served three months in prison, but I heard on very good authority that he had to do the full term on account of his disruptive behaviour, and at no time was he incapacitated because of a bad back. I believe he got his just deserts by having to serve his full sentence.

Between you and me, we would like to have given him a longer sentence but we were restricted in the sentence we could give.

Another Domestic Violence

Another domestic case involved a woman who came into court having been assaulted. Her daughter and her daughter's boyfriend were in the house at the time. We were not going to hear from the daughter who was about nine months pregnant as she did not see anything, so she sat at the back of the court. The mother entered the witness box and gave evidence that her former partner came to the house and made threats which caused her to be frightened and fear for her safety. Then he physically struck her. The daughter began shouting at her mother, telling her what to say. The words such as 'he used a clenched fist... he punched your face... you had a nose bleed... go on tell em.' I told her to sit down and stop shouting. After the third or fourth time I told her that if she did not remain quiet she would be barred from the courtroom. I was told to 'f*** o**' at which point we waited whilst the daughter was led from the court. The mother continued with her evidence which was reduced from a punch to a slap to a push. We asked the prosecutor if there were any photographs because with cases involving violence, photographs of any injuries are invaluable. There were none. The police who attended examined her face and body but found nothing to photograph.

A witness to the assault was the daughter's boyfriend and he was called next. However, before he came into court we were told that there was a need to put screens up so that he could not see the defendant because he was frightened of him. So they arranged screens in the courtroom and then told us that they required a speech specialist to be in court because the boy had learning disabilities. So we had a specialist in court to make sure that the boy understood the questions that he was being asked.

We did not stay in court whilst the screens were put in place and when we entered the court, I noticed that the daughter had returned and sat at the back. Before we started, I gave her a warning about her conduct. The boyfriend was then called. He entered the witness box and ensured that he could not be seen by the defendant. We were told that he was the father of the unborn child and although nineteen years of age, he had the mental age capacity of an eight to ten year old child. It was then explained that everybody was going to have to ask their questions in such a way that he would understand. The specialist was introduced to the court and he explained that everybody had to use really simple words, three or four letters in a word was required and he should be able to understand.

In a time consuming way, we progressed through his evidence. No, he did not see the defendant assault the mother. His girlfriend told him what to say. The defendant was against the daughter having anything to do with the boyfriend because she was just using him for her own manipulative purposes. The daughter wanted a flat and to achieve that she needed a baby. Anybody would do and so the 'so called' boyfriend was used. They would not let him move into the house because he had served his purpose, and, unbeknown to him, they didn't want him anymore. The daughter was worried that the defendant could cause trouble and thwart her plans so the assault allegation was concocted. They all left court, the defendant free, the boyfriend dumped and the manipulative daughter would get a flat and all the things that get added on to it. And that's what it was all about, a truly broken society.

Child Neglect

A woman in her twenties stood in the dock looking bored and totally uninterested, even given the fact that she was charged with neglecting her children. A single parent, she had three children in the age range of two to four years. As might be expected there was an abundance of social and welfare people to hand out masses of professional advice. The legal advisor read out the charge and she confirmed her plea of 'not guilty'. The case was outlined to us that on one Saturday night, a child was heard screaming by neighbours who went to the house but could not get anybody to answer their calls. They called the police. The police could not get the attention of anybody and so they needed to gain entry because the young child was still screaming. So with no option they forced an entry. In the house they found the three young children but no adult.

The police witness described the house as reasonably tidy. The children each had a bed. They had to quieten the middle child who was screaming and crying but they could not determine why. A call was made to Social Services as there were very young children alone and they needed to be cared for. They could not determine where the mother was and the plan was to take the children into care until the situation could be sorted out.

At this point, a woman entered the house having clearly been out on the town and was dressed for the occasion. She began shouting at the police officers and staff from Social Services demanding to know what they were doing in her house and with her children. The police asked where she had been. Out clubbing and what's it got to do with you lot, was the reply. She was asked if she left the three children alone in the house to which she claimed that she did not and had asked a girl on the estate to look after them. The girl had arrived with a boy but the defendant was not happy about the boy being there as she did not know him. The girl had said that if the boy could not stay then she was not staying. The defendant wanting her night out agreed and left them all in the house. She had been with a man at a club but at the last minute decided to go home and not take him with her. That is when she arrived to find her house full of police and Social Services people. The police cautioned her.

The Social Services people spoke to the children and the eldest was able to say that the girl and boy stayed and they all watched television.

Whilst the children were in the room, the couple started messing about and doing things. They were doing what mummy did in the bedroom. Eventually the eldest child took the others up to bed leaving the couple in the lounge. The police now needed to speak to the girl.

The girl, aged fifteen, had arrived at the house late and had a boy in tow. There was an argument because the defendant didn't want him to stay but relented. The girl told the children to go to bed but they would not go and sat watching television. The couple ended up having all manner of sex in the lounge in front of the children. When they finished the children had gone from the room. The boy, having had sex with the girl, decided to move on and left the girl at the house. She checked the children who, she said, were in bed and asleep. Now that the boy had gone she wanted to go home and she did just that, leaving the three youngsters alone.

The defendant had done the same thing before but got home as the police arrived. She was given a caution. She told the court she could not afford to pay a proper baby sitter, so made do with whoever she could find. She determined that she had a right to a social life and that involved clubbing. If it was what she wanted, it would mean men going home with her, as she was entitled to have sex with whoever she wanted. She left the girl at the house and did not know that she would not stay until she got home. If anybody was to blame it was the girl for leaving the children. The question was asked as to whether the father of the children could look after them whilst she went out. That was impossible as she did not know who the fathers were.

We, of course, had to hear from the professionals. The young woman was entitled to have a social life beyond the house and television. In fact it was her right. Clearly in this case she had made an error of judgement in leaving the couple in the house and the children might have been at risk. Yes, the girl should have stayed but the time between her leaving and defendant getting home was only about half an hour. They would not expect for young children to be exposed to sex acts, but they were young and would not have understood what was happening. It would be wrong to fine her and cause financial distress and any form of community sentence would cause distress to the children. There was the added issue of the defendant getting somebody to look after the children while she had to do unpaid work. However, Social Services could arrange for a child minder if she had to do unpaid community work. That was a first as they usually pushed for a no punishment option. The defence solicitor recommended that any sentence should be either a total discharge or a conditional discharge. The conditions could be to keep her at home so that she would be unable to go clubbing, it should be for a short period.

You would think that this sort of case is a rarity, but it's not. The police spend a lot of time dealing with domestic situations such as this and they will tell you they are police officers not social/welfare officers. Oh, what happened? For our part we would have put her in prison, but it's the children who suffer, well suffer more than they were already. We decided to request a report from the Probation Service to see what options were available. You can probably guess which option will have been recommended.

A Paedophile Case

A male defendant was brought into court and stood, emotionless, in the dock. Three solicitors comprising his defence team entered and took their places. The solitary Crown Prosecution Service solicitor looked lonely whilst waiting for them to take their places. We had been warned that it was not a pleasant case. The prosecutor outlined the situation for us. The defendant had been released from prison the day before. He had completed half of an eighteen month term in prison for paedophile offences. Having been released from prison at about 10am he had wandered from the prison gates to the main road. He began to walk towards the city but stopped outside a shop. He hung around for some time, a point noticed by members of staff in the shop. He eventually walked away but in the opposite direction to the city. He was next observed standing outside a store. Again he hung about, looking in shop windows and at people.

Just after midday a group of young children, having come from their school, went into the store. They were going to buy sweets. One young girl did not want to buy anything and so waited outside on her own. The defendant saw her and watched. The girl walked a very short distance to look in another shop. At this moment the defendant moved and grabbed the girl, forcing her down the side of the shops to an area behind them. She struggled but was unable to shout as he had his hand over her mouth. Opposite the row of shops was a garage and there were cars on the petrol forecourt being filled. A man filling his car looked up and saw the pair. The situation did not look right and he spoke to a woman who was also filling her car. She agreed with the man's assessment and whilst she went to telephone the police, he went across to challenge the defendant. At this point some of her school friends arrived. The defendant let her go and was kept at the place to await the police. The woman had joined them and took charge of the children.

The police were quick on the scene and after an assessment and the taking of details, arrested the defendant for attempted abduction and assault of a child. He stood before us on those charges but was also subject to his prison release conditions which he had breached. The prosecutor wanted the defendant to be refused bail and held on remand in prison until he could be brought before the courts for trial. Having been presented with the prosecution case we now had to hear the defendant's case which, to our surprise, was to strongly seek bail. The defence team quoted the Human Rights Act in great detail. They quoted from case law. They gave us chapter and verse about the individual before us and why we should show sympathy. He was entitled to bail and that is what they wanted for him.

We had been in court for an hour. At almost two hours we were no further forward. It appeared, according to our legal advisor, that the case being presented by the defence left us little to no room to manoeuvre. With a grim face she said that we may well have to release him on bail. The prosecutor joined in the debate and as forcibly as he could pushed for the remand. My two colleagues were getting upset and I decided that we should leave the courtroom to discuss where we stood on the matter. There was no need for discussion. They wanted the defendant remanded and so did I. Our position was clear. He had been released from prison and had grabbed a young girl attempting to abduct her. He was a convicted paedophile and, on the face of it, had breached his release conditions. There were a number of witnesses who would be called in due course. We were not prepared, knowing what had happened, to release him. We were all prepared to resign from the court rather than go back in and give him bail, even with conditions.

Three of the court's solicitors were dispatched to search the law books for a solution. It was approaching three hours later when one of the senior court solicitors arrived, carrying an ancient tome. The dust blown off, it held the answer: an Act from the 1800's that had not been repealed and meant that, for the charges the individual faced, he could be remanded into custody. Armed with the new evidence we rejected the request for bail, our legal advisor provided the appropriate legal quotation. The defence lawyers read it and very reluctantly accepted it. They did have the right to reapply for bail, but for now he was being held and not an immediate threat to young children. The defendant went to the cells, the defence lawyers departed, not at all happy. I went to thank our solicitors for their valiant work in the library. Justice was served that day. He should have had his licence revoked and returned to prison to serve his full sentence, but he would go to prison for the new offence and have the original outstanding prison time added. It would keep him away from children for a while and then he would be out doing the same again. Next time he might be successful.

What *is* going on? The Supreme Court, which is England's highest court, ruled in February 2011 that rapists and paedophiles must have the right to be removed from the national sex offenders' register if they can prove they are no longer a threat to children. How do you prove that? Who is going to give paedophiles the chance to do it again? Would any of the supporters of this obscene ruling be prepared to take responsibility for these individuals? It appears that there is support from within Parliament.

It appears that the court based its case on previous European Court rulings which enshrine the human right to privacy. It will mean that these 'individuals' get the right to appeal against being on the register fifteen years after their release from prison, because the judges said keeping serious offenders on the register for life was 'disproportionate' and a breach of their right to a private and family life. What about the victims rights? Oh, I forgot, victims have no rights.

There is an option. Those who grant an individual release from the register would have to sign to say there is no risk. However, if a further crime is committed, then those who say they are no longer a risk and are the signatories, would have to serve the same sentence in jail as the convict. Ah, there will a lot of squawking about that proposition but that will focus on the reality of the situation. Remember, because a paedophile has not been before the courts for a long period does not mean that no crime has been committed, it just means that they have not been caught. [*Daily Mail* 17th February 2011]

Yob's Rule, OK

A well-dressed male in his sixties stood in the dock. He was charged with using threatening and insulting behaviour likely to cause alarm and distress to others. Looking at the defendant you would not link him to such an offence but, as the old saying goes, you should not judge a book by its cover.

The prosecution case was that the defendant was at home working in his garden when he noticed some teenagers, male and female, outside his property and causing damage. It was not the first time as he had seen them before and so he went out to see what was happening. He could see that they were up to no good and, as he shouted at them, they ran off down the road screaming abuse at him. It was said that he chased them down the road, threatening them with all sorts of serious consequences. The teenagers were much faster than him and soon disappeared. He thought they were hiding in some bushes and shouted for them to come out. However a man came out of his house, to find out what was going on and confronted him. The defendant told the man what was happening. The man said they were only youngsters and to leave them alone. This made the defendant angry and in no uncertain terms told the man to mind his own business. He did just that and went back into his house and telephoned the police who arrived and arrested the defendant.

The prosecution was quite straightforward. Here was an individual being aggressive towards young people, chasing them down the street, threatening them and when somebody came out to find out what was going on, was abusive to him. It was quite right that the police investigated. However, did they arrest the right person or persons? The prosecution case was very dramatic but we had not heard from the defence yet.

His defence was that yes, he was at home, working in his shed when he heard his dog barking quite loudly and so went out to see what was causing the disturbance. He found a group of youngsters outside his property and they were causing damage. This was nothing new, because they had been causing damage in the area for some time. He had, in fact, called the police on numerous occasions as had others in the area, but nothing had been done to resolve the problem. The police did not investigate, monitor the situation or patrol the area. He went out and challenged the group, perhaps a very foolish thing to do these days as he could have been beaten up or worse, stabbed to death for doing so. He was greeted with a torrent of foul and abusive language and threats. He moved to the edge of his property, still telling them to go away and stop doing what they were doing. He was also trying to identify them so he could call the police. They ran off down the road, screaming abuse. He still wasn't fully sure who they were or how many, so he followed them. He was very much aware that they were a gang as opposed to him as an individual. He did not want confrontation as he was a man in his sixties.

He told us that the gang comprised of both males and females, in the age range of about thirteen to fourteen years. He followed them as he wanted to try and find out who they were and identify where they lived, but they ran away and disappeared. He reached a group of houses just down the road from where he lived. He thought that the youths had split up and that two girls were hiding in bushes so he shouted for them to come out and identify themselves. Of course nobody appeared, but a man from one of the houses came out to see what was going on. He shouted at the defendant to enquire what was going on. In reply the defendant said the youths were causing damage and he was trying to identify them. The man told him to leave them alone. At this point the defendant became angry and told the male to mind his own business. With that, the man went back into his own home and called the police. The police arrived and the defendant was arrested and taken to a police station and charged with the offence. The police were not in the slightest bit interested in the activities of the teenagers, past or present, or the damage they were causing.

The defendant produced a number of character references, including one from a former Chief Constable. Others identified that he had been involved with charity work. There was one to state that he was an active member of Neighbourhood Watch and had been in contact with the police on many occasions but that no action had been taken. The evidence showed that he had been a reputable business man until his retirement and not a man who was aggressive or part of our 'yob' culture. He was a man who was rightly trying to defend his own property, and that of others, from the 'yobs' who a society seeks to protect. Having heard all of the evidence from the police who made the arrest and a written statement from the man who was told to mind his own business, who had not been called to give evidence in court; we finally heard from the defendant. It was time for the decision making process. For the heinous crime of attempting to defend his property and those of his neighbours and for attempting to identify the 'yobs', we the bench, unanimously sentenced the defendant to a total discharge. We were not allowed to tell the man that he had done well in taking a stand against a bunch of 'yobs', but perhaps our sentence reflected that. A total discharge means that the man was not punished in any way, he did not have a criminal record and he was free to leave the court.

Afterwards in the quiet of the court when everybody else had gone we did make comment to the CPS that, perhaps, they should invite the police to look more closely and seriously at the cases that they investigate. They should explore the situation rather than bring cases like this to court where members of the public are held to ransom by 'yobs' who rule our cities and towns and country areas. But on this particular day, three magistrates felt that justice was done.

I heard of a similar case involving a Mr Alfred Tipson, aged seventy, who became so desperate with anti-social behaviour he let off a warning shot with an air rifle, but he accidentally hit a fifteen year-old yob in the neck. The incident happened after he saw one of the gang pull a wooden slat off a neighbour's fence. For some ten years, Mr Tipson and his family had suffered yobs shouting abuse, causing criminal damage, wiping excrement over residents' property and even urinating on his porch. His neighbour, who had an underlying heart condition, suffered a fatal heart attack the day after he and Mr Tipson confronted the yobs after they ripped a slat from his fence. The court was told that Mr Tipson and his wife endured a 'living nightmare' and along with all the neighbours had logged over 350 reports to the police.

The jury found Mr Tipson not guilty of wounding with intent and not guilty of unlawful wounding. It was said that he looked visibly relieved and hugged his family, who had been there to support him as he left the court. However, that is not the end of matters as he had previously pleaded guilty to possessing a firearm with intent to cause fear and will have to be sentenced on that charge.

The victim's mother, who cannot be identified for legal reasons, wept outside of the court. She said: 'I am gutted, absolutely devastated. The whole incident could have been a lot more serious. The pellet went into my son's neck right next to his jugular. He is now left with a one inch scar. He doesn't even play out that much. We had been for a family meal that night and he had only been out with his friends for about half an hour. Don't get me wrong he is no angel but this verdict is telling people that if they have a problem with local youths, to just shoot them with a gun.'

A Devon and Cornwall police spokesman said: 'Although we sympathise with any resident who has to endure anti-social behaviour, there is a process that has been proven to successfully tackle community issues. While there is no instant solution, it is wrong for anyone to take matters into their own hands.' [*Daily Mail* 4th February 2011]

It is refreshing to see that after 350 reports the police did *nothing* to stop the problem but sped to arrest the victim, Mr Tipson, for taking drastic action. Still, the police met a target with an arrest and the CPS got another target point for the prosecution. The jury got the message and did the right thing. If the mother took charge of her son and stopped him being a yob, he would not have been shot and Mr Tipson would not have stood trial. I hope the judge does the right thing at the sentencing.

Another case, not one that I was involved with, shows how employers trust their employees and when that trust is broken it can have implications that may be out of character. The case of Simon Cremer is an example, when he paraded thief Mark Gilbert through the streets of Witham, Essex, wearing the handmade cardboard sign saying: 'THIEF. I Stole £845 am on my way to the police station.'

He took him to the police station after discovering that he had written out a company cheque to himself and taken it to Cash Converters. Staff at Cash Converters were suspicious and contacted

Mr Cremer who called Gilbert into work to confront him. Gilbert admitted the crime and he was taken to the police station. It was there that Gilbert was let off with a police caution while Mr Cremer, his brother and two colleagues were charged with false imprisonment which carries a maximum life sentence. At court the case against them was dropped. But to add insult to injury, Gilbert sued Mr Cremer for his 'humiliation'. Gilbert started the legal action against his boss in a bid to claim for two years of lost earnings and the 'distress' he suffered. He claimed it had been for the trauma, distress and psychological help he said he needed after the incident. The outcome was that Mr Cremer had to pay out £5,000 in compensation and £8,000 court costs to the worker who stole from him. He said:

'He stole from me yet he is the one who is walking away with the money. It makes me so angry. This has left me with no faith in the justice system whatsoever – absolutely none.' [*The Sun* 16th February 2011]

Whilst I really do sympathise with Mr Cremer as did the court, he was technically in the wrong. I am appalled that a figure of £5000 was awarded in compensation. Victims of serious assault do not get close to that sum of money. Had Gilbert not stolen the cheque then he would not have had a case but to reward theft is wrong.

The message is clear with these cases in that normally law abiding citizens are driven to extremes because in our do-gooder society nobody is willing to deal with the real issues. It's easier to prosecute the victims than the offenders.

What's Yours Is Mine

Theft is really popular! The problem with theft is that the perpetrator thinks that when he/she steals from a retail outlet or a house that they are stealing from a very large corporate body or an insurance company. That, in their opinion, makes stealing other peoples' property quite acceptable. The person or business that has been robbed just makes a claim and everybody is a winner. We know that the holder of an insurance policy generally has to pay the first part of a claim and then, when renewing a policy, may well have to pay more to get cover. Retail outlets cover their losses by putting up prices, so the consumer pays. The only real winner is the thief who gets away with the crime.

In one case, the defendant, a young man who was unemployed and probably unemployable, stood in the dock. He was one of hundreds who pass through the courts each day. Their whole life is based on getting by on benefits and money they can obtain by stealing or handling of stolen goods. He had never worked and never would. He was on job seekers allowance but would never seek a job. If he was sent to a prospective employer, his attitude would kill any prospects of work stone dead. Who wants to employ somebody with no interest, better to employ somebody from Europe who wants to work.

Standing in the dock, he looked lethargic and quite frankly, pathetic. He was clearly no stranger to court and being there was just another inconvenience. You could read in his face that if he was found guilty he had lost nothing, after all what could we do. I know the old saying, 'you should not judge a book by its cover' but when you have seen the wasted generation stroll though the courts you get to know. He gave his personal details to the legal adviser and heard the charge read out. In a monotone voice he pleaded not guilty to theft or handling stolen goods.

The prosecutor presented an outline of the case which involved a shed on private property that had been broken into and a motorbike stolen. The shed was located in the back garden of a house close to a gate which allowed access to the street. The shed was always kept secure with a padlock.

The prosecutor called the first witness, the owner of the motorbike. The man who lived at the house had a unique motorbike which he kept locked up in his garden shed. He discovered that the shed had been broken into and the motorbike stolen. The police investigated the incident, and were soon able to identify the individual before us, but they did not recover the motorbike. Clearly the motorbike was his pride and joy and on the Saturday, he and his brother had cleaned and polished it. He was adamant that after they cleaned it, they put it back in the shed and padlocked the shed door. The back gate was closed and a bolt was in place.

On the Sunday morning the owner of the motorbike noticed that the shed door was damaged. It was a brick shed with a tiled roof and had a wooden door and a window. The motorbike was gone. The owner called the police. So it was established that there was a motorbike, and we knew when the motorbike was last seen. From the evidence we could establish that the shed had been locked correctly and that it had been broken into and the motorbike stolen. So, who did it.

The prosecutor explained that the door of the shed had been badly damaged; wood was ripped away when the door had been forced open and the police discovered two very good finger prints. One was on the wooden door surround which had been broken away and the other was found inside the shed itself. The police checked their records and found that they matched those of the man standing in the dock. The police went to his home and he was arrested and taken to the police station. No motorbike could be found.

At the police station the defendant pleaded his innocence. He didn't do it and he knew nothing about the shed or the motorbike. His defence was that whilst he lived in the area of the house where the break-in had occurred, he did not know exactly where it was and he'd never been there. The police had two very good, very clear fingerprints and the police records showed that they matched those of the defendant. With that sort of evidence our man was banged to rights, so why was he saying that it was not him.

The prosecuting lawyer made the point to him that if he was not guilty then the court would want to know how his fingerprints got on the broken wood and inside the shed. The prosecutor pushed for an answer. He asked him, 'Do you accept that the prints found at the site were yours?' He really did look lethargic and pathetic as he merely shrugged his shoulders and agreed they were. Pressed further, he was asked how his fingerprints got there. Well of course, he had no idea because he had never been there. It really was like watching grass grow, but he had to be given the chance to answer the allegations. Pushed further, he thought somebody else must have used his fingerprints without his knowledge. The courtroom went quiet, nobody spoke, nobody laughed. Everybody just looked at the young man. His solicitor had his head down looking at some papers and, was clearly thinking about his next case.

The prosecutor remained calm and asked the defendant to hold up his hands. With what appeared to be a nervous smile, he raised his hands. The scene was one of us all counting the fingers on each hand and yes they were all there. 'You still have all of your fingers,' exclaimed the prosecutor. The defendant looked at his hands as if to make sure and replied that yes, he did. 'Then can you tell the court how somebody could use your fingers which are quite clearly attached to your body without you knowing,' questioned the prosecutor. The defendant looked confused and thought about it for a moment then responded that somebody must have used them because he was not at the shed.

This now drew comments from my colleagues as to the mental state of the defendant. I cautiously raised the matter with the court. Not allowed to say, 'is this man bonkers' even though that is what we all thought. The defendant's solicitor, the prosecutor and our legal advisor all confirmed that the defendant was fit to stand trial. So the case continued.

We heard how, on the Saturday night, he had been out to a local pub and consumed quite a few drinks during the course of the evening. Under further examination he dithered but clearly stated there was a possibility that perhaps he did walk back past the house. Of course he wasn't sure because he was drunk. After more questioning he sort of relented to consider that perhaps he did see the shed, but he couldn't really remember because he was drunk. He then decided that it was possible that he did go into the garden. He might, just might have seen the shed and gone inside. But he didn't break in, because he was drunk and he couldn't really remember.

He remained adamant that he did not see, steal or handle a motorbike. Finger print evidence showed he was present at the scene of the break in, the prints being on the damaged wooden parts of the outside of the door frame and inside of the shed. It was put to him that if he did not break into the shed, and he did not steal the motorbike, please help the court by telling who did?

When put to him in this way a plausible answer escaped him. He then repeated that he had been drinking, and so there was a possibility that he did go in and look at the shed and found the door to be broken. There may have been bits strewn about, and he probably picked up a piece of the door frame and then had a look inside the shed because he was curious. Once inside he rummaged around but there was nothing in there and certainly no motorbike. So, although he was a little bit drunk, he now appeared to recall that, perhaps he had been at the shed. However, when the question was repeated, did you steal the motorbike? The answer was 'no.'

The evidence that we had was that the motorbike was stolen. We have two fingerprints that clearly belonged to him, which he did not deny. He consistently lied about his whereabouts, his access to the shed and access to the damage of the shed. Together with the changes to his story, and the proviso that he did not have detachable fingers which somebody else could have borrowed, it was quite easy for us to reach a guilty verdict.

He was not happy with the verdict and his solicitor, in summing up the case, had told us that his client accepted that there were fingerprints on the door frame and inside the shed, but he did not take the motorbike. He had arrived on the scene after it had been stolen. Therefore, whilst he might have been guilty of entering the shed, he couldn't have been guilty of stealing the motorbike!

An offence of theft from a private property generally receives community service or a fine depending on the seriousness. Now, we took the view that even though it was the shed, it was within the grounds of the property and was therefore part of it. The defence objected which we did not accept. To give a community service sentence we need the Probation Service to provide a report about the individual. The objective is to find out whether our man was suitable to undertake unpaid work and also if he is prepared to do it. He looked capable of undertaking work, but we anticipated there would be one of the usual excuses as to why he could not. Depression, bad back, ingrowing toenail, aversion to work or the need to look after an aged granny are among the long list of reasons that were regularly regurgitated. Breaking into a private property and stealing a valuable motorbike is a serious offence. He had pleaded not guilty and so was not entitled to the full discount on sentence. In this case, following conviction he did undertake a community sentence as his punishment. To this day we still do not know what happened to the motorbike, but it was probably a case of stealing to order, organised by those who recruit in the pub.

The Magic Bicycle

A woman came into court and made her way to the dock arguing with everybody about her wrongful arrest. In the dock she gave details as requested and then began a speech about why she should not be there. She was told to keep quiet as her solicitor would speak on her behalf. The prosecution case was that a lad had had his bicycle stolen. The police were called. The lad gave a description of the bike and said that an older boy had taken it and had gone to a house up the road. Armed with this information, the police went to the house and knocked on the front door. A young girl opened it and stood back. The police officer enquired if her mother was at home. The young girl pointed to what was the lounge. The officers entered the property and went into the room. A woman, scruffily dressed, smoking a cigarette was watching television. Also in the room was another young girl and an older boy. None looked up at the officers when they entered but just carried on watching television. Leaning against the wall in the lounge was a bicycle identical to the one described by the victim. The officers enquired as to whose bike it was. They got no acknowledgement. One officer went and stood in front of the wide screen, slim line television. The woman snarled at him telling him to move, as she was watching the programme. He was not going to move so she asked what they wanted. They asked again who owned the bicycle. The woman turned and looked at it.

'Whose is that?' She asked the officers. Then, before they could answer, she turned to the children and asked if they knew whose it was. 'No,' they replied. The woman looked at the officer standing in front of the television and said, 'Don't know whose it is, don't know how it got in here.'

The other officer said, 'There is a bike in your front room and you don't know whose it is.'

'Nope, no idea.'

An officer explained that it matched the description of a bike stolen from a lad down the road.

'Must be his then, aint ours.'

As one officer said 'We will take it back to him then,' the other officer asked if they owned the television. An argument began to develop and the women asked where their warrant was. Well they didn't have one but could get one and return.

The officer, not letting go of the situation, said that the TV was the same make as some sets that had been stolen. He asked where she got it.

'Don't know,' was the answer. 'One day it just sort of appeared.'

I could go on but suffice to say, this type of situation is the bread and butter of some police work. The outcome was that the bike was returned to the rightful owner and the television confiscated as one of a number stolen in a break in at a store. The woman had to do another magic trick at the pub and buy one as it fell gently off a lorry. Oh, the bicycle. A few days later the lad reported it stolen and it was found in the woman's shed, she was adamant that she did not know how it got there. Yes, the officers found her sitting in front of a new wide screen slim line television. The good fairies, elves and goblins were very busy in that neighbourhood.

Crime And The Pub

It would seem that a lot of theft and handling stolen goods emanates from a pub and that was the case with a young male who was only just old enough to be in the adult court. Like so many he looked lethargic and pathetic. The legal advisor sought his personal details and identified that he was before the court for the offences of driving a truck with no tax, no insurance, no MOT as well as a lot of faults with the vehicle. Further, he only had a provisional driving licence and nobody was in the vehicle with him. The truck had worn tyres that made it illegal to drive and the brakes were ineffective, almost to the point of not working. The truck, when stopped by the police, was piled high with scrap metal.

The prosecutor was told that it was not the defendant's truck. OK, whose truck was it? Some bloke he met in a pub. What was the person's name? Don't know. Have you seen the person before? Can't remember. What was the name of the pub? Don't know. Where was the pub? Can't remember.

'So how did you come to talk to this person?' The prosecutor enquired.

'He bought me a couple of pints.'

' What did this generous person look like?'

'Think he was a traveller and so was his mate.'

The prosecutor asked what a traveller looked like, for example was he tall, short, big, small or have dark or fair hair.

'Can't remember.'

' So how did you get to be driving a truck?'

'They asked me if I wanted to earn some cash with no questions asked. I asked what they wanted me to do. They wanted me to drive a truck from one place to another. I thought that it was easy money so I agreed.'

The prosecutor pointed out that he did not have a driving licence that allowed him to drive alone. The defendant agreed but said that it was not a long journey so he thought it would be OK. The prosecutor pointed out that the truck did not have road tax, insurance, MOT, had bald tyres and the brakes did not work properly. The truck was also overloaded. The defendant considered that it was not his problem because it was not his truck. It was down to the blokes who own it. The prosecutor then identified that he was driving erratically when the police stopped him. The defendant grinned and enlightened us that the truck had bad steering.

So we had an individual before us charged with a number of offences to which he had at least pleaded guilty. His excuse to the court was that it was not his fault that the vehicle was unsafe. He had no money to pay a fine, he had no job and no prospects. In fact he had no interest other than claiming benefits and a life of petty crime.

Whilst the man walked away virtually unpunished, the question remains as to whether the owner of the truck was identified and, unless the truck was a stolen vehicle, prosecuted for the motoring offences. The answer is no. There was a crime and one of the criminals was caught, prosecuted and convicted. Why go looking for problems elsewhere, particularly if it involves travellers and all of the potential conflicts that involves? What about the load of scrap metal? Who went and claimed it? The answer is simple, nobody, after all who is going to make a claim for stolen property and who is going to explain how the copper from church roofs and other such places ended up in the truck. Those who set up the crime lost on that occasion but there are plenty of other places waiting for them to call upon.

The Yobs' World Of CCTV

Somebody claimed that we have more surveillance cameras than any other western country. We probably need them because of our escalating crime rate. Our streets are well covered as big brother spies on us. However, where law and order is concerned they do have a value and one particular case demonstrated the value of CCTV. The case involved a defendant, a football yob who was one of two individuals in the crowd, shouting obscenities at the football players. When the stewards approached them they were subjected to the same loutish behaviour and obscenities directed at them in front of a lot of witnesses.

Two people were charged, but we only had one defendant in court on this particular day. He was categorised as a 'football yob' although this was not court terminology. The courts do not use the word yob, remember the Human Rights Act! We heard from a number of witnesses who were at the ground. They told us what had been said, told us what the threats were and identified the defendant standing in the dock as being the main perpetrator. The yob in the dock continued to say that he was not guilty as it wasn't him. Then the prosecution produced CCTV. The video pictures were absolutely brilliant because you could see the stand, see all the people in the stand and then it zoomed in to pick out the two individuals. It was good enough to show very clearly, the yob threatening, waving his arms and obviously shouting, although we couldn't hear what he was shouting. We saw the stewards moving in to try and resolve the problem and how the yobs became more aggressive. However, the stewards restrained the defendant and he was taken away and handed over to the police. He was then transferred to the police station.

The defendant stood in the dock and watched the TV screen. When the recording finished he was asked to explain his actions. He said that it was not him and he did not know who it was. So we had to watch the CCTV footage two or three times and each time, he was adamant that it was not him. In fact he became increasingly aggressive when saying it was not him and he did not know who it was. Everybody else in court, including his own solicitor who was defending him, accepted it was him. In the end he was told by me to leave the dock and go and stand beside the TV, which he did. We re-ran the footage again. There was a close up of his face and there was no question at all that it was him. I did check to see whether he had a double, a twin brother or others in the family who looked like him and he confirmed that he did not. Was he at the football match at the game on that particular day? Yes he was, very difficult to deny it in reality as he was arrested inside the football ground. We had the evidence of the football stewards, the police and CCTV footage and we could reach no other conclusion than it was him and that he was guilty. Even when we sentenced him to a fine, he was still shouting that it wasn't him and it was an injustice, and that he had been picked on. But it does show the merits of CCTV when you can clearly see events unfold.

The value of CCTV provided evidence in another situation where a female had been taken to a police station. She was drunk and disorderly and had to be placed in a cell. She claimed that during the process of getting her to the cell she was attacked by the police and assaulted. Again, it was CCTV that gave us valuable evidence. The cell area of the police station had a system installed. The coverage we were provided with clearly showed that when she was being led by one officer towards a cell, she turned and started to violently attack him. Other officers had to come to his assistance to help restrain her and get her safely into the cell and get it locked. When she saw the evidence on the TV and that it supported what the prosecutor had said, she had not realised that the custody and cell area were covered by cameras and so changed her plea to guilty.

Ideally this should have been resolved before it came before the court but unfortunately, because of the way the government of the day operated, its system of getting convictions or crimes solved and the misuse of the Human Rights Act, this sort of case came to court. I fully accept that we need to protect the rights of the individual, however, such cases waste police officers' valuable time as they had to come to court to give evidence. In turn it is a waste of court time and that also means a waste of taxpayers' money.

Good Dogs

A couple were walking through a park late at night when they saw two men by the bronze statue called 'Weathered Man', which was lying on its side. It had cost £3,000 to create and a further £500 to install. They then saw a four-by-four vehicle being driven up to the statue and they realised it was about to be stolen so they telephoned the police. A male attempted to escape by jumping over a fence near where the couple were watching from a hiding place. As soon as the police arrived they told them where he had gone. The police then let German Shepherd police dog Zak loose to apprehend the fleeing individual. The dog followed the scent to a nearby courtyard where the defendant was hiding and then detained him by biting his left buttock.

On hearing how the criminal was caught, Judge Julian Lambert who has criticised the justice system for being soft said in court: 'Good! I hope it hurt. Well done Zak!'

At the time of the statue offence, the male was subject to two suspended sentences totalling twelve weeks which had been imposed for burglary and handling stolen goods. Judge Lambert then sentenced the male to six months in jail for the attempted statue theft and three months consecutively for breaching his suspended sentences. He then publicly commended the couple who had spotted the theft and called the police. He ordered that they should receive rewards of £100 each. [*Daily Mail* 18th February 2011]

I was sent this next story and thought that it was poetic justice. The police in their pursuit of criminals often use dogs which are well trained. They have the purpose of deterring crime and where that fails, assisting in the apprehension of criminals. One case brought before Greenwich Magistrates' Court involved a fleeing burglary suspect and a large German Shepherd police dog.

The police were following up on a series of burglaries when officers went to investigate the suspicious activities of a man who was seen in a back garden. In addition to police on the ground, a helicopter was called in and having located the individual tracked him and guided police officers with dogs to the area.

Officers keep the dogs on leads until they have a defined target as they cannot have dogs going after law abiding citizens. So the police dog officer will shout loudly, a number of times, for the person to stop and stand still or the dog will be released from its lead. Anybody with any sense will know that you cannot outrun a dog, a big one at that. Everybody knows that police dogs are trained to bring down an individual who runs away. The individual did not stop and so the dog was set free to chase him. When the dog caught up, it pounced. Police dogs are trained to go for arms but in this case the dog bit the individual's ear. The dog was not impressed and spat out the ear which was recovered allowing the police to pack it in ice. The male was taken to hospital where it was sewn back on.

The police retraced his escape route through a number of gardens, and found a rucksack filled with suspected stolen property. Following four days spent in hospital, the male appeared in court charged with burglary. He sported a large white bandage covering his right ear. The chairman asked if he could hear properly whilst in the dock to which he replied he could, just about. Following the hearing he was remanded in custody.

The individual is now threatening to sue and it is said that if successful he could get as much as £50,000 compensation and because he is jobless he would qualify for Legal Aid. If found guilty and there was justice, he should have to pay for the ambulance and the hospital treatment. We have yet to see if the do-gooders are on the trail of the police dog, demanding that it be put down on the basis that it is dangerous. It must be only a matter of time!

Crime On The Highway

The courts get lots of cases where a vehicle has gone through a speed camera and has been 'flashed' for speeding. The police then identify the address registered with the DVLA for the vehicle owner. The vehicle owner is then sent a communication which asks who was driving the said vehicle on the particular day at the particular time?

Initially the owner of the vehicle would write back and say they had no idea who was driving on the date and time the offence was committed. It would be claimed that two or three people drove the vehicle and they could not say who it was that was driving at that time. It was cause for concern at the courts as clearly vehicles were going through speed cameras exceeding the speed limit. The owner of the vehicle was using as a defence that he or she didn't know who was driving. If you don't know who was driving there is no way you can actually prosecute anybody, fine them or put points on their licence because nobody is named as an offender.

In order to overcome this, the authorities took the view that a system had to be put in place to ensure that when a car was identified by a speed camera for an infringement of the speed limit, the owner of the vehicle would be brought to court. They would be asked to give a reason why it was not known who was driving at the given time. Their answers would determine the way the court dealt with their case. For example, a driver might have insurance that allowed only named drivers to drive, so that cuts down the potential defendants. In some cases the defendant is the only person who is allowed to drive that vehicle and therefore, unless the vehicle is reported stolen, one would consider that the defendant would be the guilty party.

In one case, a man had been summoned to court for failing to disclose who was driving a sports car on a given day at a given time, at a speed that warranted the camera to record a speeding offence. The owner of the vehicle pleaded not guilty, as he didn't know who was driving. His argument to the court was that it could have been him, or it could have been his partner. It was duly noted that his partner was with him in court and whilst he was a well built male, his partner was a very slim petite blonde lady sitting at the back of the court. It was clarified that there were only two people allowed to drive the vehicle, the defendant and his partner. We were presented with a photograph of the offence. It was a photograph taken by a speed camera and it showed a sports car with the hands of the driver visible on the top of the steering wheel. We could not discern who the driver was by facial identity.

So it could not be determined if the driver was male or female, large or small. The defence made a very strong case that clearly there was a picture but it could have been either of the two people. Neither could remember who had been driving the vehicle on that day at that time. As we sat looking at the photograph, one of my female colleagues leaned over and whispered that the picture we had been presented with showed a man's hands, not petite female hands. The case ran its course and the defence said that there was no case to answer. We were then given the opportunity to ask questions. I asked the male in the box to hold up his hand as if he were holding the top of a steering wheel, which he did. I then asked the young lady to come forward and to do the same thing. We compared the two and the evidence in the picture. It was very evident that the photograph showed that it was a man's hands at the top of the steering wheel. We pointed this out to the prosecutor and to the defence solicitor. They examined the photograph and the hands of the couple. It was evident that we had found a weak point in the defence. The defence solicitor consulted with his client and he changed his plea to guilty of failing to provide information as to who was driving on that day.

Following on from that he would be convicted for a speeding offence but we only had to deal with the matter of who was driving at this particular time. It would of course been more prudent to have paid the £60 fine and taken the points on the license, but when we checked the license he already had a considerable number. He felt it was worth trying to get out of the prosecution offence, but on this occasion he failed to do so. Magistrates do not just sit and take things as they are presented to them, they do think, they do consider and they do have minds of their own and are able to invoke justice as and when it's required.

Driving without due care and attention cases are generally interesting, particularly the view point of the defendants who plead not guilty. In one case the prosecution solicitor outlined the circumstances to the court, which involved a man who had left work late at night, on his motor scooter. He came out from where he worked on to a main road which was well lit, and drove up the road to a cross roads with traffic lights. When the lights changed to green he noticed there was a car on the opposite side of the road which was going to turn right, across his route of travel, but he had his lights on and was wearing a fluorescent jacket, so he was sure the driver could see him and he had the right of way. They began to go across at the same time and the other car pulled forward and started to turn right, however, it didn't stop and hit the scooter with him on it. The driver was knocked off and injured and was taken to hospital for treatment. The police arrived and took all the details at the scene of the accident.

On the day we were sitting in court the defendant, a lady, was standing in the dock and the injured party, who clearly still had injuries, sat at the back of the court. The prosecution put forward the case in detail, it was very straightforward and clear to the court, and would have been obvious to even a person with no knowledge of the court system, that the defendant was guilty!

But hang on a minute, we haven't heard from the defence yet!

Once the prosecutor has finished outlining the case and used the immortal words, 'and that is the case for the prosecution' she sat down. That is the end of the prosecution case.

The defence lawyer stood up and to our surprise, instead of hearing a defence case he said, 'Sir, I have to submit a case of 'no case to answer'. In simple terms, my learned friend, indicating to the prosecution solicitor, has not in the prosecution case, actually identified that my client was the driver of the car at the time of the incident.'

We turned our attention very quickly to the prosecutor who had a look of horror on her face. She held her head in her hands before she stood. She stated to the court, 'My learned friend is absolutely correct and on that basis, there is no case to answer.'

Our legal advisor confirmed the situation. I asked the defendant to stand and explained what had happened. As an outcome of failings in the prosecution case, there was no case to answer and she was free to go. The injured party was sitting at the back of the court and had heard a very good prosecution case, and looked pleased with the proceedings. That is until he heard that the defendant was free to go. He sat with his mouth open before shaking his head and leaving the court with the assistance of those who accompanied him.

This case emphasises the vulnerability of the prosecution and the defence in putting their cases. It is particularly important for the prosecution to get the facts right and delivering them to the bench in the appropriate manner. We were certain that the woman was driving; we were certain that she knocked the man off the scooter, but she hadn't been identified and therefore could not be found guilty.

Careless Driving Or Dangerous Driving

A defendant stood in the dock charged with careless driving. The public seating area was filled with people seemingly keen to hear the case. Our legal advisor confirmed the defendant's details, the charge and that he was pleading guilty. The prosecutor gave brief details of the case and whilst doing so caused some agitation with those in the public seating. When he finished he sat, allowing the defendant's solicitor to put forward mitigation on behalf of his client. The information provided to us by the prosecutor and the defence was the case. The penalty was a financial one and we fined the defendant along with awarding costs to the prosecution. The defendant offered to pay the fine immediately and in a great hurry went with the usher to the pay office.

The people sitting in the public area erupted and began to shout at us. I repeatedly asked them to be quiet and when they calmed down I asked what the problem was. It transpired that the driver was arrested for dangerous driving. That was the initial charge but the driver was going to plead not guilty so the CPS and the defence came to an agreement, the driver would accept a charge of careless driving and plead guilty. The prosecutor offered that, in some cases, they would accept a lesser charge (do a deal) to spare the family having go through the trauma of a trial. This sort of deal should be done with the agreement of the defendant and the victim. However, a man screamed that they had not been consulted and no deal was agreed with them. He then added that dead people didn't matter so long as the targets were met.

I asked the prosecutor why the family had not been contacted but he could not answer as he just prosecuted the case as given to him. I then asked if somebody had died in the incident and he confirmed they had. Those in the public seating were incandescent and quite frankly, I sympathised with them. However, I explained that because the case was downgraded to a guilty plea we only heard about the careless driving. On that basis we could only sentence for the lesser crime. We departed the courtroom to a barrage of abuse but there was no point in confronting them further as they had not got their day of justice. I was told that they were given advice on who and where to lodge a complaint. On that day, crime did pay and I was embroiled in it. Neither I or my colleagues were happy playing the political game.

Drink Driving

I always despair at those charged with a drink driving offence who arrived at court and expected sympathy. Well tea and sticky buns were served in the little café in the court but I am sure the staff would not want to hear their bleating. One such case involved an individual who was caught a number of times over the legal limit. Our bench sentencing guideline book identified that prison should be seriously considered. It was not the first time he had been charged with a drink drive offence and each time he had escaped a custodial sentence. He clearly thought that he would do so on this day.

The case was revealed to us, witness gave evidence and documentary evidence was added. It was a straight forward case, he was guilty and had pleaded guilty. We then heard the mitigation. Mr X was a business man employing a small number of people. It was put to us that because it was a small enterprise he was the sole person in charge. If he was not there then the business would collapse and the staff would be thrown on the pile of the unemployed. Did he have a wife or partner who could stand in? No. He had marital problems and that was why he was drunk when driving his car. This cat and mouse game went on for some time until I intervened and asked Mr X what arrangements he had for covering the business if he had an accident. Well in that situation he could make arrangements and gave the name of a person who knew the business and could stand in and keep it running. The staff knew what to do so it would be OK.

I then had notes pushed over from my colleagues asking what was the difference between an accident and going to prison. The argument he put forward was that an accident could not be avoided but we need not send him to prison. So it was his contention that we could not send him to prison because the business would fold. He would not be able to undertake a community sentence because he could not spare the time. He also pointed out that as a disqualified driver he could not get to a place of work. He could pay a small fine but his wife was taking him to the cleaners over the pending divorce, so he may not have any money. We looked at all the options in the context of the evidence and the seriousness of the offence and decided that with all the evidence and to be consistent, prison was the justifiable option. We awaited the arrival of the cells staff and I then told him that he was going to prison for eight weeks. If he behaved he would only serve half of that time inside and that he would be released on licence.

As the cells staff attempted to get handcuffs on him he screamed at me 'You f****** bastard, you've destroyed me and my business.' He was still screaming the same obscenities as he went down to the cells. Three of us made the decision and we reflected on the old adage, 'don't do the crime, if you don't want to do the time'.

Driving at Work

Now when you get in a vehicle and drive it on the public highway you are responsible for the vehicle and that includes anything being carried in it or on it. The fact that the driver is at work and driving a company vehicle does not matter. The driver is responsible. However the business also shares that responsibility in that the vehicle must be in good working order and safe to drive.

The man in the dock was driving a company pick-up truck to take him and the equipment he needed to undertake a day's work. The equipment was too large for the vehicle and hung out from the vehicle in a dangerous manner. He was stopped by the police and highways agency staff who deemed that he could not continue to travel with an unsafe load. The man explained at the time that he was told by his boss to load the items on his truck as the bigger truck was not available. He was charged with an offence of driving with a dangerous load.

In court he explained to us that he was told by his boss to do it. When he raised concerns he was told to either drive the vehicle as it was or be fired. Now I know the law says that you cannot fire somebody just like that, but many smaller businesses do not bother with the law and hire and fire as they please. So employees do not complain because word gets about that you are a trouble maker and you do not get employed. That is a fact. Our man had a family and could not afford to be fired, so he drove the vehicle in the hope that he did not get caught.

So there is a dilemma. Technically the man is guilty of an offence which would warrant a fine and points on his driving licence. I asked the prosecutor if the company had been investigated and faced any charges. He asked the Highways man, who said no, because it was not their job to do so. I raised the matter of him being ordered to take the equipment by his boss and if not he would be fired. Did that not matter? Again the focus was on the fact that he was the driver and he was responsible.

My colleagues were as uncomfortable with this as I was. Our legal advisor was consulted in open court, to determine what sentence options were available. I cannot remember what sentences we gave but it was probably a total discharge. I then addressed the Highways prosecutor to say that we understood the law and their approach, but if companies are breaking law and hiding behind the threat of sacking staff, then something needs to be done. We all departed the best of friends. Of course nothing was done to change the situation.

Death by Dangerous Driving

I was approached by a solicitor to consider if I would be able to provide an expert report. It was for a pending case in which a man had been charged with the serious offence of causing death by dangerous driving. It was a subject that I knew little about and doubted whether I could be of help. It then transpired that it was an 'at work' accident and it was thought that the company, who had not been charged with any offence, was failing both their employee and the person who had been killed.

When reading the case file it took very little time to discover that the company who employed the defendant and provided the vehicle, trailer and equipment, or lack of it in this case, played a major part in the cause of the accident which caused the death of a pedestrian. It became obvious that neither the company nor its managing director were investigated or prosecuted. I began with the question, why? The police had what they considered to be an open and shut case and the driver was to blame. It later emerged that although there was a meeting with the Health and Safety Executive who could have assisted with any investigation of the company, the police failed to obtain their support as defined in guidance titled, Work-Related Deaths – A Protocol for Liaison. It was later in court that we learned that the police failed to provide minutes of the meeting. In fact the managing director was actually called as a police witness having made declarations in his statements that showed that he had clearly breached health and safety legislation.

Not being an expert on road traffic offences, I understand that for the act of causing death by dangerous driving the following sentences could apply:

The maximum prison sentence is fourteen years but in a case such as this it could have been immediate custodial sentence of between two and five years. To avoid that there would have to be exceptional circumstance. There would be a minimum driving disqualification of two years. So the defendant who was pleading not guilty faced a high tariff and prison would be inevitable if found guilty. In his favour there was an excellent solicitor and barrister forming his defence team.

The case involved the defendant who was driving a works van and was 'at work' at the time. He was accompanied in the vehicle by three other employees and the van was towing a trailer containing plastic drainage pipes and equipment required for the work project. Attached to the trailer was a steel cage that kept the pipes and other items in the trailer. It had an access gate at the back which spanned the width of the trailer and could be opened so that it could reach the side of the trailer.

The prosecution case was based on the allegation that the gate had not been securely closed and had swung open during the journey, striking a pedestrian causing a fatal injury. However, the defendant stated that the gate was closed and secure before departure and was still closed upon arrival at the work site and he maintained that position. In fact he told the court that he closed and secured the gate every day and did so on the day in question.

The police investigation began with a search for the vehicle that caused what was considered a hit and run incident. The following day at the site of the accident they stopped vehicles travelling along the road to seek any information about the incident. They stopped the van and questioned the defendant who was driving and the passengers who all said they knew nothing about it. It was about three weeks later when the van was stopped again on the same road because the police were looking for a blue vehicle and the van and trailer were blue. The outcome was that the trailer was impounded and samples of paint taken. The principal evidence were specks of blue paint removed from the skull of the deceased and samples of paint taken from the trailer that matched. In addition the injuries that caused the death matched the gate profile. The driver was arrested for causing death by dangerous driving.

The trailer gate was held closed by two-drop catches and a piece of frayed rope that was tied round as an added safety precaution. In theory with the catches closed and the rope tied, the gate should have been secure. The defendant told the police and the court that on the day of the incident he closed the gate, dropped the catches in place and tied the rope. He did it every day and he did it on the day of the incident. Of course in reality he would never remember what he actually did on the day as it was a repetitive action and he should have said that he normally secured the gate but could not remember for that specific day.

It transpired that the drop catches in this case were well worn and could if the trailer hit a bump in the road, jump up and open. To make the catches really secure, safety clips should have been put in place but they were not provided. However, even if the catches had come open, the rope even in its very poor state, if tied, would have held the gate closed.

A gate swinging free on the trailer as it bounced along the road would have been seen in the wing mirrors or heard as it crashed into the side of the trailer. Well none of those in the van noticed or heard anything or any noise that would have been made by a swinging gate. If the gate was free then it swung open and then wedged itself closed for the remainder of the journey.

The focus has been on the defendant who appeared to have failed to close the gate securely but are drop catches that could jump open and a piece of frayed rope sufficient? The answer is no. The drop catches should have been fitted with safety clips which would have ensured that the catches could not open. The issue now turns to the company and its managing director who should have ensured that the safety clips were provided. The safety clips would then be attached to the trailer by chains that stopped them being lost when not being used. This simple device was missing and was a factor in the death of an innocent pedestrian.

The managing director holds responsibility under the Health and Safety at Work etc Act 1974 and accompanying health and safety regulations. This means that his duties included ensuring that all employees under his management are provided with the necessary information, instruction, training and supervision to enable them to carry out their work without risk to their health and safety, or to the heath and safety of any other person not employed but who could be affected by the company's activities.

The company, on its website, stated that it has its own comprehensive health and safety policy, risk assessment, method statement and that safety was a priority. Evidence from the managing director and general manager in court clearly showed that this was not the case. The company had in the past engaged a consultancy to provide some health and safety information and create a number of documents and forms for use by the company. However, only blank copies were provided to the court which indicated that the documents and forms were not used at the time of the incident. This meant that the managing director had not complied with his legal duties regarding health and safety.

The general manager who had been appointed the health and safety officer had received no training in the subject which was evidenced in court when questioned by the defence barrister who clearly exposed his lack of knowledge. The general manager told the court that he had issued every member of staff with an Employee Health and Safety Booklet. The managing director, when giving evidence, also claimed that every member of staff had received a copy. Nobody who gave evidence had ever heard of or received a copy.

During that police investigation the managing director made a statement in which he states: 'Each team has an unofficial team leader.

The team leader isn't in charge of the rest of the team' 'X (mechanic) is in charge of the vehicles and all paperwork in relation to the vehicles...X made the cages for the trailers to carry the pipes to the sites, I don't know what dates they were made... Any new team members that join the company get verbal training and advice from the other team members in relation to loading the trailers; there is no formal training.'

In a second statement to the police the managing director states: 'There is no written policy instruction in relation to any training, it is given verbally. It is the driver's responsibility to report anything that isn't secure, or anything that isn't roadworthy with the vehicles to the company... Since this incident I have spoken to the other teams and advised them, once someone has secured the trailer gate, get another member of the team to check it.'

He then states: 'The cages are built by X to fit the trailers, and are built to our own standard, which I feel is an appropriate standard for the work they are used for.'

[The managing director cannot say that he 'feels' that the cages are made to an appropriate standard. He cannot generalise, it either is or it is not. If it is an appropriate standard then the company should have the drawings and details available for inspection.]

In a third statement the managing director states: 'The employee's health and safety handbook is something that employees are given a copy of when they start with the company. They are given it when they first start as part of their induction which they take away with them and read... When we take on work with a company we issue a method statement and a risk assessment which covers our work while we are on a customer's site; this doesn't cover the transport or the pipes from [the company site] to the customer's site... The blue rope that teams use to tie round the gate and post of the cages was already in use when I took over the company; I don't know who introduced the use of the rope but I have allowed this procedure to continue as I know the gates are secured by other safety/security devices other than the rope.'

[The court heard from witnesses that there were no inductions, no health and safety handbooks issued and none had seen risk assessments.]

There was a risk assessment form that had been prepared by the consultants for the loading and securing the trailer. The form identified the possibility of the trailer gate opening but was totally ignored by management. It also stated that a visual check was required by another employee prior to driving the vehicle. This was in conflict with the reality because the managing director stated in evidence that: 'Since this incident I have spoken to the other teams and advised them, once someone has secured the trailer gate, get another member of the team to check it.' Another failure is that it should be an 'instruction' or 'directive' not advice and it should have been in place and acted upon. None of the employees who gave evidence had ever seen or heard of a risk assessment.

It is understood that it is the responsibility of the driver to check his vehicle and trailer to ensure that it is roadworthy and that any loads are safe and secure. However, the driver is required to follow company requirements and if a system of work is not defined and the appropriate equipment provided then the managing director has failed in his legal duty. In this case, employees were left to do what they considered to be correct and acceptable and it was clear that that there was absolutely no health and safety management. It is the responsibility in a workplace activity for the employer to provide instructions and training as to what the company requires its drivers to do and for the company to provide the equipment to be able to do it. Following such instruction a record of all employees must be recorded and kept on file. There was no evidence of any records being kept.

The managing director told us that there were no formally appointed supervisors but there were what he terms as unofficial team leaders but as he revealed, the team leader isn't in charge of the rest of the team. This means that because there were no supervisors appointed, the unofficial team leader has no responsibilities and was not empowered to take any leadership role.

The company mechanic told the court that he did not make the trailer cage but that he maintained all of the company's vehicles, trailers and equipment and he decided what should be recorded on his maintenance cards. He told the court that the trailers were only serviced every five to six years and because there was no maintenance programme in place, he did not know when the trailer in the case was last serviced. The managing director had the responsibility of identifying what records of maintenance and repairs should be kept and ensuring that they are completed and kept up to date.

The trailer was taken onto rough fields and tracks and when inspected by the police engineer it was found that the brakes did not work, no grease had been used and it did not conform to the legal requirements for it be on the road. It was in the words of the police, un-roadworthy. However, no prosecution of the company was forthcoming on that matter.

After a trial lasting a week, the jury spent some time deliberating the case to reach a verdict and in the end found the defendant guilty of the offence. The problem was that the defendant was adamant throughout that he closed and secured the trailer gate when clearly he had not. He had, in the eyes of the judge and jury, lied.

The trial judge was very experienced and certainly had a sound grasp of the case and its failings. He sentenced the defendant to a nine months prison sentence suspended for a year. There was a requirement to undertake 240 hours of unpaid work. His driving ban was reduced from the usually mandatory two years to six months. The judge made it clear in sentencing him that he had not been at all impressed with his behaviour during the investigation, and all the lies he had told. He sentenced him for being negligent on that single morning in failing to secure the gate properly and that he bore the criminal responsibility for the death.

He then went on to make it clear that his employer's attention to health and safety issues left much to be desired. He said that they had in place a poor maintenance regime and used poor design and had a poor training and instruction system. He said that the company's attitude was embodied by the unattractive and complacent way in which the managing director gave evidence. It is most regrettable that he took the view that the company could not have done more with regard to health and safety issues. There should have been in place a much better training and instruction system.

The judge clearly identified the serious failing on the part of the company and the managing director in particular when sentencing. The police had a meeting with inspectors from the Health and Safety Executive where it was decided that they would not play a role in the investigation. In court the police officer responsible for the case was unable to tell the court what information was provided to the HSE and why their assistance was not required in the investigation of the company. It was said that it was not known who took minutes of the meeting, if indeed any were taken. No records of the meeting were available to the court.

If the company had adopted even basic health and safety procedures the accident would not have occurred, a pedestrian would not have died, the defendant would not have been prosecuted and punished. This case had all the ingredients for Corporate Manslaughter and whilst one person carried the burden of the crime, the other got away with it. That is not justice!

Foreign Defendants

The influx of people coming to the UK in recent years resulted in many more foreign people coming to court. This means that foreign names can be a challenge and on occasion getting the right pronunciation can be a problem. However, it's not just names that cause problems.

In one case a Russian appeared before us on a criminal charge. He just stood in the dock and stared at us. The legal advisor asked him his name and to confirm his address. With a lot of difficulty due to his very strong accent we were just about able to get the information. However he was making it very clear that he didn't understand and didn't speak English. The response to every question asked of him resulted in a shrug of the shoulders and a comment we did not understand. As interpreters are not readily available in court the only option open to us was to put the case off until we could get both the man and an interpreter into court at the same time. It is not a problem getting an interpreter to court, however, it does cost you and I as tax payers about £300 a time and we don't get that back, even if the defendant is found guilty. We gave the Russian a document and asked him, as best we could, to go and check it and be back in court on the date stated. A happy chap, he left the court. I did a quick check to see if Russia had joined the EU and found that it had not so why did we have a Russian in the UK, on state benefits and requiring us to spend money on an interpreter? How can that be? Why was he not sent back to Russia? Oh sorry, don't ask, human rights!

However, it got better, because when returning to the court at lunchtime, I rounded the corner of the court building and noticed a man was standing with his back to me talking on a mobile phone. As I got closer, I could very clearly hear him speaking, with an accent, but in good English. When I looked, I realised that it was the Russian defendant from the morning court. He could clearly speak English. Now, I was not empowered to actually say or do anything at this point, so I went into the court and asked if he was still outside for somebody to get the police and arrest him. He could be brought straight into court so he could be dealt with. I also wanted to adopt a charge of perverting the course of justice by him indicating that he did not speak English. However, I was advised that this would be infringing on his human rights! He had been asked to come back to court on another day, with an interpreter, and we had to be satisfied with that. You see crime does pay in the UK.

Nicky [see Church Minister JP] had a case where there was an immigrant with no insurance on his car who didn't want to pay the fine.

He told the court that he came from Zimbabwe but of course there was no proof. Oh, he had no money and he had a wife to support. Nicky's colleagues on the bench didn't want to fine him because he hadn't got any money. Nicky raised the point that he still had his car and claimed that he was going to ship the car to Zimbabwe so he had got enough money to do that. Then the defendant claimed he was getting income from Zimbabwe every month to cover himself being here as a student. The fact is that you cannot take money out of Zimbabwe. Nicky wouldn't back down and wanted him fined the full amount. If he couldn't pay it he could sell his car. Then she faced the same old reaction, 'oh well, what about his wife'. Nicky's view was he committed the crime so he had to pay the fine and that is what happened, he was fined and he paid it.

There is the case of a foreign criminal who has cost the taxpayer at least £500,000 in an extraordinary deportation farce and pocketed a huge compensation payout. The convict was a Somalian who arrived in Britain claiming asylum. Since his arrival he had thanked us by committing crimes and been jailed for more than a dozen offences including violence, burglary and robbery. He has spent almost eight and a half years in prison at a cost to the British public of more than £300,000. The man, who had been receiving legal aid throughout his criminal career, re-offended within days or weeks each time he was released.

He was first told he was being considered for deportation in 2001, but officials failed to deport him. From 2004, when his last jail sentence was completed, to 2007, he was held in an immigration detention centre to stop him fleeing at a cost of around £40,000 a year. Judges decided that for two months of that period he was being held 'illegally' and he should receive a compensation payout which, in other similar cases, has averaged £16,000.

He was not happy and wanted more. He appealed the case through the court system, assisted by legal aid. He is still in Britain and anybody facing deportation to Somalia can claim their human rights will be breached, so there is no guarantee he will ever be repatriated. His various court cases are believed to have cost £200,000. Why can't he be deported back to Somalia? He has abused our system beyond belief so why should there be one ounce of sympathy for him, or indeed others who abuse the UK and its people. Send him back and perhaps in Somalia they know how to deal with criminals.

In May 2011, magistrates in Manchester jailed a fifteen-year-old Romanian criminal. He comes from a family sponging off the UK State benefits. He has been locked up six times in the past for repeated thieving while posing as a beggar, taking money from victims at cashpoints. They locked him up for a seventh time after hearing evidence of eight new offences, including stealing a family's Christmas present money. In court the youth showed no emotion as victim statements were read out, interpreted by a translator. He admitted six counts of theft and two of attempted theft. The magistrates sentenced him to a detention and training order for twelve months but then refused to allow him to be named because 'it was not in the public interest'.

The chairman of the bench said: 'We feel it would also be harmful to this young man if any rehabilitation becomes necessary.'

In my opinion it is in the public interest and it is vital that people know who this person is. It seems that he is past rehabilitation and actually needs urgent repatriation to his home country. No other country in Europe pays benefits to non-nationals as they are expected to work or support themselves. However, the UK with loads of money to waste pays out no matter the situation. This case exemplifies one of the reasons that I felt the need to resign from the bench. It is the pandering to criminals instead of dealing with the problem. [*Daily Express* 26th May 2011]

Deportation of Criminals

The defendant entered the dock and stared at us with a slight grin. He was from a non-European country but spoke sufficient English to enable us to conduct proceedings. He had entered the country illegally and was not new to the court system. He was before us on a new charge as well as a list of unpaid fines. We were not allowed to ask why he could stay in the country without permission whilst undertaking a personal crime spree. It transpired that he was wanted in his own country for numerous crimes and was seeking asylum in the UK. Clearly our criminal justice system was a better option than the one in his own country. Perhaps real justice may have been meted out where he came from.

The prosecutor gave details and provided evidence of the present charge and the outstanding fines. Then it was the turn of the defence and the defendant's solicitor stood. He regaled us with the breaches of the Human Rights Act his client had suffered and indeed continued to suffer. Look how many times he had been pursued by the police and brought before a court. Yes, he had been found guilty or had pleaded guilty, but he was a victim, not only of the UK injustice system but that of his own country, where he was persecuted and imprisoned. Yes, it had been for criminal actions, but the punishments were severe. In the UK we were more understanding and sympathetic. He had fled to the UK to start a new life and hoped to stay. I almost shed a tear but then soon returned to reality. As a bench we were considering prison or lengthy community sentence however, the solicitor proposed a total discharge so as to give his client a chance to redeem himself. Or, if we were minded it could be a conditional discharge. We were completely stunned when the prosecutor stood and said that he agreed with the discharge option and that we may wish to be sympathetic and order a full discharge. Normally the prosecutor would have been pushing for the highest possible tariff but was now going for the lowest option. We left the courtroom for our retiring room to consider the case and the options.

Our legal advisor joined us to explain that the prosecutor wanted the defendant released because immigration officers were present with a warrant and order for deportation. We went back into court and at the announcement of a discharge, the solicitor smiled, the man laughed, now no longer a defendant and free to go. Neither were aware of the pending doom that awaited. The man left the dock and hugged his solicitor who was looking rather full of himself. They walked to the door of the courtroom which suddenly opened and in walked an immigration officer and a plain clothed police officer. The man, sensing trouble, stepped back and looked around, no longer laughing, but looking for an escape route. Whilst the immigration officer read out the deportation order, the police officer handcuffed the man and he was then led away. His solicitor, who had been so full of himself, had no idea of what was to happen. He turned to the bench and saw three straight faced magistrates. If he was going to say something he didn't and departed. The prosecutor stood and explained that the man was on the run from the immigration authorities and this was the opportunity they had waited for to catch him and deport him. He was, we were told, being taken straight to an airport and flying out that very day. The trouble is, some do-gooder will let him back into the country.

We are now told that the abuse of the system will end and that thousands of foreign prisoners are to be sent back to serve their sentences in their own countries. David Cameron will tear up agreements that had meant that convicts could not be returned home without their consent. As the number of foreign inmates in Britain's jails approaches one in seven, the Prime Minister wants them sent back to serve prison terms in their countries of origin even if they insist they do not want to go. [*Daily Mail* 8th November 2010]

There will be problems because lawyers will misuse the Human Rights Act to put forward cases for convicts to stay in this country. In the future, foreigners found guilty of offences involving the use of official documents such as a fake passport or destroying a passport may be given 'conditional cautions' rather than jail sentences, barring them from returning to the UK. They would be thrown out of the country so they do not end up in prison here in the first place.

I found some figures that suggested there are currently 11,135 foreign inmates serving time for offences including murder, manslaughter, robbery, assault and drugs. Convicts from Jamaica top the list followed by Nigeria and the Irish Republic. There are 364 Chinese nationals in UK jails. The huge number of overseas nationals held in our jails reflects the number of immigrants here.

A real problem will be faced because countries accounting for large numbers of inmates will not want these people back, so better to leave them in the UK to undertake their criminal activities. What about those where human rights need to be taken into account? The UK does not send prisoners back if they are possibly going to be tortured or killed. Should we worry about them? They have come to the UK, abused our hospitality and committed crimes serious enough to receive jail sentences. They only came because of their criminal activities and the severe penalties in their own country. No, if they have committed a crime send them back. The removal process involves the right of appeal, which can delay or abort the process. So remove the appeal process and return them regardless. At last there is an EU prisoner transfer agreement, which takes effect from December 2011 which does not require the consent of the prisoner and should ensure the return of many more people to EU countries.

Things are getting serious because we now hear that foreign murderers, rapists and other criminals are being offered cash bribes of up to £1,500 to return home after serving their sentences. The coalition government has trebled the amount of money offered to prisoners who go back to their country of origin voluntarily. Those who agree to return with up to nine months left to serve will receive a bigger payout than those who go at the end of their sentence, in an attempt to create more space in prisons. Hundreds of criminals who have no right to remain in the country are likely to take advantage of the offer each year, costing the taxpayer millions of pounds. However, critics have attacked the payouts as 'obscene' when law-abiding families and victims were facing higher living costs, falling wages and widespread austerity measures.

Philip Davies, a Conservative backbencher, said: 'People say crime does not pay but obviously it does if you are a foreign criminal. It seems quite obscene that criminals are basically being given £1,500 bribes for abusing our hospitality and committing a crime.' [*Daily Telegraph*, 9th November 2010]

That's quite right, and when they go back to wherever they came from they will obtain false documents and return to the UK. We will then pay them another £1,500 or not bother because the scheme has been abandoned. Should being deported apply only to those convicts who serve time in prison? How about any foreigner who is convicted of offences such as acts of violence, repeated acts of theft, begging or occupying land or property illegally. They should be deported and any property or money they have should be used to pay court costs, fines and the cost of transport.

Pay Your Fine – Now!

Careless driving is reasonably common and where it involves a car it can be serious but in the case of a large articulated lorry it can be devastating.

The defendant was a lorry driver from Europe and, having come off a by-pass and heading towards the city, he realised that he had taken the wrong route. The road was wide and there was nothing coming towards him and he could see nothing behind him so he slowed and swung the lorry round in a u-turn. In fact a car was following the lorry and when it braked to slow down the car driver pulled out to overtake. The car driver was then confronted by the lorry moving across in front her. The lorry caught the car and swung it round. The lorry driver, having completed his turn, did not stop but continued up the road to re-join the by-pass. The car driver phoned the police and the lorry driver was apprehended. He was charged with careless driving and failing to stop after an accident. Apparently, there are often collisions between cars and large articulated lorries where the driver is unaware of any incident. The driver pleaded not guilty on the basis that he did not see a car or hear a collision. The manoeuvre was deemed dangerous and he should have seen the car in his mirrors. He was found guilty and the penalty was a fine. I asked if he had the money to pay to which he replied that he did not. He said that we could send the fine to his company somewhere in the depths of Europe, or he could pay it when he was next in England. Hang on, does he thinks we are stupid? Don't answer that! I said that we wanted the fine paid in full before he left court. He shrugged and started speaking in a language that we did not understand. He had been speaking very good English up to this point. After consultation with the legal advisor and a more senior member of the courts legal team we had a plan.

I asked again if he had any money. No, but he did have a credit card but was loath to use it because it was for fuel only. So he could go to a bank and use the card to get some money. 'Yes'. Would it cover the fine. 'Yes'. He said that he would go to a bank and get the money but he first had to go to his lorry. Thinking that he may depart in his lorry without paying the fine we confiscated his lorry and everything in it. We then asked a police officer who had been called as a witness if he would accompany the man to the bank and back to the court under a court order. He checked that this was in order and confirmed that it was. The defendant was then bailed to leave the court, get the money and return. This was done and when the money was paid over his lorry was released and he departed for wherever.

Dodgy Landlord

There are days when there is a blatant disregard for the law, all in the cause of greed and profit. One such case occurred for me in February 2006 which resulted in there being a fair trial and justice was done. A landlord, Morteza Saffar, rented many of his properties to foreign workers. He pleaded guilty to eight offences relating to a six-bedroom, three storey house. The fire detectors in the property had been blocked with tape, seals on fire doors were broken and fire extinguishers had not been serviced. The property had worn and loose floorboards, no hot water in the bathroom and damage to the flooring around the bath. Mr Saffar claimed he had not known the law about renting out houses where more than one tenant was living.

The local press highlighted the case quoting bench chair Mike Welham: 'You have owned this property for ten years and there was a total lack of fire safety procedures. You own around forty-seven properties yet it appears to us that you do not know about property law.'

Following the case the local newspaper ran an article in which it was said by Mr Welham that Mr Saffar's case was the worst he had ever come across and was especially bad as Mr Saffar had also been exposed for exploiting vulnerable people, including asylum seekers.

He stated: 'We handed out maximum penalties for three of the eight offences relating to houses in multiple occupation.'

Mr. Welham added: 'These offences have to be publicised in the newspapers so people know that they don't have to put up with such conditions. Before, maybe, people did not know who to go to if they had a problem with landlords, but now they do. It's especially bad because asylum seekers will have been persecuted in their own countries. They are maybe not the type of people, when they come to a new country, to rock the boat and complain. As you have identified, the problem is more deep rooted and needs exposing.'

Since then, the newspaper has reported how Mr Saffar also had tenants in his houses living in cramped and poor conditions while charging them £500 a month for the privilege. Mr Saffar had converted six two-storey houses into twelve flats and rented them to migrant families who were desperate for somewhere to live.

In the case Mr Saffar was fined £10,250 and ordered to pay £3,000 towards the costs of the case. A plea was made that if the heavy fine and costs were imposed then Mr Saffar may have to sell a property to pay the court. The response from the bench was that if that was the case then Mr Saffar needed to sell some of his forty-seven properties, sooner rather that later. It is probably the only case that I have sat on where I expected the full wrath of the Human Rights Act to be used against me and my colleagues for being tough on one immigrant who was exploiting asylum seekers.

The City Council subsequently announced an investigation into Mr Saffar's property portfolio, after it emerged that he had illegally converted six small two-storey houses into flats without first gaining planning permission. Council officers discovered that the badly converted flats lacked fire precautions or insulation ... The City Council is insisting that the houses be turned back into single house. However, another issue that was not addressed is that the tenants were having rents paid through welfare benefits. No checks were made by those handing out the money as to the condition of the property.

Assets Please

Probably about ten to fifteen years ago, in an attempt to get people to pay their fines, there was a trial in our area where reluctance to pay meant we could impose points on the driving licence. The original offence did not have to be a driving conviction so it covered the whole spectrum of cases that we dealt with. It worked, but was not adopted into the system. Take the yob who has failed to pay up. He or she comes to court with a multitude of reasons why he or she has not paid. They can go out boozing, using a mobile phone and driving a car, but cannot pay a fine imposed for a criminal offence. So bringing back to court they had to pay up or have three points added to their licence. Back to court four times and you are disqualified from driving. Points already on a licence were added to. In some case that tipped the balance and the convict found he or she had reached the magic twelve points, for disqualification. Word soon got out and people came to court to pay fines to avoid the points.

A judge or magistrate can take property to meet unpaid court fines for offences like criminal damage, anti-social behaviour or affray. Like most things introduced under New Labour the process was slowed down by bureaucracy which meant that defaulters were not dealt with for months. A change in the rules [December 2010] meant that bailiffs are able to go straight to the offenders' houses and take away their high-value assets such as a car, the day the fine is overdue. A senior government source was quoted as saying:

'This is specifically designed to wipe the smile off smug yobs' faces. Taking their wheels hits their attitudes as well as their pockets.'

On the face of it this is a good idea but experience in court was that when the bailiffs went to a property either, the convict no longer lived there or nothing in the house belonged to the convict. The bailiffs generally left empty handed. Even in the case of cars, they were always owned by somebody else with the convict being allowed to drive them.

I was involved with one case where the defendant arrived at court in a very smart and expensive sports car. He lived in a very grand house and was well dressed. He pleaded that he could not pay the fine because he did not have any money. Everything was in his wife's name and he owned nothing. The situation was put before a judge and it was soon sorted out. He suggested that if the defendant and his wife divorced then he would be entitled to half of all the assets. So a calculation of the wife's assets was to be made and that would reveal a figure. The defendant's half was calculated and the judge set the fine and court costs to realistic figure and ruled that payment was required now...perhaps he would like to consult with his wife on method of payment and it would not include payments by instalments. A flexible friend was taken to the payment office and a transaction made. OK, crime did not pay on this occasion!

You're in Safe Hands

Young barristers are sent to the courts to represent clients and gain experience. Often a client is pleased that he or she is represented by a barrister as opposed to a mere solicitor. What they don't know is that, unless you have bags of money or can fiddle the legal aid system, you do not generally get a very experienced barrister. That said, I have been with superb and very experienced barristers who work on legal aid cases. In many situations it was because they favoured the case. In court most of the cases I sat on, the new barristers came from London. They would get the early morning train, arrive at court, look at the case file, enter the courtroom and act for the client. Then, if that was the only case, a dash back to London looking for their next case.

One morning we sat in court when a defendant was called and entered the dock. The prosecutor was ready, we were all ready, but the person representing the defendant was not in court. The prosecutor said that the missing lawyer was new to the court, and so he would go and see if he could find him. The prosecutor re-entered the court followed by a young lawyer, flustered and out of breath. He apologised but the train was late arriving. The legal advisor confirmed the defendant's details and that it was a guilty plea. After that the prosecutor provided the prosecution case. The new barrister stood and stated that in mitigation Mr X, the defendant, had pleaded guilty... There was a stunned silence in court as Mr Y stood up in the dock. The prosecutor began to stand but I was ahead of him. I addressed Mr new barrister, to point out that not only was he not using the defendant's correct name, but had got the wrong charge. He looked at me and then at his client who said that his name was Mr Y and what he was charged with. He turned back to the bench and said he was soooooh, sooooh sorry, but he had the wrong case file. Could we possibly allow him some time to acquaint himself with the case. We could have said no, but told him to go with his client and evaluate the case then we would fit him in where possible. He then had the cheek to explain that he had to get a train, to get him to his next venue, where he was appearing in court in the afternoon. I told him that he may need to make other arrangements and that we would deal with his case in due course.

Is It Racism?

One thing I found some difficulty with in court was determining when some situations were racist, and when they were not. Some cases are straightforward but because of extreme political correctness the line becomes blurred. I found that in court the ethnic origins of an individual did not matter. It is about the crime and the decision of guilt or not was what mattered. Evidence would clearly reveal if there was a racial, sexual, religious or other motive. If a crime was truly racially motivated then it carried the appropriate sentence for a guilty person.

One case I sat on involved the assault of a female by a male who were both immigrants. The male pleaded not guilty on the basis that where they came from it was normal practice for men to keep women in line and that may incur a slap or punch. In fact the Human Rights Act was quoted as part of his defence as his right to expression and the right of freedom of conscience. It had to be explained that whilst such actions may be acceptable in other countries they were not in the UK. It was pointed out through the interpreter that it was against the law, and that was why he was being prosecuted. Such a decision can draw criticism of being racist by some who argue that they should be allowed to do what their culture allows.

Another case involved road rage. The prosecution case was that a car was going along a main road in the correct manner when a van was seen by a number of road users to be overtaking dangerously. It passed the car in an erratic manner and because of oncoming traffic it had to pull over sharply with the result that it cut the car up. The driver of the car responded by sounding the horn. The van came to an emergency stop, causing the vehicles behind to stop. The van driver got out and walked to the car. He was shouting abuse which continued when he reached the car, including a remark that was considered racist. The driver of the car was of Indian ethnicity. He then went back to his van and drove off. The offences he had been charged with involved his sub-standard driving and the threatening and abusive behavior. The charges were made worse because of the racist remark which gives the reason for an action to be racially motivated. In this particular case the standard of driving put many people at risk of injury. There were the threats of violence which could have been made at any driver, male, female, young or old with accompanying derogatory remarks. Some question that did a word shouted in anger in this situation make it a racially motivated case?

Judge Christopher Elwen was accused of using a 'racial slur' against gypsies when he told the fraudster he had 'gypped' a student out of money on the eBay website. The slang verb 'to gyp' means to defraud or steal. However, the *Travellers Times* editor commented:

'Gypped is an offensive word. It is derived from gipsy and it is being used in the same context as a person might once have said they "jewed" somebody if they did an underhand business transaction. Basically what Judge Elwen has done is ascribed thievery to an entire ethnic group.'

A spokesman for the Judicial Communications Office defended the judge's choice of words, saying: 'Gyp is defined in the Oxford English Dictionary as an act of cheating, nothing more. There is no evidence to connect this term to any ethnic group and this is certainly not how it was used in court.'

In fact the Oxford English Dictionary defines gyp as a late-19th century verb of unknown origin that means to cheat or swindle someone. One other suggestion given by the Dictionary in an entry published in 1972 is that it derives from "gyp" "pain" (as in to "give someone gyp").' [*Daily Mail* 9th June 2009]

Judge Elwen is not alone. I was sitting on a case that had no racial content whatsoever. In court the prosecutor and the defence solicitor were in contention over some matter of law. It was evident that the defence was making a point on behalf of his client that even to us non-lawyers seemed dubious. It seemed like a good time to retire and let them sort themselves out and then call us when they had done so. We made our way to the main retiring room and made ourselves a cup of tea. Another bench of three were also in the room waiting for their case to be sorted out. Our legal advisor came to tell us that the lawyers were ready to continue.

As I stood I said to my two colleagues, 'I wonder if the prosecutor will find a chink in the defence armour.'

Then from behind me a loud voice announced. 'That is racist, what you have just said is racist. You are being racist about Chinese people. If you were a teacher at my school you would be suspended immediately. (I found out later that he was a school headmaster) In fact I shall report it to the chief clerk of the court.'

My two colleagues stood open mouthed, looking at the man who had made the remark. I looked at them and enquired what had I said wrong. 'Nothing, nothing at all,' was the reply. We left the room and returned to deal with the case. It is very difficult to concentrate after an incident like that. The use of the word chink is an everyday term and in the wrong context it could be derogatory but like Judge Elwen the terms were used in a totally different context.

As a matter of interest the Collins English Dictionary and Thesaurus identified the term chink as a small narrow opening such as a fissure or crack. It actually quotes, "chink in one's armour". I did speak to the chief clerk when I saw him next. He would not say if a complaint had been made but said that some people are very sensitive to every word that is spoken. So you see extreme political correctness permeates every aspect of society and because of misuse, it has actually become a subject of ridicule.

Travellers Rule OK

I do not have any objection to where people live and how they conduct their lives as long as it does not impact on others and they abide by the laws of the land. The situation is that many travellers seem to put themselves outside of conventional society. They don't help their cause and the public only see the down side. It's the rubbish that they dispose of with total disregard of the countryside, the defiance of the law with vehicles untaxed and uninsured and the illegal occupation of land. There is evidence that reports of theft increase when travellers move into an area. They claim to be travellers but want to take over land and build on it without planning permission. They do not contribute financially to society but expect everything in return. Perhaps worse is the impact of the official and unofficial organisations who actually support and condone these activities. Say a word out of place and you are racist. In my experience there are not many travellers prosecuted. I was told by a senior police officer that they give false names, have no fixed address and have a total disregard for the law. This means that it's virtually impossible to prosecute a traveller. Those that do appear in court are often there facing charges arising from the illegal occupation of land or motoring offences. It seems to be a situation where there is a crime but if it involves travellers avoid it, why go looking for problems?

I lived in a small English village that comprised of a general store with a post office. I knew the shopkeeper very well and we often chatted, putting the world to rights. One day when I called at the shop he was quite upset. The problem was that travellers, who had moved into the area, had visited the shop. He explained that about seven of them came in and separated. Staff could not watch everybody and by the time he became involved some of them had grabbed goods and departed without paying. He was able to look at CCTV to get an idea of how much stock they had taken. He called the police but being in a rural area it took time before they arrived. They took the CCTV tape and the names of staff and customers who were present and said they would be in touch. The shopkeeper explained that they probably came from the site close by which they were illegally occupying and that, if the police went round now, they may find and recover the goods.

The shopkeeper was taken to one side and a police officer gave a gentle warning. Accusing travellers of theft, even with CCTV footage, was seen as a form of racism and he could be charged with an offence. He explained that the officers had looked at the CCTV and seen people take goods off a shelf, put them in a bag and walk out of the store. Find the person and you have a criminal. The officer explained that it was not that easy. First, the police were not allowed onto a traveller's site without the presence of an armed response unit. Why? Well it is alleged that the travellers are generally armed. Second, the police [beat officers] have to get permission from senior officers as well as warrant from the court to enable them to search property. Sorry can't do that. Why? Well they are a diverse group of people and we have special procedures we have to go through before we take any action, if indeed we do.

The only immediate action the shopkeeper decided he could take was to ban the travellers and he would put a sign up to that effect. Sorry, that would be discrimination and illegal. He then said that he would place a guard on the door and stop them entering. Sorry, that could result in a disturbance of the peace and therefore, illegal. Further, if force was used that would be illegal. Our shopkeeper, trying to remain calm, spelt out the situation. Those people can come round in their vehicles, which have no road tax or insurance, enter my shop and steal whatever they want. Even with evidence the police are not allowed to investigate and there is nothing that can be done. That about sums it up. So our shopkeeper had his store robbed in broad daylight by half a dozen people. There were witnesses and CCTV coverage and the police would not do anything about it. I only went for a newspaper and a few grocery items but was bombarded by a real tale of woe. What was I, as a magistrate, going to do about it? Well there was nothing I could do. We both agreed that the concept of one law for all does not exist, because there are exceptions.

In another situation, picture the tranquil scene of rural England where a couple move their family into a converted barn, with a plan to get back to nature and enjoy their horses amid beautiful countryside. Then a group of travellers arrive and set up camp next door. It is alleged that dead dogs were thrown into their property, their teenage daughter was subjected to obscene abuse and threats and violence became an almost daily occurrence. Some of the men they passed on the road made shooting gestures with their fingers. It is alleged that one of the travellers claimed that the family would all be found dead in their living room. Complaints to the police fell on deaf ears, and the local council granted the site legal status, with permission for the travellers to stay indefinitely. A £500,000 property became virtually worthless and this is yet another example of one law for us and another for them. It is quite clear that the local council are to blame because they do not want to confront illegal activities and it is a situation that will come as no surprise to law-abiding homeowners up and down the country who find themselves confronted with the ever-growing problem of illegal traveller encampments. [*Daily Mail* 2nd June 2009]

An elderly couple who suggested that gipsies and travellers should contribute towards the cost of cleaning up any mess they make have been branded racist. However, rather than objecting to proposed gipsy and traveller camps, all the couple did was to point out that the planned sites might be messy. At present, travellers give nothing to the community where they stay; indeed they create expense such as rubbish clearance after they have departed. The couple received a letter from the council that cited the Race Relations Act and concluded that their opinion 'could be construed as offensive' and would therefore be ignored.

If you think that the illegal occupation of land, building without planning permission and intimidation and threats of violence are bad, then how about a group of travellers who, allegedly, wrecked a multi-million pound police helicopter which was being used to observe their site. A gang used axes to smash the £5million aircraft, having climbed over a four foot wall surrounding Surrey Police force's helipad at Fairoaks airport, near Woking in Surrey. They threatened staff working in the operations room and then set about wrecking the helicopter, smashing six of its windows and causing tens of thousands of pounds worth of damage. The incident happened after weeks of aerial surveillance on a travellers' site, where detectives believed stolen goods had been hidden and officers were getting ready to raid the site after collecting evidence from a camera fitted under its nose that beamed broadcast-quality footage to the control room. The aircraft is the only police helicopter in Surrey and is used mainly for chasing crime suspects in their cars, finding missing people and pre-planned surveillance operations. [*Daily Mail* 14th May 2009]

Police were told that they could not object to a planned travellers site because to do so would be 'racist'. The council chiefs have ruled that the local force's professional opinion 'breaches the Race Relations Act'. The decision meant that councillors considering the planning application were not told how officers had been called to another local camp 109 times in just two years. Police had joined local villagers objecting about a travellers' site by writing a letter to the council. The letter identified that over a two-year period to January 2008, officers had visited the three sites a total of 210 times. The police were called out to deal with reports of fights, arson, assaults, stolen vehicles, violent disorder, anti-social behaviour, theft, child abduction and use of weapons. However, the local council refused to take the letter into consideration when deciding whether to approve the site. Officials claimed that including it in the summary given to councillors would leave the authority open to a prosecution for racial discrimination. The council's act of censorship is another illustration of how the politically correct appear to be appointing themselves as our 'thought police'. [*Daily Mail* 2nd June 2009]

Then we learn that gipsies and travellers were paid £60 each of taxpayers' money to attend a conference. Dozens turned up at the day-long event after they were offered the fee. It advised them how to find a GP, dentist and a school for their children while moving between illegal sites, and please note the word illegal. Organisers of the Traveller and Gipsy Awareness Day handed out the money because they feared that there would be a poor attendance without the financial incentive.

The County Council paid £2,500 to hire a venue for the day. Whilst food and drink for each attendee at the conference cost £67, taking the overall cost of the event to many thousands of pounds. We are told that participants were given a coffee and Danish pastry on arrival, followed by more coffee and shortbread biscuits later on in the morning. At lunch they were served a large buffet, followed by mid-afternoon coffee and strawberry scones. Bottled water, biscuits and sweets were also provided. Many of those attending did not stay for the afternoon once they had eaten their lunch and picked up their money. No surprise there then! [*Daily Mail* 8th July 2009]

There are so many stories of illegal activities by travellers that they would fill a book in their own right. It is tragic that so many decent, law abiding tax payers are on the receiving end of such activities. Even more tragic is that the criminal activities are fully supported by councils, as well as a growing number of do-gooder action groups. For me it destroys the concept of a fair and just society because the evidence is that criminals and the crimes of a minority are rewarded by the State. Again, it is an abuse and misuse of the law and crime pays.

Don't Offend Offenders

Many of those attending court involve repeat offenders who, even when offered a helping hand to get them on the straight and narrow, arrogantly ignore it. The soft approach has been tried and failed, it now needs a new tougher system for dealing with the problem. That is not the view of everybody because some people thrive on disorder and make outrageous suggestions such as that put forward by Frances Crook, head of the Howard League for Penal Reform. Crook stated that criminals should no longer be termed 'offenders' because the term is insulting and demeaning. She considers that someone who commits an offence is not an offender, but 'someone who has done something'. She wrote in *Criminal Justice Matters*, the magazine of the Centre for Crime and Justice Studies, that it had been easy for politicians to treat some sections of society as less than human. Well Ms Crook, those people who 'have done something' and have been found guilty of a criminal offence are convicts until their sentence is completed. As for convicts being treated as less than human, I suggest she goes to court, sees some of the victims and hears their evidence before making such a statement. I doubt that Ms Crook would change her mind but people who seek justice may well consider the actions of some convicts as being evil and less than human.

3

Crime and Punishment

Lies, Damned Lies and Statistics

I have no intention of getting bogged down with figures but I do have to raise a very important point. When government officials or a minister states that the evidence about crime comes from statistics, then it is probably a lie. You have to remember that there are three kinds of lies: lies, damned lies and statistics and this was adopted particularly by the New Labour government, who in more recent years, developed a great skill at fudging the figures. I fear that the ConLib coalition will fare no better.

Remove the spin and the reality is as Ken Pease, Professor of Crime Science at University College London and Loughborough University says: 'You can use crime statistics to 'prove' just about anything you want about crime. The overall trend seems to me to be certainly up, but you will find statisticians who will question that claim. My view is that the overall trend is less important than the fact of nasty things happening on the streets... some of the things which happen on our streets today are extremely nasty.' [*Daily Telegraph* 2008]

The Ministry of Justice (MoJ) figures showed only one in four of the most serious crimes reported to police were solved. Of the

4,338,604 notifiable offences recorded in England and Wales in 2009, only 1,204,967 offences were marked as action having been taken and only half of those resulted in criminal charges. More than a fifth, 269,552 offences, were dealt with by police cautions and just under one in ten led to penalty notices. In all, 1.7 million defendants had their cases taken to court in 2009, with only 94,586 being sentenced in a Crown Court. Of these, 51,801 were jailed, with an average sentence of 24.3 months. Then 19,749 were given a suspended sentence, 16,174 received a community sentence and 2,300 were fined. Of the 1.3 million cases dealt with by magistrates, 943,194 people were fined, 179,593 were given community sentences and 48,389 were jailed. [*Daily Express* 22nd October, 2010]

The MoJ statistics also showed the number of defendants found guilty of violence rose by 4.6% to 43,300 in 2009, compared with 41,500 the previous year. The number of offenders found guilty of drugs offences also rose by 7.4% from 52,900 to 56,800. However, overall crime recorded by the police fell by 8% in the last year. (That does not mean that there were less crimes, it may well mean that less crimes were reported.)

What this means is that all the millions invested with the prisons and the Probation Service to sort out offending behaviour has been wasted. Following time spent in prison, thousands of offenders return to a life of crime. The evidence shows that more than a third of people convicted of burglary and 36% of those convicted of theft and handling stolen goods had fifteen or more convictions or cautions.

In June 2007 it was reported that an extra two million violent crimes a year were committed in Britain than previously thought. This arises because of a distortion in the government's crime figures. government distortion...can this be possible?

The basis for the claim is made in a report by Professor Graham Farrell of Loughborough University and the former acting head of the Home Office's Police Research Group, Professor Ken Pease. They have calculated that if the overall number of British Crime Survey (BCS) crimes is more than fourteen million rather than the current eleven million a year estimate. Their research found that across all types of crime, three million offences a year are excluded from the BCS. The reason is that the figures are capped so that the number of times a victim can be targeted by an offender, is only five incidents in a year. So if anyone interviewed for the survey says they have been targeted more than five times a year, the sixth incident or more are not included in the BCS. [*www.independent.co.uk*]

The report identifies that violent crime is 82% higher at 4.4 million offences compared with 2.4 million in the BCS. Domestic violence is 140% higher, up from 357,000 incidents a year to 857,000. There are nearly three million common assaults a year rather than the 1.5 million estimated by the BCS, a rise of 98%. Burglary is 20% higher than currently estimated at 877,000 a year and vandalism is 24% higher. Robbery is 7 % up on the official estimates, or an extra 22,000 crimes bringing the yearly total to 333,000. The authors quantify their research by stating:

'If the people who say they suffered ten incidents really did, it is capping the series at five that distorts the rate.'

The authors add:'It is truly bizarre that the victimisation survey, based as it is on the assumption that people will, by and large, tell the truth about what happened to them... suddenly withdraws its trust in their honesty when what they are told does not chime with their own experience. Yet the reality is that some people are very frequently victimised, and that frequent victimisation is what they suffer rather than being an invention or exaggeration.'

The cap of five crimes for repeat victims has operated ever since the inception of the BCS in 1981. It is interesting that Ministers claim the survey, which polls 40,000 people a year about their experiences of crime, is the most reliable indicator of crime levels. This has led the authors of the report to state:

'The unwillingness to believe the facts of chronic victimisation means that crime control, police training and criminal justice action are now substantially misdirected. In particular, the system means that the most vulnerable people in society may not be getting the police protection they require from repeat offenders.'

The New Labour government blamed inaccurate police record keeping for a 22% rise in the number of the most serious violent crimes in England and Wales. [*The Guardian* 23rd October 2008]

The fact is that crime is on the increase, particularly violent crime, and it has become a blame game with nobody wanting to take ownership of the problem and deal with it. After all we are only talking about victims and as we have seen, they don't count.

Court Fines

Fines are probably the most common punishment handed out in the Magistrates' Courts because it is a simple option for much of the petty crime that comes before the courts. When a person is found guilty we need to determine how much money they have available to pay a fine so we can work out a level of fine to impose. We ask the individual to fill out a means form and show us the amount of money coming in and from where and the amount of money going out and for what. This has always been an issue for me as often the person filling in the form has been convicted of theft or a linked offence. We now ask them to tell us the truth by filling in a form. Now fines are a priority debt because Magistrates' Courts have the power to send a person to prison for non-payment. This means that fines come before luxuries and that includes such things as money for cigarettes, a mobile phone, entertainment and clothing from catalogues. This has to be explained in great detail because what might be considered to be luxuries to the court are seen as essentials to those convicted of an offence.

So it is by a process of elimination that we progress our way through the form. That said, it becomes a case of looking at the total amount of money available, take off the essentials and that leaves a figure and that is the one upon which to base the fine. Another factor is that generally a fine should be imposed that is cleared within a period of say a year to eighteen months. This means that a convict does not have an outstanding fine hanging over them for years.

Once the fine is imposed it can be added to any other fines that are being paid off. A notice of the fine and the repayment rate is sent out. If payments are missed, or not made at all, a reminder is sent out. If those payments are not brought up to date the convict is summoned to the court to explain why the fine has not been paid. Generally the individual offers some pathetic excuse and agrees to pay as originally agreed. If they pay any arrears up to date and continue to pay at the correct rate, in most cases no further action is taken. If they don't, action can be taken against them.

Those who fail to attend a court hearing are issued with a *Warrant with Bail* (private bailiffs will give the individual another court hearing date) or a *Warrant without Bail* (private bailiffs would arrest the individual and bring them before the court) or a *Committal Warrant* to commit the individual to prison (if there is a suspended sentence already on the fine). This means that either the police or bailiffs will arrest the individual and bring them before the court. At court they will have to explain why they have not paid their fine. The court does have the power to search an individual and remove all the money they have with them.

Often people have genuine reasons for not paying the fine such as a drop in income, loss of job, a relationship breakdown, a baby or illness. The problem is that they do not contact the court and explain the situation. They just stop paying and hope it all goes away. Faced with the prospect that the fine payments cannot be met, it only requires a visit to the court or a letter sent to the court which holds the fine to tell them about the situation and make an offer of repayment. It would be a good idea to have or enclose a copy of any information that supports the situation to show how the change has impacted on the ability to pay.

The Magistrates' Courts have the power to make an attachment of earnings order to make deductions from an individual's wages if they are employed and this can be done even without agreement. The court can apply to the DWP to make weekly deductions from those on benefit of a set amount if they are on income support, income based or contributory job seeker's allowance or pension credit. They can do this when they set the fine or when an individual falls behind on payment arrangements. Those being fined can find themselves in trouble if they do not give the court correct details of income and outgoings when ordered to do so.

If there is continued failure to pay an outstanding fine the court can use bailiffs to recover the money or goods to the value of the outstanding sum. Bailiffs have the power to break into a home or other premises to take goods. Some household items like beds and bedding, clothes, books and/or tools of a trade are exempt and cannot be taken. Goods that belong to other people cannot be taken either.

The court can remit the fine in part or 'write off' a fine. The problem with this is that it becomes a game. A person is fined and does not pay but drags out any action by the use of pathetic excuses. Then they get caught for another offence and fined. The outstanding fine and the new fine are added together. They do not then pay off any of the new combined fine. Caught again they are then fined but with the new fine added the total due is above what they can realistically pay. In this situation the court is faced with remitting some of the original fine to reduce that total amount owed. I have known this to go on and it became an issue for many magistrates not to remit fines at all. The problem was that there was no alternative punishment. That situation may have changed now.

Before we could send an individual to prison, the court must establish 'wilful refusal' which means that the magistrates think that there is a deliberate refusal to pay; or that there is 'culpable neglect' which means the individual has been careless or thoughtless in not paying. In this situation, to avoid a prison sentence, the individual must convince the court that there is a genuine reason for not paying. The excuses for not paying would fill a book and provide a great deal of amusement. Remember, there is no room in prison so why worry! Whilst the court can write off fines it cannot write off court costs. If an order was made to pay compensation, the court may write to the person who is owed compensation to ask them whether they are willing to write it off, as this can only be done with their consent. I always found this to be a really offensive action. If anybody is awarded compensation they are the victim of a crime so what they are due should get paid regardless.

Community Punishment

You may well have heard the statement that a community sentence (the new term is community payback) is a really tough alternative to prison! Well don't make me laugh. The simple fact is that they are not. From my own personal knowledge and in discussion with numerous people with first hand experience, it is said to be a joke. The concept of a community sentence is well intentioned and is used where an individual has committed a crime, but a prison sentence is seen as unwarranted. It means that a person is given a set number of hours to do unpaid work in the community. Of course everybody has to be assessed to ensure that they are fit and able to do the work programme.

It has to be said that many people just go and get on with it and some actually do a good job. But there are those for whom the word 'work' has no place in their brain or understanding and the excuses leave magistrates in despair. 'Can't do the work cause I suffer from depression,' or 'can't do that sort of work sir, cos of 'elf and safety,' or 'can't work during the week sir, cos I'm on job seekers' allowance and I need to be available for work,' or 'can't do the work because my girlfriend's got two kiddies and I need to be available to take her shopping.'

'What everyday?'

'Yes sir, she aint got no fridge.'

We then quiz the individual further to find that he does not live with the female and she already has another male living with her.

'Well Mr X it seems that you do have time for work.'

'But it's not easy as I have to pop round and see the children.'

Of course the man is entitled to see his children, but we are told that they are not all his children, but he treats them as such. We then discover that his girlfriend has moved a considerable distance away.

'Mr X you will undertake the unpaid work.'

'But I will become depressed.' I always wanted to say, 'then go and do some work and be depressed doing it.' But I never did, not in court anyway.

How about the boss of a taxi company who, having been found guilty of a criminal offence, received a community service order and was directed to undertake unpaid work. He was assessed for work that would be suitable for him. He could drive a car and so he was tasked with delivering local government leaflets to hundreds of houses. For this he was unsupervised and so whilst pounding the streets popping notices through letterboxes he added a leaflet advertising his taxi firm. Having completed half the assignment he went to see his supervisor to report the number of hours he had worked. The figure he gave was the total he was required to do and not what he had actually worked. Without any checks he was signed off as having completed his sentence. Let us be very clear, a community sentence is the next step down from going to prison and it is for serious offences. It is not an opportunity to assist a business expansion plan.

There was a case where three young male convicts were given community sentences. Two of the convicts attended and when the probation officer asked where the third convict was, he was told that he was late but would be with them shortly. The officer in charge set them a task of planting young trees. One would dig the hole, another would plant the tree and the third would fill the hole. They would work as a team and the officer provided them with the tools and trees. They were told to get on with it and he would be back later to check on them. Later the officer found a long line of the locations where soil had been dug and replaced, but there were no trees. He caught up with the two convicts and asked what they thought they were doing. They replied that they were following orders. One dug the hole, another planted the trees and the other filled the hole. The officer enquired as to where the trees were. He was told that it was the job of the missing convict to plant the trees, but he had not turned up that's why no trees were planted!

In October 2010 figures released showed that more than 13,000 criminals who had committed thirty or more offences were given community penalties in the space of a year. The figures emerged after Kenneth Clarke, the Justice Secretary, reiterated his stance on the need to reduce the number of short jail sentences. He told prison governors:

'The army of short term prisoners we have at the moment, who have a particularly bad record of re-offending within six months of being released, is too big and we've got to find some sensible community sentences.'

The new figures, which relate to 2008, were disclosed by Crispin Blunt, the Justice Minister, in response to a parliamentary question and were reported by the Tory backbencher, Philip Davies, who branded the criminal justice system a 'joke', adding: 'You have to work very hard to get into prison nowadays.' Almost 2,700 community sentences were issued to people who had more than fifty previous offences, while 315 serial criminals who had 100 or more previous convictions were spared jail. [*Daily Mail* October 2010]

So how about this for so called justice? One repeat offender avoided going to jail after a judge said she did not want to 'spoil' his forthcoming wedding to his long suffering fiancée. Michael Furlong was due to marry his partner, but had been 'caught red-handed' stealing whilst subject to a suspended prison term for burglary. A Crown Court heard how the couple had been saving every penny for their marriage before Furlong had put the ceremony at risk by taking a discarded £5 TV stand. Furlong, whose latest victim was a magistrate, was facing up to nine months behind bars with more on top, after flouting the suspended order a second time. Judge Beverley Lunt, who said she had told the defendant in 'clear English' last time he would go to prison if he did it again, told him:

'Why this lady still stands by you I have no idea. She is too good for you, quite frankly. She has come to support you again. I am not going to spoil her wedding, although it's you who would have done that, not me.'

Being on a suspended order means that if a convict commits another crime, then the order is actioned and the convict returns to prison. No if's and no but's. Otherwise why bother to issue a suspended order in the first place? It is also noted that this was the second breach of the order. I do hope the judge got invited to the wedding and was maid of your honour!

* * *

Is there real action at last? Please do not hold your breath. We are told that multimillion-pound industrial projects will be undertaken by a land army of 100,000 convicts as an alternative to custodial sentences. The government wants to completely re-brand community service. We are told that offenders will be expected to undertake unpaid work for up to seven hours a day, in a major plan for them to 'pay something back' to society. They will do labouring work on building projects, carry out industrial cleaning and clear towns and cities of the blight of graffiti. So instead of the 'soft touch' option of doing several hours community labour a week road-sweeping, window cleaning and planting trees, convicts will work full-time thus serving their up to 240-hour sentences more quickly. The 'soft option' will be replaced by harder manual work, saving the public purse millions of pounds. A Whitehall source stated:

'Putting it simply, it is payback time. This policy will send out a very tough message that there is no easy ride and that it is everybody's responsibility to rebuild the economy and the country. One hundred thousand is a big workforce, almost doubling the 55,000 now sentenced to community service or unpaid work.' [*Sunday Express* 26th September 2010]

The Probation Service, which has run community sentencing since 1974, says the proposals could break health and safety legislation and threaten the future of paid workers. Harry Fletcher, assistant general secretary of the National Association of Probation Officers, said:

'This is all about punishment and not rehabilitation but clearly it is essential that there is an element of rehabilitation, otherwise individuals are likely to carry on offending.'

Whilst I do not want to knock some of the very good work of the Probation Service and the successes that they do have with administering community work, the current system does not work. Convicts given unpaid labour as opposed to prison should work very hard and rehabilitation has been tried and does not work in its current form. Most convicts see it as justice being soft.

Then the headlines screamed: SOLDIERS TO TAME THUGS – Battle-hardened army veterans are to be put in charge of violent criminals serving community service sentences.

Community service was established in 1976 as an alternative to custody. A third of those sentenced are given unsupervised work. The other two-thirds are supervised in work groups of up to eight, with a supervisor employed at £8.50 an hour. However, the plan is for the system to be privatised. Then the private sector organisations will recruit Afghanistan and Gulf War veterans to form the central plank of a new get-tough policy. In addition, civil servants believe they can save up to £20million a year by offering retired sergeant majors and other non-commissioned officers the minimum wage of just below £6 an hour, because they are already receiving Army pensions.

The change is to save money and is a result of hundreds of reports showing that staff have been attacked or threatened by gangs of offenders doing unpaid work as part of the current 'soft touch' sentences. One example from a National Association of Probation Officers (NAPO) survey tells how a convict told a supervisor he was going to kill him and rape his four-year-old daughter. Shootings have even taken place, with convicts targeted by rival gangs while on community service. The use of retired army sergeant majors who have always had an awesome reputation as disciplinarians is considered to be an inspired idea. It is accepted that NCOs throughout the present-day Army are well used to dealing with teenage recruits, who often come from tough backgrounds, and moulding them into first-class soldiers. However, the problem is that dealing with soldiers under military law is one thing. Dealing with civilian convicts and the Human Rights Act will be an entirely different matter, even for men who have survived Afghanistan and the Gulf Wars.

The probation service, which runs community service, is naturally opposed to privatisation and believes the scheme is an insult to retired Army staff. Harry Fletcher, the assistant general secretary of the NAPO, said:

'Community service, or unpaid work as it is now called, has been successfully run by the probation service for thirty-four years.'

I have to say that I disagree with Mr Fletcher on this point because there is ample evidence to show that community service really is a soft option and not a success. Take another example to support this. It was in November 2010 when a convict was ordered by a court to do 100 hours of unpaid work after a nightclub attack. Twice he failed to turn up and he also tampered with his electronic tag when he broke an 8pm curfew. He was summoned back to court.

He was asked by the judge: 'Would you rather go to prison than get out of bed and do unpaid work?'

He replied: 'It's not that I want to go to prison it's just that I don't want to do unpaid work.'

The judge activated the remainder of the six-month suspended sentence imposed in September when the man was in the dock for headbutting a man. Perhaps we should go back to hard labour where convicts break rocks for twelve hours a day and see what impact that has. [*Sunday Express* 19th September 2010]

Orange Bibs

Crime adviser, Louise Casey, identified that the criminal justice system is seen as 'too sympathetic' to criminals, and that many people working in the criminal justice system instinctively side with offenders, because they want to give them a second chance. The outcome is that the public think that the system is set up to meet the needs of criminals, rather than the victims of crime and the wider public. Ms Cassey is spot on. You only have to sit in court and hear what the offender organisations have to say for it to be very clear. Criminals matter, victims don't.

Ms Casey said: 'I think if you spend a lot of time with offenders you start to hear that they have had tough lives and you start to understand why they have ended up offending in the first place. You are a human being and you start to feel for these people. That is human.'

However, Ms Casey added: 'I think they miss something. The public want a criminal justice system that is not the criminal's justice system. They really want a public justice system.' [*The Times* 19th October 2009]

Again, spot on. This is, in part, one reason why I had to resign as a magistrate because to tackle the do-gooders was becoming impossible. So, how can it be that one person, appointed by the government, undertakes research which shows that two thirds of the public think the criminal justice system respects the rights of the offender more than the rights of victims and nobody in government takes one ounce of notice?

To make criminals more accountable for their crimes, Ms Casey proposed putting the outcome of court cases on websites and in leaflets as one way of letting people know when a person has been convicted of a crime in their neighbourhood. That has met with resistance from the do-gooders, who argue that it is not a proportionate response to offending and could breach a criminal's human rights. You will note that in every case of criminal activity the focus is on human rights.

When there is a victim, a breach of their human rights are never quoted.

You can see the problems that face magistrates and, indeed, judges on a daily basis and why the public consider that the system falls far short of delivering justice. It's all quite simple. If you don't break the law, you won't end up in a courtroom, you won't end up wearing an orange bib with 'Community Payback' on the back. You won't end up with your name on a leaflet being put through somebody's door and you won't be pointed out as a bad person. But, for those who break the rules there are some identifiable consequences and the public needs to know who the people are, and that they are being punished for their misdemeanors.

The assistant general secretary of the National Association of Probation Officers, told the BBC's Today programme:

'Wearing the so-called 'vests of shame' introduces unnecessary risk... there was no evidence that shaming worked and that if offenders were concerned for their safety, compliance would drop and cases would end up back in the courts. The real intention of the vests is to make the government look tougher on crime and to demean the offenders.' [*BBC1* 8th December 2009]

We then have the good news that probation chiefs will be working very closely with our diverse communities to ensure that High Visibility Vests (HVVs) are appropriately implemented, to reduce re-offending and protect the public. If any group claims that wearing a vest will adversely affect them, then they will not have to wear one. Any reservations raised about the practicality of implementing high visibility uniforms across the board, or questions about their suitability in some instances, must be addressed. However, it must not be forgotten that there is one rule of law in the land, and it applies to everybody, and I do mean everybody.

Young offenders helping to clear a towpath by the River Thames, near Hampton Court Palace in south-west London, were some of the first to wear the new bibs. One told *BBC Five Live*:

'We have got a board... already saying who we are, so why should we be pointed out like saying we are all criminals and stuff? People know it already, so why make it even worse.'

Somebody should have told this person that he/she is a convict having been convicted of a crime and everybody should know. If he/she was not happy about it then they should not commit crimes. We all have choices.

It was interesting that another offender did not object, saying the group had already been wearing yellow ones anyway. He said: 'It is better then being inside [prison] so anything will do.'

[*BBC1* 8th December 2009]

ASBOs

Anti Social Behaviour Orders (ASBOs) will reduce crime and be an effective deterrent! Sorry the jokes are not very good. ASBOs are, for the most part, an absolute waste of time and effort. There will the occasional case where the system works and I think the concept will change to reflect the failure.

One day when I was in court a male stood before us, guilty of a crime and virtually begging us to give him an ASBO. It transpired that all his mates had one and so he wanted one. It was seen as a badge of some sort of pride. Even though he demanded he be treated like his mates we were adamant that he was to be ASBO free. That was one very upset young male who departed court that day!

However, it was in July 2004 that I became part of what was described as a landmark legal case. It involved a drunk who regularly shouted and swore at people in the city centre and became one of the first people in the city to be made the subject of what was then a new style of anti-social behaviour order (ASBO). The individual who was aged forty-nine, had fifty-three convictions for eighty-five offences. Standing before us he admitted three charges of disorderly conduct and breaching a conditional discharge imposed for a similar offence. We thought prison was an option but that the new punishment would be better. So we banned him from a number of areas in the city between noon and 6am every day. We heard that he helped market traders set up their stalls and ran errands for them and was not a nuisance until the afternoons, after he had been drinking.

The media stated: Chairman *MichaelWelham* told the defendant, 'In reaching our decision we decided that you have behaved in an anti-social manner and that has been ongoing. The cases before us and your antecedents involve behaviour representing a trend which is unacceptable.'

We then banned him from certain areas, prohibited him from behaving in a threatening or abusive fashion. If he breached the order he would face a jail sentence. A police constable who had dealt with the individual on a number of occasions and had looked into his offending record, states:

'He has frequently been drunk and swearing in particular areas. He has a prolific pattern of offending in the city centre, the majority of those offences being public order orientated.'

The prosecutor told us that the defendant had been given a six-month conditional discharge. Four days later he committed the first of the offences for which he was before us in court. A member of the public pointed him out to police when he was swearing repeatedly. He clenched his fists and was shouting and swearing, despite being told to calm down. Then he was again found shouting and swearing in front of shoppers in the city centre. The next evening police were called to a disturbance and found the defendant, who had clearly been drinking, being very abusive. He was told to stop, but continued swearing and clenched his fists. He had to be prevented from moving towards a group of youths.

His defending lawyer said: 'He cannot recall the circumstances in any detail of any of the offences. He has a problem with drink and at times when he has been drinking behaves in this way.'

In court I spelt out the terms of the ASBO and provided him with a plan of the city with the areas that he was not allowed to enter clearly marked. I told him he was very fortunate that he was not going straight to prison but that he had to comply with the order. He just had a wry smile and said, 'Thank you sir.'

As he left the courtroom we all knew he would be back and would then go to prison.

During the lunch break a colleague who had sat with me on the case earlier in the morning, came in and reported that he had seen the defendant in the city centre, drunk and being verbally abusive and offensive to women and those with children. I advised the court so that the police could be called. Had the police been notified he could have been brought back to court and sent to jail. But nothing happened. The next time I was in court, a fellow chairman told me that he had sat on the following Saturday, when an old friend of mine came to court and was one of the clients. Yes, it was the defendant. My colleague told him that he had been warned by me about going to prison, to which he agreed. He was then told that was where he was going and that was where he went.

One witness to the activities of the defendant summed up the individual when he stated that: 'He was an alcoholic and as soon as he got a drink in him he was away. I have seen his record of previous convictions it's as long as my arm. When he is sober I have all the time in the world for him. He never turned violent though, he was just verbally abusive to people. I don't think we have seen the end of him. The police have tagged him in the past but he just took that off and threw it in the river. He is the kind of man who will go where he wants to.'

An officer of the law said: 'We've had a central problem with individuals who either persistently get drunk or who are under the influence of drugs who congregate on the city centre locations and act in an inappropriate manner. Police, for a number of years, have arrested these individuals for disorderly behaviour and drunkenness and they have been placed before the courts, and on the majority of occasions the individuals are fined. The government has passed laws which allow, in certain circumstances, for the court to impose anti-social behaviour orders on offenders; in effect banning them from the areas where their behaviour is affecting others.'

He continued: 'Some of the offenders have been given strict bail conditions to prevent them from offending in the area prior to their court appearance. However, some people have failed to keep to their conditions, so it's with these type of people that we will be seeking anti-social behaviour orders. People who continue with this type of behaviour will be targeted. The effect of an anti-social behaviour order can be far reaching, effectively banning people from areas for a maximum of five years.'

Tagging

One form of punishment that I, as a magistrate, have always had concerns about, is that of tagging. For those who don't know, tagging is where an electronic device is worn around the ankle of a person convicted of a crime and is often used instead of sending an individual into prison or some other form of punishment. It might be that an individual is unable to undertake work in the community with a community punishment order and so tagging offers an even softer alternative.

Generally, tagging means that an individual has to have a home with a telephone in the premises and through this telephone system he or she is restricted to the confines of the house. If they leave the house the device will indicate that they are no longer within the vicinity and therefore they are subject to arrest by the police.

The tagging scheme was introduced in 2000 and it covered such people as drug dealers, burglars and thieves who were forced to observe a night curfew with the magistrates being flexible on timings. Generally it would be a twelve hour period from say 7am to 7pm. To keep a person tagged costs about £42 a day to operate and it relays offenders' movements via satellite to a control room which are run by private firms. The aim is to alert the authorities if the criminal should enter an exclusion zone, such as a paedophile entering a children's play area or if the individual is not where he should be as part of these curfew requirements or if the equipment is removed this would be rapidly identified. However, what has been shown is that this system does have failings because buildings can provide a screen which means the system doesn't always work properly.

When you are looking at tagging an individual, which could be for as long as six months for those that are seriously bent on committing further offences, it holds absolutely no deterrent whatsoever. It has become evident that, for example, crimes by prisoners released early from jail wearing these electronic tags have increased quite dramatically to a figure quoted as being 400%. The one thing it is not is any form of effective deterrent to stop further crime.

Corporal and Capital Punishment

I have in my global travels, been on aircraft where, prior to landing in Vietnam, Singapore, Borneo, and Malaysia, there was an announcement made by cabin staff stating that the carrying of drugs into the country was illegal and that anybody found with any would face the death penalty. When passing through the immigration and customs checks, large notices provided a vivid statement to deliver the message. It is interesting to see people, having heard the announcement, make their way to the toilet prior to landing. Then on the ground others make for the first toilet they see, possibly unaware that they are observed by the authorities.

In China a mixture of police and soldiers were on guard outside a court building. Enquiring of our guide what was happening, he explained that it was punishment day for drug dealers. A family were persistent dealers and had received previous punishments. Having not heeded past warnings they now faced the final punishment. The entire family: grandparents, parents and children were to be shot. The authorities even made them pay for the bullets. Our guide considered that they caused misery and destruction to others for reward, so they had to pay the price for that greed.

I do not have a problem with the actions of these countries. They have a drugs issue and other serious offences and they deal with it. Because of the poverty of some and the greed of others, people take the risk but they know the penalty if they are caught. I understand that those caught can do deals with the authorities and have their life spared, in return for good reliable information about the drug operations. One thing is certain, most of those involved with drugs, if caught, will not do it again because they are dead.

Corporal Punishment

The Borneo jungle was hot and humid as our guide, a formidable lady, led the way pointing out things of interest. She never went anywhere without a very sharp machete which she wielded with skill. We came to a halt and I heard her call to me. I went forward to find her at the front of our small group. We had chats about crime and punishments, comparing the actions of the two countries. Her view was that the UK had a welfare system that provided everything, so why did people need to commit crimes and, why were punishments so soft. In her country there was no welfare system and there were very poor people. Many committed crime out of real necessity and the punishments were harsh. I found our guide standing alongside a tree with long vines creeping up it.

'This is what you need in the UK,' she exclaimed. She explained that it was rattan and from it came the *rotan* cane. She told me: 'We have a number of crimes where the punishment is the cane and this is what we use. Those who have been punished say they never want to be caned again.'

We had a long way to go and so the trek re-commenced and the subject was dropped until latter.

In the evening our guide again raised the subject of punishments. The conversation began with Turtle Island. We had made a visit to the island which was a small land mass comprising sand and vegetation with a research centre as the main building. Accommodation for visitors and staff was sited alongside. It was the place where great numbers of turtles came and laid their eggs. Because of theft by poachers, after the turtle had laid the eggs and gone back to the sea, the staff dug up the eggs. They were then taken to the hatchery where they were incubated and stayed until old enough to be released back into the wild. Without this conservation programme, one particular species of turtle would now be extinct. Our guide explained that the army had a camp on the Island and the reason was to protect the turtle population from poachers. Once it got dark we visitors were confined to the centre and the army were on patrol. They would take prisoner any trespasser and if they fled or fought then the army would and did shoot them. The poachers came by boat from another country with one intention and those captured were taken to the mainland and to court. They received four months in prison with four strokes of the *rotan* cane. One stroke was given for each month. So, just as a convict got over the pain, they received the next stroke. Once they had served their sentence they were deported. I asked how many repeat offenders there were.

Without hesitation she said: 'None really, but other people try. They have nothing in their own country and so they become desperate.'

I told her that one big problem for the UK is the use of drugs. She pondered and then said, 'Drugs are a problem here and they are illegal. If you are caught dealing or carrying a saleable quantity then it's the death penalty. There is no debate about it, you die!'

If you are caught with a small amount of drugs you go to prison and get the cane. The number of strokes will depend on the seriousness of the crime.

In addition to Malaysia (Borneo is part of Malaysia), Singapore and Brunei have caning as a punishment. It is for males only and they can be sentenced to a maximum of twenty-four strokes of the cane on the bare buttocks; the punishment is mandatory for many offences, mostly violent or drug crimes, but also immigration violations, sexual offences and in Singapore caning can be ordered for over thirty offences, including hostage-taking, robbery, gang robbery with murder, drug use, vandalism and rioting. Caning is also a mandatory punishment for certain offences such as rape, drug trafficking, illegal money-lending, and for visiting foreigners who overstay their visa by more than ninety days, a measure designed to deter illegal immigrant workers. The punishment is applied to both locals and foreigners. Prisons may impose corporal punishment not exceeding twelve strokes of the cane for aggravated prison offences. Inmates of Drug Rehabilitation Centres may be caned in the same way. A *rotan* cane has a length of 1.2 metres [four feet] and is 1.27 cm [half an inch] thick. The cane is soaked in water beforehand to make it heavier and more flexible and is treated with antiseptic before use to prevent infection. A lighter cane is used for offenders aged under eighteen.

Caning is always ordered in addition to a jail sentence and never as a punishment by itself. It is administered in a separate area within the prison, out of view of the public and other convicts. Those present are limited to the convict, prison officers, medical officers, the caning officer and sometimes other prison officials. An inmate sentenced to caning is only notified on the day his sentence is to be carried out. In the caning room, he is ordered to strip naked and given a medical check by the prison doctor to ensure that he is medically suitable to receive the punishment. When the doctor passes the convict as fit, the punishment is given. If the doctor finds him unfit for the punishment, he is sent back to the court for his prison term to be increased as an alternative.

A prison official confirms the number of strokes the convict is to receive. He is then taken to the A-shaped frame where his wrists and ankles are secured tightly to the frame by strong leather straps, in such a way that he assumes a bent-over position on the frame with his posterior protruding. Protective padding is placed on his lower back to protect the vulnerable kidney and lower spine area from any mis-strokes. Only his buttocks are exposed to the cane. The officer administering the caning takes up position beside the frame and delivers the number of strokes specified in the sentence. He is required to put his full force into each stroke. If more than one stroke is given, the medical officer can stop the caning because of the convict's physical condition. In this situation the rest of the strokes are converted to additional prison time. After the caning, the inmate is released from the frame and receives medical treatment. An antiseptic lotion is applied to the wounds which are left to heal and, where a large number of strokes are given, there is long-term scarring of the buttocks.

In bygone days the UK did not use the *rotan* cane but adopted the birch. This was comprised of a bundle of leafless twigs, bound together to form a device for administering corporal punishment. The birch is not always made from birch twigs, but can also be made from various other strong and smooth branches of trees or shrubs, such as willow. However, a hazel cane is said to be particularly painful. It was a device of four or five hazel twigs that was used in the 1960s and 1970s on the Isle of Man, the last jurisdiction in Europe to use birching as a judicial punishment.

Another factor in the severity of a birch is its size e.g. its length, weight and number of branches. Birches were soaked in brine, a heavily salted water, before use which greatly increased the weight, flexibility and strength of the twigs, making the punishment more severe in terms of pain. There was also damage to the victim's flesh in the form of cuts and weals but because of its antiseptic properties, the brine helped prevent infection developing in the wounds following the punishment.

Birching as a judicial penalty, in both its juvenile and adult versions, was abolished in the UK in 1948, although it was retained until 1962 as a punishment for violent breaches of prison discipline. The Isle of Man with its own legal system continued to birch young offenders until 1976. The birch was also used on offending teenage boys until the mid-1960s on the Channel Islands of Guernsey and Jersey.

There are many who advocate the return of the birch to deal with the mass of violent offenders who are a scourge of our institutions who, when released, continue their rampage against society. From what can be ascertained, where a cane is used in other parts of the world it is effective in crime reduction. Of course the re-introduction of such a measure would be strongly opposed by the growing army of do-gooders who seem to love criminals and their violent crimes. But its re-introduction could well help with our growing crime problem.

Capital Punishment

Court open days were one of the positive outcomes of court work. This was a busy time with every aspect of court activities on display with the public free to walk round and chat to people who deal with the subject on a daily basis. It was a good time to ask all those awkward questions. Visitors even got to see the cells and inside one of the prison vans that transport convicts between courts and prisons.

I opted to be on the front desk to meet and greet visitors, a job shared with a colleague. Before the visitors arrived I liked to have a look at the exhibits and have a quick chat to people I often only saw on the other side of the court. On one particular day, I entered one of the courtrooms dedicated to punishments over the years. The exhibit had been put together by one of our court legal advisors and her husband, a defence solicitor, both keen and excellent people. As I walked in I noticed some of our legal advisors standing chatting. They turned to see who had entered. But my attention was drawn to the dock where a gibbet and hangman's noose had been erected. As I smiled the legal advisors in unison said: 'No Mr Welham, hanging has not been brought back, it's only for display.' I think I must have had a reputation!

In his book, *Hangmen of England*, Brian Bailey writes of The Royal Commission of 1949 who were provided with a memorandum by the Home Office which said:

'Some twenty minutes before the time fixed for the execution, the High Sheriff, or more usually the Under Sheriff, arrives at the prison and, a few minutes before it is due, proceeds with the Governor and medical officer to the place of execution. The executioner and his assistant wait outside the condemned cell with the chief officer and officer detailed to conduct the prisoner to the execution chamber. On a signal given by the Sheriff they enter and the executioner pinions the prisoner's arms behind his back. He is escorted to the drop with one officer on either side. The Sheriff, the Governor and the medical officer enter the execution chamber directly by another door.

The prisoner is placed on the drop on a marked spot so that his feet are directly across the division of the trap doors. The executioner places a white cap over the prisoner's head and places the noose round his neck, while the assistant pinions his legs. When the executioner sees that all is ready he pulls the lever. The medical officer at once proceeds to the pit and examines the prisoner to see that life is extinct. The shed is then locked and the body hangs for one hour. The inquest is held the same morning. Burial of the body takes place in the prison graveyard during the dinner hour. The chaplain reads the burial service.'

But what of the hangmen whose job it was to carry out the task. One of the more well known was Albert Pierrepoint who was an executioner for nearly twenty-four years. It was on 23rd February 1956 that he submitted his resignation to the Prison Commissioners. Later, having retired, Pierrepoint published his autobiography. In the preface he wrote:

'The fruit of my experience has this bitter after-taste: that I do not now believe that any one of the hundreds of executions I carried out has in any way acted as a deterrent against future murder. Capital punishment, in my view, achieved nothing except revenge.'

In the main body of the book he wrote: 'I now sincerely hope that no man is ever called upon to carry out another execution in my country. I have come to the conclusion that executions solve nothing, and are only an antiquated relic of a primitive desire for revenge which takes the easy way and hands over the responsibility for revenge to other people.

I have seen prison officers faint on the scaffold, strong men weep and women prison officers sobbing helplessly. I have known prison doctors who could not examine the body after execution because the beat of their own heart was obliterating anything they could distinguish. I have felt overpowering sorrow for the victims of crime, for little children murdered, for the families of all concerned, for the special worry which policemen's wives always suffer and for the tragic occasions when it is justified. Yet I have had many friends in the police and in the prison service who also feel very strongly against capital punishment.

It is said to be a deterrent. I cannot agree. There have been murders since the beginning of time, and we shall go on looking for deterrents until the end of time. If death were a deterrent, I might be expected to know. It is I who have faced them last, young lads and girls, working men, grandmothers. I have been amazed to see the courage with which they take that walk into the unknown. It did not deter them then, and it had not deterred them when they committed what they were convicted for. All the men and women whom I have faced at that final moment convince me that in what I have done, I have not prevented a single murder.'

Geoffrey Robertson, a Barrister, has a chapter in his book, *The Justice Game,* in which he provides a description of hangings as described by a prison warden who had seen many:

'When the trap springs the prisoner dangles at the end of the rope. There are times when the neck has not been broken and the prisoner strangles to death. His eyes pop almost out of his head, his tongue swells and protrudes from his mouth, his neck may be broken, and the rope many times takes large portions of skin and flesh from the side of the face that the noose is on. He urinates, he defecates and droppings fall to the floor while witnesses look on. A prison guard stands at the feet of the hanged person and holds the body steady, because during the first few minutes there is usually considerable struggling in an effort to breathe.'

The National Campaign for the Abolition of Capital Punishment gained momentum and in December 1969, the Houses of Commons and Lords approved total abolition of the death penalty for murder. In 1974, when the House of Commons debated bringing back the death penalty for acts of terrorism, those voting in favour numbered 217 of Members of Parliament, and included the Prime Minister. The move to reintroduce capital punishment was defeated then, and has been again since, but 218 MPs, again led by Mrs Thatcher, still voted for its return in 1988.

It is without doubt a fact that capital punishment permanently removes the worst criminals from society. It means that those executed will never be released to commit further serious offence. It is also without doubt cheaper that keeping a convict in prison for long periods. Support for the death penalty in Britain seems to have remained steady and is particularly strongly supported by young people. It is claimed that it would be politically impossible to reintroduce capital punishment given our membership of the EU and our commitment to the European Convention on Human Rights.

One issue that is always quoted, even by those who want some form of capital punishment, is the concern that innocent people have been, and could in the future, be executed. That said, DNA has gone a long way to redress the balance in favour of correct identification of convicts. The fact is that the police, the courts and the legal system generally cannot be trusted to get things right. They never have been able to previously and it is doubtful that they would today and so would juries be willing to convict in capital cases where they have to make the decision as to whether the person in the dock should live or die? Even more importantly will governments who are in power for five years, be willing to carry out death sentences. Criminals and the anti death penalty lobby would use their vote for the government that will not execute. It is also very unlikely the very worst murderers would be deterred because they are typically psychopaths or of such dubious sanity, that they are incapable of rational behaviour. They often take their own lives immediately after the crime, as in the cases at Hungerford, Dunblane and Cumbria. Terrorists will not be deterred from their cause of mass murder. Drug traffickers may be deterred because they have a clear option knowing the risks. However, it would not deter those drunk or on drugs from kicking somebody to death. Then there is the situation where a person has a serious argument with their partner and in the heat of the moment, fearing more violence, picks up a carving knife and uses it to kill.

The question is, does the death penalty deter? Well in countries such as Singapore which almost always carry out death sentences, there is a claim that the death penalty is a deterrent, but only where execution is an absolute certainty. Statistics were kept for the five years that capital punishment was suspended in Britain (1965-1969) and these showed a 125% rise in murders that would have attracted a death sentence. Would there have been less if capital punishment had been an option?

Despite what the government states, we are in a period of ever rising serious crime, and it is going to get worse. On a daily basis we hear of people being stabbed, shot and kicked to death and the public in general has become concerned about what is going on. They see those caught receiving derisory punishments and the do-gooders crowing for better prison conditions, less custodial punishments. Those who stop at the re-introduction of the death penalty see whole life imprisonment as an answer for the worst murders with suitable sentences for other murder cases. This means that there would need to be degrees of murder, such as in the USA that would distinguish between pre-meditated killing and those killings that, whilst still homicide, are much more understandable to the public. Therefore, juries would find it easier finding a prisoner guilty and judges the ability to pass sensible, determinate sentences based upon the facts of the crime as presented to the court.

One very real problem is that we see murderers being able to 'get off' on the grounds of diminished responsibility with their alleged psychiatric disorders or by plea bargaining by going guilty to a lesser sentence of manslaughter. It removes peoples' faith in justice which is very dangerous. People want terms of imprisonment that removes convicts from society for a given period, and in my opinion where life is given, it should mean life and the convict dies in prison.

Thankfully at this time, some parts of society still view murder as a particularly heinous crime which should justify the most severe punishment. Putting people away does not provide a guarantee because do-gooders in future governments may release such offenders. As time progresses it is very difficult to remember the awfulness of an individual's crime and easy for the do-gooders to claim that they have reformed. You only have to look at the killers of Jamie Bulger, adopted by the do-gooders as good citizens, given new identities costing the nation millions, to see where we are headed. [*capitalpunishmentuk.org*]

4

Mrs Windsor's Hotels

Take Him or Her 'Down'

When I first sat as a magistrate the sending of a convicted person to prison began with the sentence, 'For the offence you have committed you are going to prison for six months'. This was immediately followed with instructions to the cells officers to 'take him or her down' because the cells are generally below the courtroom. Do-gooders complained that 'take them down' was not politically correct and the convicts were upset by the words. So we were advised to say 'Unfortunately you have to go to prison for six months, but you will only be in prison for three months if you are good and do as you are told. Will you please go with the officers, thank you'. So convicts have been asked nicely to serve only half of the original sentence and whilst inconvenient, they are happy that they have been asked nicely to leave the courtroom. The do-gooders are happy that a court client, in the real world a convict, has been given reasons for his/her unfortunate incarceration and been invited to go and do what the nasty magistrates and judges have imposed.

The people I sent to prison deserved to go based on evidence and a fair trial. Most had used violence of some form and being polite was the last thing I had on my mind. Often, it was a case of 'if I had more than a six months sentence available that is what you would be getting.' Once sentenced, the convict would wait in the court cells until a van conveyed them to prison. Sending a convict down generally left a family to get by whilst the individual was away. For some it was a normal event and just down to the bad luck of getting caught. For others, where criminal activity was not a regular occurrence, it brought hardships. That said, being sent to prison is reserved for serious offences and generally linked to a record of numerous previous offences. A newspaper article describes the impact on the family where one of their number serves time in prison:

Rachel Jenkins says that she will never forget the four years that her stepfather served in prison and the devastating effect it had on her, her mother, sister and brother. She was fifteen at the time and recalls many harrowing Saturdays spent travelling from the family home in Neath, Glamorgan, to Cardiff and, later, Parc prison in Bridgend.

'I remember every other Saturday spending hours on a bus, then a train and then another bus to get to the prison, then coming home in the dark, exhausted. We were always terrified of sniffer dogs because there were rugby fans on the train smoking drugs and we thought the smell might get on our clothes.'

Rachel's stepfather has since been released, settled back into the family home and found a job. Looking back, Rachel cannot believe that her mother was not given any help. 'The cost of the transport for the visits was about £50 a time for all of us and she was on benefits. I would also have really loved someone to talk to, someone who had been through it or at least knew how to talk to a child about what it was like. It is very tempting for children to put a brave face on so they don't upset their other parent, but it was really hard for us.' [*The Times*, 19th October 2009]

Well Ms Jenkins, the problem is that your stepfather committed a crime and I would imagine that the full sentence was about eight years as prisoners only serve half the sentence in prison. Now to get a sentence of that length the crime would have been quite serious. I know it's not your crime, but you, as do many other families, suffer the consequences of somebody else's actions. It was a situation where your mother would not be entitled to any financial help for travel as the argument was why should the state, ultimately the tax payer, hand out money when somebody has been imprisoned for a criminal act. The good news would be that her stepfather upon release found a job and hopefully has a settled life.

However, I then discover that relatives who claim benefits can claim cash to make visits to convicts in prison. They can spend the money on petrol, hire cars, taxis, trains, ferries and even plane tickets. It can also pay for child care, food and drink and overnight stays. The Ministry of Justice's Assisted Prison Visits scheme cost more than £3 million in 2010 to fund 73,000 visits to prisons in England and Wales. The idea is to help prisoners maintain family ties through visits every two weeks, in the hope it will help them go straight when they are released. Oh how nice and thoughtful!

TaxPayers' Alliance campaign manager Charlotte Linacre sums it all up when she said: 'With many law-abiding people struggling to pay for their own travel because of high fuel prices, it's worrying the costs of this scheme run into such large sums. It's unfair to expect taxpayers to fund taxis and planes for criminals to see their families if they can't afford to travel that way themselves to see their own relatives.'

If that is not bad enough we find that the application form for the cash is translated into ten languages. That's nice! [*The Sun* 1st February 2011]

Ms Jenkins' family were obviously unaware of these generous handouts. Perhaps the forms are not in the English or Welsh languages.

What's It Like in Prison?

I have visited prisons and they are certainly places that I would not want to stay in and I fail to understand why anybody would be prepared to return again and again. I received an article from an unknown source that was dated 2001. It was written by Erwin James and titled '*Does prison work?*' I have taken the liberty of reproducing it in full as it provides one persons view of what happens once a convict is sentenced and goes to prison.

'…my first day as a prisoner. I'm walking along a gantry-style landing on the long-term wing of a large London prison. I'm on the third floor – 'the threes'. I'm carrying a plastic bucket inside which clatters a plastic cup, knife, fork and spoon. Under my arm I have a 'bedroll': two flannel sheets rolled up inside two coarse blankets. I'm guided to my cell by a large prison officer sporting a handlebar moustache. The peak of his cap has been 'slashed' so it fits low over the bridge of his nose. We reach the cell and with a noisy rattle of his keys he unlocks the door and pushes it open. He's smiling, "In you go son, don't be shy." The door slams shut behind me.

The cell is dimly lit by a small, grime-covered fluorescent light. The walls are covered in cracked and flaking emulsion. There's a table, a chair and a metal bed, with a stained mattress and half a foam pillow. The heavily barred window high up on the wall is closed, and the urine-tainted air makes me want to retch. I sit down on the bed. Time to collect my thoughts – but no, I hear a sound like rolling thunder approaching fast, and suddenly the cell door is unlocked and pushed open again. "Slop out and get your tea," instructs handlebars…'

It is certainly a grim picture of life behind bars and begs the question, why would anybody want to commit an act that would expose them to the possibility of being locked away in that environment?

Then there were the views of Jonathan Aitkin, a former cabinet minister who was jailed for perjury and perverting the course of justice. He was sentenced to eighteen months in prison for each offence, with the two terms running concurrently. His legal counsel told the court his client had already suffered enough and said:

'The fall from grace has been complete, his marriage has broken down, he has lost his home, he is one of only three people this century forced to resign from the Privy Council, he is bankrupt and his health has suffered.'

However, the sentence could have been far harsher. Perverting the course of justice carries a maximum sentence of life imprisonment, while perjury can be punished with a seven-year jail term.

'...prison, for him, was a distinctly uncomfortable experience. He considered that an inmate would be unwise to whinge about the discomforts that they experience which include non-stop noise, stale tobacco odour, dodgy drains and intense overcrowding alongside some awkward, occasionally aggressive fellow prisoners...' [*Daily Mail*, 15th May 2007]

I offer no apology when I say that I have no sympathy whatsoever with the convicts who serve time. As the saying goes, you do the crime so you must be prepared to do the time. Why should it be comfortable and cosy? Why should the food be better than in hospital and why should the conditions be better than many old peoples' nursing homes? Prison should be a place that, once you have been in, you do not want to go again. So why do people commit further crimes that send them back?

Prison Staff – a Softer Approach

There was a study by Her Majesty's Chief Inspector of Prisons which concluded that prisoners [convicts] were not living in a good environment and recommended that staff should soften their approach. This means that when officers want to search cells for drugs and weapons, they will have to ask permission before entering cells. Can you believe it and it's not April 1st? This applies to prisons that house murderers, rapists and robbers as well as those convicted of other serious crimes. To add insult to the victims of serious crimes, prison management have set up teams to ensure the Report's recommendations are carried out.

One prison officer was reported as stating: 'We are in a constant battle against drugs and mobile phones being brought into the prison. To have to ask permission to enter a cell stops us from doing our job. Those extra few seconds delay could be crucial because the prisoners know how to hide pretty much anything.'

Yet the government of the day, you know the tough on crime lot, encouraged the new recommendations. This is all part of the absolute madness of the drive to continue with the misinterpretation of the Human Rights Act. After all, what is a prisoner in prison for? Are they not convicts, having been convicted of a crime, often a serious crime? If prison officers have to become nannies and be nice to the inmates, it is an insult to those who do a difficult job.

It doesn't get any better. How about Colin Gunn, who was sent to prison for thirty-five years in 2006 after he ordered the execution of Mr and Mrs Stirland at their Lincolnshire home because they were related to someone who had crossed him. Gunn, who had headed a drug empire, claimed that guards were not treating him with enough respect. So he complained to the ombudsman while he was being held at Whitemoor Prison and won a ruling in his favour. In his complaint, he demanded that he be called 'Mr Gunn' and can you believe it, the Prisons and Probation Ombudsman upheld his complaint.

Gunn then wrote a letter to the prisoners' newspaper, *Inside Time,* from his cell. He called on other inmates including murderers, rapists, paedophiles and drug dealers to stand up for their rights and complain to the ombudsman if they were humiliated by rude, ignorant prison staff. He wrote:

'The law is on your side, so do not give in. It is no longer acceptable to address prisoners by surname alone. Staff address me as Mr Gunn, although they were very reluctant to do so at first. None of the prison staff like it but that's tough because they do not have a choice.'

This is the same set of laws that he and those like him rejected when they committed their heinous crimes.

Colin Moses, national chairman of the Prison Officers Association, the POA, responded: 'It's political correctness gone absolutely barmy. Gunn has rights but so do staff and the public and I believe it's wrong that staff have been put in a position where they can be complained about if they forget to call Gunn 'Mr'. The next thing I can see happening is the ombudsman asking us to call them 'sir'.'

He added: 'The ombudsman should be looking at how to protect law-abiding prison officers, not to pander to murderers.'

However, the Prison Service guidelines say prisoners should be addressed in the way they prefer and also instruct guards to knock on doors before entering cells.

A Prison Service spokesman said: 'Previous director generals have made clear that as part of the process of treating prisoners decently, staff should be encouraged to address prisoners in an appropriate manner. This will generally mean addressing the prisoner by his or her forename or by the use of 'Mr'.' [*Daily Express* 6th December 2010]

Then the insanity increased when a convict paid £33 to change his name to 'Sir', so that is what prison officers would have to call him over the tannoy and when dealing with him on the landings.

Mr Blair and Mr Brown allowed and encouraged this sort of thing to happen and no doubt Mr Cameron and Mr Clegg will continue to do so. Respect has to be earned and the sort of people being dealt with only understand that respect is via a gun, knife or some other weapon. Prison is not working and it's not reducing repeat crimes. The rehabilitation aspect of the bizarre lovey dovey approach is an even bigger failure. What is the point of magistrates and judges sending people to prison if this is what happens?

Food, Glorious Food

In August 2009, the media revealed that some hospitals spend less on meals than is spent on a convict. In fact it appears that ten hospitals spent less on breakfast, lunch and an evening meal than the £2.12 a day allocated for food by the prison service. One spent just £1 per person. However, in fairness most hospitals do spend more than £2.12 but prisoners end up better fed than patients. Experts from Bournemouth University studied the food offered to inmates and across the NHS and found patients fared less well than convicts.

This is supported by Professor John Edwards who was quoted as saying: 'If you are in prison then the diet you get is extremely good in terms of nutritional content, the food that is provided is actually better than most civilians have, there's a focus on carbohydrates, then there's the way they prepare the food, it's very healthy. They don't add salt and there's relatively little frying of food, if you have a burger then it goes in the oven. Hospital patients don't consume enough.' [*Daily Mail* 30th August 2009]

If you think that's bad then how about the actions of Prisons Minister, Crispin Blunt who says: 'Prisoners must be given a choice of at least five different dishes for dinner... Under new rules quickly dubbed 'Porridge à la Carte... Inmates will be presented with a menu from which to select their desired meal from the five on offer. Governors must change the menu regularly to ensure the same options do not appear more than once a month.'

The order dictating the changes even insists that prisoners are 'consulted' about the quality of meals served. This is the same prisons minister who previously gave the go-ahead for Halloween and Christmas parties for inmates. The rules, issued by the Ministry of Justice, have been sent to every jail in England and Wales and they came into force on 1st October 2010.

The 'Catering – Meals for Prisoners' section in Prison Service Instruction number 44/2010 states:

'A multi-choice, minimum five choices, pre-select menu including a minimum of one substantial hot meal choice per day will be provided for the lunch time or evening meal.'

Food must meet the 'cultural, nutritional and diversity needs' of inmates, the order states. It adds: 'The menu provides information which enables prisoners to make decisions about their menu choice. The menu cycle will be for a minimum of four weeks.

Prisoners are consulted about and can make comments on the catering provision. Officials said each menu would include a hot meal, a cold meal, a vegetarian option and one that is free of dairy products.' [*Daily Mail* 16th October 2010]

The directive requires drug addicts trying to get clean to be given hot chocolate because it is 'comforting'. Every menu must also include a halal meal that complies with the Islamic code on how animals should be slaughtered. New inmates must be given an arrival pack containing tea and coffee, sweets and cigarettes. And late arrivals, such as newly-sentenced prisoners, must be given a hot meal even if they arrive at the prison after all the other inmates have eaten.

I have to say that I agree with the comments of Fiona McEvoy, campaign manager at the Taxpayers' Alliance, who stated:

'While many ordinary, law-abiding taxpayers struggle for cash and brace themselves for cuts in services, these convicts are getting five-star treatment on the public purse. The amount of effort and planning going into these menus is just insulting – it seems criminals are being fed better than patients, school children and the elderly in many cases. No one would deny inmates a decent meal, but this is just ridiculous.'

Then Mr Blunt is said to have told the House of Commons that undersize fruit handed out at jail canteens could create 'issues of order and control'. He claims: 'It is worth remembering that discontent about the quality of food, changes to menus and failure to deliver what was previously promised have been known to be the catalyst for serious disturbances… An undersize apple handed out at the servery will create issues of order and control, so we use suppliers that are sensitive to that need and that use their sourcing ability to maintain consistency from their supply base.'

It is the same Mr Blunt who lifted a ban on taxpayer funded prisoner parties and comedy workshops for high security inmates.

Fortunately somebody with an ounce of sense in Downing Street reversed the decision the following day. But Mr Blunt continued his exploits when he said convicts could get their jail sentences slashed if they said sorry. The insanity did not stop because newly released prisoners were being offered free mobile phones in a taxpayer-funded 'welcome pack' when they arrive at bail hostels. Again, it seems that Downing Street stepped in and reversed these actions. I am sure that there is a better job for Mr Crispin Blunt, preferably one that does not require him to make any proper decisions and nothing to do with convicts and possibly on the other side of the world.

Tory MP Philip Davies said: 'At a time when the government is looking for ways to save money, it's quite extraordinary that the only people who look like they are going to be better off are prisoners. As far as I'm concerned, it's absolutely unacceptable and I think the public will be outraged.'

A Prison Service spokesperson said: 'The choice of meals that are available to prisoners reflect both religious and medical requirements, including halal, dairy free and vegetarian options. In practice this means a number of prisoners only have one choice.'

Whatever happened to porridge? How did we get into a situation where convicts are pandered too. A term in prison is a punishment for wrong doing, remember only the serious cases involve going to prison. It should be a place that nobody wants to return to.

As if all that is not bad enough convicts are getting upset because canteen goods prices at prisons' in England and Wales have risen by up to 71%. Convicts complain that that food inside, now costs more than at supermarkets on the outside. An outside contractor provides prisons with 'canteen goods'. Many of the 750 items on its supply list have soared in price since a new contractor took over. They include: Tuna chunks £1.49 (were 87p, up 71%); Branston Pickle £1.55 (£1.05, 68%); Heinz Baked Beans 75p (58p, 29%); Kellogg's Cornflakes £2.19 (£1.69, 29%). Equivalent supermarket prices are tuna 78p, pickle £1.20 and beans 53p. A 500g box of cornflakes is £1.93.

One convict is reported as saying: 'Prison grub isn't up to much, so we look forward to our canteen orders, even if it's just a jar of pickle.'

A prison source said: 'Prisoners get only around £10 a week for 32 hours' work, so these rises really hurt.' [*Sun* 8th Oct 2009]

Perhaps it is a perverse justice when convicts are at the receiving end of what they no doubt see as a criminal act. However, it all combines to provide the evidence that confirms that the convicts are running the prisons supported by political lunatics who run the asylum.

They Want Compensation

A group of 164 convicts fell ill after eating egg and cress rolls infected with salmonella. That found lawyers filing a claim demanding £1,800 compensation for each of the rapists, paedophiles, killers and drug-dealers. The money is for 'pain, suffering and loss of amenity'. Those sound like some of the symptoms suffered by their victims. Oops, sorry, victims don't count.

We are told that the writ says: 'All suffered diarrhoea and vomiting shortly after their consumption of the contaminated egg and cress sandwiches. Most were confined to their cells for the duration of their symptoms, in consequence of which they were unable to exercise, make phone calls, socialise or meet visitors.'

Oh dear what a shame, however, Whitehall commented: 'There is no doubt that compensation will be paid, but the amount of money the prisoners are after will be contested vigorously.'

They then added the understatement of 2010: 'There will be very little public sympathy for this.'

Well they got that bit right, £300,000 worth of no sympathy. The only sound advice to be offered to the do-gooders who allowed eggy rolls in the prison is that if the prisons stuck to porridge there would not be the problem!

Customer Satisfaction

Nanny state England is so concerned about the welfare of those arrested by the police that a night in the cells is now followed by a 'customer satisfaction' survey, with those detained in custody being asked to rate the 'services' on offer. Now, I fully accept that not everybody who is arrested is charged with an offence. Those who are held for interview or possible court action are innocent, until charged and proven guilty. This is particularly so when the media reports so many cases of the wrong person being arrested. A system where a complaint against poor treatment is one thing but a customer satisfaction survey is another.

I did check the date to see if it was April 1st, alas, it was not.

The survey form was part of a pilot scheme undertaken by Devon and Cornwall Constabulary who stated they are committed to providing the best possible service to people who are detained in custody. They ask: 'We would be grateful if you could complete the following survey and return it to the custody centre.'

Best described as a hotel-style questionnaire it asks for their views on the quality of a variety of aspects of their incarceration, including the food, how 'safe' they felt, brightness of the cells, cleanliness, lighting and air temperature and the provision of towels.

One officer in the force said: 'These people are in the cell for a reason, it's not like they've come here on holiday. They are starting to treat the emergency cell buzzer like a room service hotline.'

He added: 'We are getting asked all sorts – to get them celebrity magazines, to put aircon on, to bring them a salad.'

But Chief Inspector Ivan Trethewey, the force's head of custody who is behind the project, told *Police Review* magazine:

'It does not mean we will be providing steak dinners as a result. There could be some valuable learning points however, I wanted a reality check: what I think the service is that we are providing versus what detainees tell us we are giving them.'

Dave James, secretary of Devon and Cornwall Police Federation, said: 'You would not get a questionnaire that detailed in a Holiday Inn.'

Superintendent Chris Brown, head of the force's criminal justice unit, said 'We must also be mindful that not all those in our custody are charged with a crime and, indeed, for some the custody centre is used as a place where members of the public, not guilty of any crime, can be assessed under the Mental Health Act.' [*Daily Telegraph* 13th August 2009]

So if you are travelling in Devon or Cornwall and need a place to stay try a local police station, you will be welcome and very well looked after. If not you can complain and no doubt bags of compensation will be forthcoming.

Measure A Prisoners' Quality Of Life

There is no money in the countries coffers. Thousands are to lose their jobs. Vital projects to keep the country operating are stopped. Schools cannot be upgraded. The list is a long one but you can be comforted with the knowledge that the Ministry of Justice is to continue with an annual survey (started in 2002 as another New Labour money squandering exercise) despite massive cuts to its budget. It is expected to cost taxpayers an astonishing £449,000. What is the survey? It is to measure the quality of prison life. Oh yes it is! It's the real do-gooders charter. Inmates at almost half of the country's jails will be asked if they feel looked after and how well they get on with prison officers. Are they treated as a person of value in the prison. Is the prison good at placing trust in prisoners. Do inmates have opportunities to relax and be themselves. What are their washing facilities like. Are they allowed enough time on the telephone. Do they sleep well. Does their stay 'feel like a punishment'.

The Prison Service actually defended the survey as they claim it helped prison governors make sure facilities were acceptable. The MoJ says that the results from the Measuring Prisoners' Quality of Life survey, help prison governors ensure they are reforming offenders in an environment that is safe and secure. What a lot of twaddle. Prisons already have Her Majesty's Chief Inspector of Prisons reports and Independent Monitoring Board reports. And each jail also has members of the public who can enter prisons without permission to check prisoners are not being mistreated.

The final word goes to John O'Connell, research director of the TaxPayers' Alliance, who said: 'Taxpayers will be annoyed that they will have to foot the bill for this. It's important that prisoners are safe and healthy while serving their sentences, but there are already measures in place to ensure that's happening. With necessary reductions in spending on the way, it's more crucial than ever that the prison service finds value for money and cutting back on these kinds of surveys is a good place to start.' [*Daily Mail* 2nd March 2011]

Smoke Alarm

As of the 1st July 2007, there was a smoking ban introduced in the UK as part of the workplace health and safety legislation. This meant that people were not allowed to smoke in any public building, shop, office, hotel, restaurant etc. It seems that the rules do not apply to prisons because convicts are allowed to smoke and prison officers are not. Convicts are able to smoke in their cells, even though the ban has been introduced, because it is classified as being their home. Their home? They are incarcerated in a prison. It appears that a convict who doesn't want to share with a smoker is able to move to a non-smoking cell. This has resulted in governors having to juggle convicts around in what is already an overcrowded place.

As with workplaces throughout the country, prison officers are forced to leave the building to have a cigarette because it is their place of work, whilst the convict can remain in his/her cell smoking to their heart's content. To accommodate this, money, which neither the prison service nor the government has spare, had to be spent to ensure that cells are smoke proof to protect the health of inmates who don't have the habit. It has to be asked why should the tax payer pick up the cost of moving convicts about and the expense of providing smoke extraction equipment. Convicts give up certain rights when they go to jail, and smoking should be one of them. Smoking should be banned completely within the prison which is a work place because prison officers have to access all areas. Prison officers should be provided with suitable smoking areas outside of the building like other workplaces in the UK. If the convicts don't like the rule then don't commit the crime.

Illegal Drugs

Most prisons are swamped with illegal drugs and many convicts are released from prison without any form of treatment being given to them. In fact, the British Medical Association called for hit squads of prison and police offers to go into every prison in England and Wales to assess the extent of the drugs crisis. What about the infringements of their Human Rights? I was told that the prison authorities don't clamp down too hard on drugs because when prisoners are high on their drugs they are generally not offending. What this means is that they are less of a problem to prison staff when they are spaced out and not inclined to be disruptive. The real problem is that prisons become swamped with illegal drugs and that creates an environment where it is almost impossible to get somebody off a drug habit. Drug dealers have a free reign in prison, anybody entering prison who doesn't take drugs can rapidly be induced to taking drugs as part of expanding trade. Once you are on drugs and hooked, you are part of the system and all the problems that go with it. Why does nobody want to deal with the problem?

Pay for Crime

It costs the tax payer £33,000 a year to keep a person in prison and for most of them, once in prison, they virtually sit on their behinds and do very little. In fact they contribute nothing to society. Some do work and some undertake training because it's a way of gaining some sort of income to buy cigarettes and other luxuries. Others do physical exercise in their purpose built gyms.

One answer came from Mrs Blair who wanted to pay convicts £10,000 a year for working. What this means is that a large multinational company would put work into a prison and a sum of money would be paid by that company to the prison. That is fine but the money must not go into the pockets of the convicts who perpetrated the offences so he/she can buy goodies and drugs. It must be given to the victims, so that they can get their lives in order, get damaged or stolen property repaired or replaced and injuries treated. After that, any money earned should go to the prison to pay for the convicts board and lodging whilst inside. In other words, the convict pays for the privilege of being inside and the prison becomes self-funding.

Convicts who fail to work or refuse to work should get basic food and no benefits. That means no television, no DVDs, no cigarettes, no special food, absolutely nothing. That would certainly focus the mind and give them an incentive to work and contribute. We know that they will claim this is an infringement of their Human Rights however, the answer to that is quite simple, they are convicts in prison for breaching the laws of the land. Nobody made them do it and they should pay as a consequence.

Prisoner Reward Scheme

It gets worse, oh yes it does! At Bullingdon jail, near Bicester, in Oxfordshire, convicts get £5 for every hour-long training session they attend. The reward scheme, the first of its kind in the country, was introduced at the category C prison by governor Andy Lattimore. It is said that the 1,000 inmates, including killers, paedophiles, robbers and drug dealers, can earn up to £100 a week if they sign up to various courses on offer. With the country in financial meltdown and thousands becoming unemployed with little chance of financial support, this hair brained scheme could cost the taxpayer more than £5million every year. [*Daily Express* 8th October 2010]

Convicts are already compelled to attend anger management and rehabilitation classes to secure early release. But this is the first time that prisoners have been paid to attend. This comes at the same time that the Ministry of Justice announced it could slash 15,000 prison staff jobs in a bid to save £2billion from its £9billion budget.

Prison Service spokeswoman Georgina Mear said: 'Under prison rules, convicted prisoners are required to work and are encouraged to participate in education and to attend courses designed to address their offending behaviour. Those who refuse to work do not receive any pay.'

Emma Boon, spokeswoman for the TaxPayers' Alliance, denounced the prison pay scheme as 'scandalous'.

'These payments are disgraceful… There is no way that prisoners should be paid to be rehabilitated. Criminals are already incarcerated at great expense. We should not be making crime pay by giving them money on top of this… Rehabilitation is not an added extra that prisoners should have to be bribed into. The Ministry of Justice needs to scrap these scandalous payments immediately.'

It is a fact that many of the prison population cannot read or write. One answer is to make it mandatory as part of the prison programme that they learn to read and write. This will in many cases, help them to get on a more stable track when they are released. From personal knowledge, it follows that if an individual can read and write they are more likely to get jobs and hold them down.

It's Party Time!

What do you do when you have a pile of cash to waste and a bunch of unhappy yobs? You throw a party and so convicts at the Rochester Security Training Centre in Kent were treated to a Hawaiian party paid for with taxpayers' cash. The centre was the first of its kind in the UK and houses some of the country's most hardened young criminals, many of whom have dozens of previous convictions. They are there for 'retraining' as an alternative to being sent to young offenders institutions. The offenders, who cost £3,000 a week to be locked up, enjoyed a weekend long party with hula hoops, bongos, limbo dancing, coconuts, pineapples, palm trees and even an alcohol-free punch bar. There were DJ decks and games including a scalectrix car racing set.

An un-named source at the centre said: 'It's unbelievable. They wanted something to keep the inmates spirits up and offered them a choice and they came up with a Hawaiian party... It looked more like Butlins in August than a rehabilitation centre... The victims of these offenders' crimes would have stood there dumbfounded, there was very little in the way of remorse being shown.'

The centre, which is run by the private firm Rebound, was criticised in an official report after at least a dozen disturbances in the years since it opened in 1998 and has also come under fire from Social Services inspectors. To be sent to the centre, convicts need to have committed at least three imprisonable offences and breached a supervision order. Inmates at the centre include those serving so-called Section 91 sentences, the equivalent of a stretch of up to fourteen years which would be handed to an adult criminal. They are handed down for offences so serious that they can only be dealt with at Crown Courts. [*Daily Mail* 2nd January 2009]

Well we can all sleep better knowing that the young convicts are being looked after so well.

Crime Amnesty

It gets worse, yes it really, really does. Ministers have secretly declared a 'crime amnesty' for the 84,000 prisoners in England and Wales, a confidential Whitehall document has disclosed. Prison governors no longer have to report to police thousands of crimes involving assaults, drugs and theft. The memorandum of understanding between prison governors and the Association of Chief Police Officers, says prisoners caught using class B and C drugs do not have to face arrest and prosecution; neither will they automatically be prosecuted for attacks on prison staff, criminal damage and disorder. That's all OK then! [*Sunday Times*, 23rd August 2009]

Bed and Breakfast for Criminals

In January 2008 it became known that some 200 towns and cities in the UK were earmarked to provide bed and breakfast accommodation for criminals. The list was drawn up by the Ministry of Justice and passed to Clear Springs, a private organisation paid to house a range of offenders. The objective is that the hostels would ease prison overcrowding by giving a bed to those who would otherwise be kept in jail because they had nowhere suitable to live. The system works in that Clear Springs rents the properties from private landlords in residential locations through a contract alleged to have been worth more than £15 million. That gives Clear Springs a profit of £2.4 million. So crime really does pay in more ways than one.

Residents in one area knew little about the criminals living amongst them until there was an outbreak of violence. Gangs of teenagers, high on drink and drugs, were seen fighting day and night outside two offender hostels. The local population claimed that Clear Springs which runs the properties had not consulted them about their plans. The police had to be called out because of problems and even they admitted that they had not been told what the house was being used for. I think this is called joined up government?

As one resident in the area stated: 'One night there was a gang drinking and fighting in the street all night, it was terrifying we were awake all night, these people should be locked up, not living next door to pensioners and young families.'

Then the do-gooders did even better when in February 2008, the government came up with another 'new' scheme. It was decided by the government that they would evict more than 600 prison officers from their homes. They could then move in convicts to ease the overcrowded jail's problem. So the Ministry of Justice told the prison officers to leave their state owned properties so they could be used to house convicts released on electronic tags. It was just before Christmas 2007 that the MoJ served notices to quit on the remaining officers in prison service quarters. Leaflets, some nailed to front doors, ordered them to find alternative accommodation or face eviction. Yes, this meant that more than 100 of the homes ranging from one bedroom flats to large town houses, which are located in prime sites across London, were made available to convicts. The outcome was that prison officers, whose rents were heavily subsidised, said that they could not afford to buy houses because of their low incomes and were made homeless. The MoJ then decided to sell the homes to the private sector, raising an estimated £150 million. Oh, that's really nice!

Nobody Goes to Prison

The Prison Reform Trust has said that the government should establish a Royal Commission to investigate the best options for the future in a non-partisan way. The government must reach beyond party politics, and instead of arguing about who can spend most money on jails, it should establish a review of the nature and purpose of imprisonment.

Oooooh alarm bells ringing! Somebody is going to come up with an alternative where nobody actually goes to prison and we don't need that. It is quite alarming that England and Wales is probably the biggest open prison in the world with the number of people that commit crimes who are released early and continue to commit crimes.

Enter the new Justice Secretary, Ken Clarke, who states that: 'Prisoners will work a forty hour week recycling, computer processing and furniture making. If they refuse, they will lose their privileges. They will be jobs that have not been filled by the normal workforce. The tough regime is being drawn up to give repeat offenders a work ethic, so they don't go back to a life of crime. Prisoners would get the £5.93 minimum wage but it would be paid to them over a period of time after their release. It means prisoners could earn almost £240 a week. Around one fifth of their earnings would go towards helping victims.'

The tough regime will not be tough, it's what millions of law abiding people do every day to get by. It's called the world of work. It will not stop re-offending. Convicts should pay more to help victims and pay for their exotic menu choices. Why should the taxpayer pay? Everything they get whilst inside should be a privilege and earned. Those who do not conform, should be segregated and allowed only the basics. Prison must not be a nice cosy place. The problem is that the do-gooders rule outside the prisons and the convicts rule inside.

£10m Prison Rampage

In 2010, two wings at Moorland Prison near Doncaster, South Yorkshire, were destroyed. The trouble began in the youth wings before spreading to the adult wing. Prior to the real trouble in the youth wings three members of staff were assaulted, and a female officer sustained a fractured jaw when more than 40 young convicts refused to return to their cells after a fight broke out at 7pm. One young prisoner was taken to hospital after trying to hang himself when rioters lit a fire outside his cell because he refused to join in the violence. Officers fought their way through the mob to carry him to safety. The rioting convicts surrendered more than eight hours later after officers in riot gear were called in.

A Prison Service spokeswoman said: 'A third incident of indiscipline occurred... at Moorland prison, on the male adult category C side. It began at 6.30pm on Houseblock One when prisoners started throwing objects and causing damage on the wing. Prison Service Tornado teams arrived at the prison and intervened at 1am. By 1.25am all prisoners had surrendered and 166 were removed to other establishments in the area. One prisoner was reported to be suffering from serious injuries and was taken by ambulance to outside hospital... The houseblock has been damaged, although damage to individual cells is not considered serious.'

Glyn Travis, a spokesman for the Prison Officers Association (POA), said that all the prisoners in Moorland's adult wing, up to 100 inmates, were involved in the riot. He confirmed that no prison staff were injured, but said extensive damage was caused. He said: 'Apparently the juveniles and young offenders were locked up and the adults were allowed to come out and when they refused to go back to their cells it all kicked off... It is horrendous inside. They have caused at least £10million of damage. It's an absolute wreck...'

Tom Robson, acting chairman of the POA, blamed the violence on street gangs gathering in our jails. He added: 'They continue in the only way they know, which is in a violent and anti-social manner. Our members confront and manage this on a daily basis.'

So in times when the taxpayer is suffering with daily increases in the cost of living and additional taxes, they now have a bill of £10 million to repair a prison, replace the televisions and other luxury items just because convicts were not happy about being sent back to their cells. I expect that the trouble was brewing before that. The problem is identified by many commentators in that convicts do not have anything to do apart from hang about in gangs, plotting and planning their next venture to disrupt the system. The do-gooders will be pleased, because it allows them to reiterate their the case that prison is not good for convicts. Perhaps not, but what is the alternative? Well, hard work, otherwise known as hard labour for long hours, then they will be too tired to riot. Take away all the things that make the good life, television, cigarettes, drugs and all the extras. That will not happen, the do-gooders will see to that!

Violence broke out in B wing of HMP Ford, a Category D men's prison, near Arundel, in West Sussex. About forty prisoners began smashing windows and setting off fire alarms. They then set fire to accommodation and facility blocks, forcing prison officers to evacuate. Five of the prison's blocks were initially set alight with another three torched after. The damaged blocks included a mail room, a gym, a snooker room and a pool room with ten newly-installed pool tables. Prison officers equipped with shields and helmets secured the perimeter of the prison with Alsatian dogs. Inside, a number of convicts were detained and searched, before being led away. It took more than ten hours for police to regain control of the first of two accommodation blocks and a further five hours to regain control of the second. Six prisoners were identified as the alleged ringleaders and about 165 prisoners were transferred to other prisons as a result of the damage caused. The trouble began when staff tried to breathalyse inmates following fears that large quantities of banned alcohol had been smuggled onto the premises for the New Year's Eve celebrations.

Mark Freeman, deputy general secretary of the POA, said: 'In the early hours staff tried to breathalyse a number of prisoners because they suspected they had been drinking, which I think we can say with some certainty because of the amount of alcohol found over recent days and weeks. Staff have been running around trying to breathalyse prisoners, it's been reminiscent of the end scenes of The Benny Hill Show, the only thing missing was the music. A total of forty bottles of alcohol have been found empty. When the prisoners refused to be breathalysed they became violent along with other prisoners and went on what we call a mutiny, a prison mutiny. One of the officers, a very experienced officer, could see how it was going to unravel and withdrew the officers.'

Mr Freeman reported that there were only two prison officers and four support staff on duty at the time to manage a total prison population of 496. There were 290 inmates in B Wing, the side of the prison where the trouble erupted.

Ford prison specialises in housing non-violent offenders who are nearing the end of their sentences and have a low risk of absconding. Good job there were no violent convicts in residence!

In March 2009, the prison's Independent Monitoring Board issued a report criticising staffing shortages and an outdated CCTV security system after it was found burglars had broken into the prison to steal equipment from workshops. The report also found that drugs, alcohol and mobile phones were being smuggled into the prison for convicts. Then some two months later, an inspection report from Her Majesty's Chief Inspector of Prisons found that convicts were leaving the prison at night to buy drink. They really were little devils weren't they! [*Telegraph January* 2011]

Then the convicts at Littlehey, near Huntingdon, Cambridgeshire, a Category C prison, set fire to a wing, smashed windows and vandalised residential units by smashing tables, chairs, TVs, windows, in fact anything they could break. Prison officers in full riot equipment fought to bring the prison under control. Two officers were reported to have been injured when they were attacked whilst trying to bring a riot under control. The convicts assaulted a woman prison officer and threw a jug of scalding water into her male colleague's face in an outbreak of violence at a young offenders' wing which houses around sixty prisoners aged eighteen to twenty-one. These are the nice people who should not be in prison but doing unpaid work in the community. [*Daily Express* 11th January 2011]

Pagan Prisoners Worship the Sun God

I fell off the chair when I read that hundreds of convicts are to be given four days a year off prison work to celebrate pagan festivals. I am not sure if it was anger or with laughter and I did check that it was not April Fools day. No, it was for real, prison governors have been issued with a list of eight annual pagan holidays and told inmates can choose four to celebrate. The new guidelines entitled 'Religious Festival dates for 2011' state that all prison staff must be made aware of the pagan festival dates. It is the latest in a series of rulings to protect convicts' rights and ensure equality among different faiths.

The festivals include Imbolc which is The Festival of the Lactating Sheep which falls on 1st February and is dedicated to the goddess Brighid. There is the festival of Beltane, which falls in early May; devotees are urged to celebrate the Sun God with 'unabashed sexuality and promiscuity'. Then there is the Yule festival which involves pagans 'casting spells' and dressing up as ghosts. Pagan inmates will be allowed special food and drink on their days off and prisons have been told that they must prepare specific foods if it is a requirement of a prisoner's religion. But the guidance states that the food should be prepared inside prison kitchens and the cost must be 'proportionate to the number of prisoners involved'.

A Prison Service spokesman said: 'The Prison Service issues annually a list of religious festival dates for the year ahead – this includes key dates on which prisoners registered in that affiliation can be excused from work.' [*Daily Mail* 7th December 2010]

Back on my chair, I reflect on the situation. Why is Nicky [see Church Minister JP] harassed by government officials because of her Christian religion, when her only crime is to help alcoholics, drug addicts and those with mental problems? How many of these Pagans' actually play an active part in that society when not in prison? Or is this just another scam by convicts to manipulate the system?

Jihadist Prisons

The big problem for the authorities is that images of beheadings, torture and Jihadist propaganda are being freely circulated on illegal mobile phones in British jails. It is estimated that 9,000 illegal mobiles are in circulation, but in reality the figure could be far higher. It is a major campaign to radicalise Muslim prisoners and the investigation has found that the nation's 140 prisons have been turned into a madrasa by inmate extremists bent on a terror war on the West and that there are some 8,000 Muslim convicts who are key targets for radicalisation.

An example of the problems occurred when four prison officers at Feltham Young Offenders Institution in Middlesex were assaulted by Islamic prisoners chanting Jihadist slogans. It is said to be a prime example of the radicalisation being practised on a regular basis in Britain's jails. [*Sunday Express* 12th December 2010]

Prison Contraband

A *Sunday Express* investigation has identified that the prison computer system is unable to quantify or properly log details of contraband, including drugs, mobile phones and weapons that are smuggled into prisons. Apparently the Local Inmate Database System which was installed in 1989 and used in all our prisons, is no longer fit for purpose. It appears to be the oldest computer system in the public sector and should have been replaced. The new Prison-NOMIS (Prison-National Offender Management Information System) went online but only keeps a record of inmate details. It cannot record or track prison crime and so reliance is still with the old system, the one that does not work. That's convenient.

The whole problem is that the judicial system has been taken over by do-gooders who see crime as the fault of everything or everyone apart from those committing the crime. Criminals are well aware that the chances of them getting a custodial sentence are very slim and even if they do then it is no big deal because it's like a holiday hotel. Now, it is easy to criticise but there have to be solutions.

The first is that you have to keep drugs, phones, weapons and other contraband out of our prisons. Some will remember in the past that when convicts had visitors they sat either side of a glass screen and used either a telephone or a hole with mesh over it to speak through. That way no contraband passes through. Anybody found with a mobile phone, drugs, weapon or inciting any form of intimidation is segregated and all extras, entertainment etc. are removed for periods of six months or more. Depending on the seriousness of the offence the convicts should lose the opportunity of early release and serve the full sentence. Every non-British born person should be deported upon release regardless of any claims for any reason to remain. Those who have been granted citizenship should have their British passport revoked and be deported. The country cannot continue to be run by convicts with more being allowed in. Prison must first and foremost be a punishment and somewhere that once you have been there you never wish to return.

Convicts Get the Vote

The European Court of Human Rights ruled in October 2004 that a blanket ban on prisoners voting breached their rights to free and fair elections. The judgment was upheld by the courts' Grand Chamber the following year.

It began with John Hirst who was jailed for a minimum of fifteen years for the unprovoked attack on sixty-three yearold Bronia Burton, but went on to serve twenty-five years. Barbara Calvert QC, who prosecuted Hirst, told the jury:

'On the evening of June 23rd they were watching television when Mrs Burton asked the defendant to collect some coal from the shed. He went to the shed, got the coal and at the same time picked up a heavy hand axe. He returned to the living room, put the coal on the fire and then approached Mrs Burton and hit her, perhaps seven times, on the head with the axe. He then went to the kitchen to make coffee and drank it, waiting for Mrs Burton to die.'

After finishing his coffee, Hirst, then twenty-eight, walked six miles to the nearest police station from Mrs Burton's home in Burghfield Common, Berkshire, where he gave himself up. He denied murder, but pleaded guilty to manslaughter on the grounds of diminished responsibility. He was released in 2004 after serving ten years more than his original sentence due to a number of violent crimes committed in prison.

John Hirst was born to a Latvian mother in Bradford in November 1950 but was soon put into a Barnardo's children's home and had an unsettled childhood. Hirst became involved in crime early in life and was convicted of arson, burglary and deception in 1971 before being sent to jail for five years. However, eight years later, Hirst committed his most serious crime by killing his landlady, Bronia Burton, with an axe and claimed to feel no remorse. Prison did not reform him and in 1989, he was put into a unit with the most dangerous prisoners after attacking a prison officer. After suing prison governors over his belongings going missing, he began issuing written complaints up to nine times a day, making him Britain's most litigious prisoner. In 2001, he took his case on voting rights to the High Court, failed but then managed to win in the European Court of Human Rights in 2006. [*Daily Telegraph* 11th February 2011]

Diminished responsibility is one of three special defences which exist for the criminal offence of murder. The defence of diminished responsibility is set out in Section 2 of the Homicide Act 1957 as amended by the Coroners and Justice Act 2009. When the defence is successfully pleaded it has the effect of reducing a murder conviction to manslaughter. There are three requirements which must be established by the defendant:

1. There must be an abnormality of mental functioning
2. This abnormality of the mind must have been caused by a recognised medical condition
3. The abnormality of the mind must substantially impair the defendant's mental responsibility

The question of whether the defendant is suffering from an abnormality of the mind is for the jury to decide after hearing medical evidence. However, the jury are not bound to follow medical opinion and it is ultimately their decision as to whether the defence should succeed. Abnormality of the mind is assessed by reference to what a reasonable man would regard as abnormal. It has a wide meaning and encompasses the inability to exercise will power and control.

Hirst used 'diminished responsibility' as a defence against murder, so who decided that he no longer had an abnormality of his mind? With his fervour for complaints whilst in prison, he certainly showed that his mind was capable of understanding and so should diminished responsibility have been allowed at his trial? His claims are on the basis of human rights but what of those of Mrs Burton? Ah, she is dead and she was a victim therefore she does not count.

Hirst brought the case to the European Court of Human Rights which ruled in 2005 that the ban breached the right to free elections under the European Convention on Human Rights. [*Daily Telegraph* November 2010]

Sentenced prisoners were originally denied the right to take part in ballots under the 1870 Forfeiture Act, and the ban was retained in the Representation of the People Act of 1983. Prisoners on remand awaiting trial, fine defaulters and people jailed for contempt of court can vote.

We then see Hirst on YouTube popping a champagne cork and smoking illegal drugs, saying he is toasting the 70,000 convicts who will now get the chance to help elect the next government.

He says: 'Well, I've got the joint, I'm going to celebrate. I've got the bottle of champagne and I'm going to celebrate because last night it was announced that prisoners have now got the vote, which I'm really chuffed about. I'm now going to celebrate for the 75,000 prisoners who will be getting the vote. That includes murderers, rapists and paedophiles... all of them will be getting the vote because it's their human right to have the vote...I don't think the taxpayers will be too chuffed that the government's left them with a £135million (legal) bill.' [*Daily Mail* 3rd November 2010]

So what is the situation in other countries? Many developed countries have some form of prisoner voting, including twenty-eight other European nations such as France, Germany and Italy. There is a full ban in Azerbaijan, Armenia, Bulgaria, Estonia, Hungary, Romania, Moldova, Georgia, Turkey, Russia, Latvia, Liechtenstein and Slovakia. Some prisoners are able to vote in Austria, Belgium, Greece, Italy, Luxembourg, Malta, the Netherlands, Norway, Poland and Romania (Note the EU countries). There are full rights in Canada, Albania, Bosnia and Herzegovina, Croatia, Czech Republic, Denmark, Finland, Macedonia, Iceland, Ireland, Lithuania, Portugal, Slovenia, Spain, Sweden, Switzerland and Ukraine. In France and Germany the courts can revoke voting rights as punishment.

However, the Strasbourg-based court said that each country can decide which offences should carry restrictions to voting rights. Ah, now a ruling can be made to exclude all those in for the nasty crimes such as murder, manslaughter, GBH, rape, pedophilia, terrorism etc, etc.

MPs mounted a historic defence of Britain's sovereign right to make its own decisions by defying demands from the European courts to hand prisoners the vote. They voted overwhelmingly to maintain a 140-year-old ban on convicts taking part in elections because, they said, those who commit a crime have 'broken their contract with society'. It followed six hours of impassioned debate. MPs voted by 234 to 22, a majority of 212 to defy a ruling from the ECHR that the ban must be overturned. This has set Parliament against the European Court of Human Rights in that they are telling the unelected Strasbourg judges that they have overstepped their authority.

Experts said the vote left Britain's relationship with the European court in 'uncharted territory'. It places the Prime Minister under intense pressure to launch a defining challenge against Strasbourg. Proposing the cross-party motion which 'supports the current situation in which no prisoner is able to vote', former Tory shadow home secretary David Davis said:

'The general point is very clear in this country: that is that it takes a pretty serious crime to get yourself sent to prison. And as a result you have broken the contract with society to such a serious extent that you have lost all of those rights, your liberty and your right to vote.'

Dominic Raab, Tory MP for Esher and Walton has said: 'It is time to draw a line in the sand. It's time we send a very clear message: this House will decide whether prisoners get the vote, this House will decide the laws of the land.'

The Prime Minister said: 'I just think that if you are sent to prison and you have committed a crime then you give up the right to be able to vote. I don't see why we should have to change that…'

Only twenty-two MPs supported the European Court of Human Rights' insistence that British prisoners should have the vote. Parliamentarians realised they can support human rights, but oppose the flawed way the human rights court works. Britain has taken a small but significant step towards regaining control of her destiny.

Attorney General Dominic Grieve insisted that Britain, as a signatory of the European Convention on Human Rights, would be acting 'tyrannically' and in breach of the rule of law if it simply rejected rulings from the court. But he admitted that there was in fact no mechanism to enforce the court's will, telling MPs he anticipated a 'drawn-out dialogue between ourselves and the ECHR'. Mr Grieve said Parliament had to show why it would be 'reasonable and proportionate' to retain the ban, adding: 'That gives us the best possible chance of winning the challenges which may then occur thereafter.'

Former Labour Justice Secretary Jack Straw, said: 'Of course it is important that Britain observes its treaty obligations and upholds the rule of law. But in attempting to overrule British law on prisoner voting rights, the unelected judges in Strasbourg have exceeded the limits of their authority.'

Tory MP Priti Patel said: 'It's appalling in this day and age that we're actually talking about the rights of convicted criminals rather than putting the rights of victims first. We've got to start saying no to Europe bullying us and dictating to us on issues of this nature.'

Mr Cameron could, of course, withdraw from the European Convention on Human Rights, a move which would be cheered by many of his MPs. But it would lead to high-profile resignations from the government and a possible fracturing of the Coalition. Government lawyers can attempt to negotiate a compromise with the court, arguing that one of its key objections to the ban that Parliament had not expressed a view on the issue for decades has now been addressed.

One proposal being examined by Downing Street is simply to defy the European court ruling. It is not clear whether compensation orders made by Strasbourg are enforceable. Alternatively, compensation awards to inmates could be clawed back through a charge for their prison accommodation. Prisoners released following miscarriages of justice are routinely charged board and lodging to cover the time they spent in jail. Doing the same for prisoners suing over being deprived the vote would be a neat solution. [*Daily Mail* 11th February 2011]

Then came some really good news. In February 2011, convicts were trying to make money out of the voting ban on prisoners. The first cases failed when the High Court Judge, Mr Justice Langstaff, ruled that European judgments should never be allowed to trump laws passed at Westminster. It was a decisive victory for the authority of Parliament over the European Court of Human Rights. They each sought £5,000 in compensation but the judge, in addition to throwing out their claim, ordered them to pay £76 each towards the costs of their action.

Thousands of prisoners had been expected to try to sue the government because it has not bowed to Strasbourg and presented them with the right to vote in elections. Lawyers estimated that if it had been successful it would have left the taxpayer with a bill of close to £150million.

However, the threat evaporated following the ruling as none of the 588 convicts involved had been able to retain the services of lawyers to represent them, because they were denied taxpayer-funded legal aid by the Legal Services Commission and no lawyer was willing to take on the case on a no-win no-fee basis. Without legal aid they must pay the costs of their lost action themselves. So the risk of having to pay costs appears to have affected the willingness of prisoners to pursue their claims once they realised they would not be given legal aid. No doubt the do-gooder will be swinging into action to help them. [*Daily Mail* 19th February 2011]

TaxPayers' Alliance campaign director Emma Boon said: 'This is a victory for taxpayers. There is a growing compensation culture here and it is worrying taxpayers could pay the bill running into tens of millions in this case. The decision on whether or not prisoners should have the vote should be made in the UK. It shouldn't be foisted upon us.'

Transsexual Prisoners

Have we now reached a new height of insanity? First, let me be very clear in that I do not care what people do in private, providing that it does not transcend the law or invade the privacy and respect of others. I do not care what sexual orientation people want to be so long as it does not impact on others. That said, at the time of writing, the latest remit to slurp out of Kenneth Clarke's Ministry of In-Justice is for me, as indeed it will for the majority of people in the UK, more evidence that prison is not a punishment to be endured, but a place of some enjoyment and comfort.

Why do I say this? Another prison policy document has put our minds at rest and this one sets out the rights of sex change convicts and it's all in a twenty-page guidebook which is issued to prison governors. At what cost to the taxpayer I ask? You can bet it's printed in about 50 languages. The document provides advice on problematic issues when dealing with transsexual convicts, such as access to prison showers and urges officers to contact the Ministry of Justice's dedicated 'gender recognition policy team' if they have questions about the policy. The country is well on its way down the drain with thousands of people being put out of work because there is no money, but there is a 'gender recognition policy team'!

So a prison must permit convicts who consider themselves transsexual and wish to begin gender reassignment to live permanently in their acquired gender. This means that convicts are allowed to dress in clothes appropriate to their acquired gender and adopting appropriate names and modes of address. The guide says that transsexual people, particularly those who have not undergone surgery or extended hormone therapy, may use various items to assist with their presentation in their acquired gender. These can range from sophisticated prostheses to padded bras and, in the case of those changing from male to female, make-up to cover beard growth.

Unlike other male convicts, transsexuals will not be expected to wear prison uniform if they are punished by being moved to the basic privileges regime. In other words, allowing male to female transsexual convicts to wear their own clothes is not a privilege and the guide tells prison staff that it may be helpful to explain this to other prisoners who are required to wear prison uniform. Any prison which attempts to stop transsexual convicts from having such items could be taken to court for judicial review. [*Daily Telegraph* 5th March 2011]

We then hear that a convict who killed a prostitute after she mocked his performance is to have a sex-change operation in prison at a cost of £45,000 and it will funded by you, the taxpayer. He has to undergo hormone treatment as he builds up to the costly operation. The Department of Health spokesman said: 'Transsexual prisoners have the right to receive the same range and quality of NHS treatments as anyone else, including treatment for gender re-assignment.'

A spokesman for the TaxPayers Alliance said: 'It is unfair that law-abiding patients face a postcode lottery for care.' [*Daily Mail* 14th March 2011]

Sorry To Keep You Waiting

Drunken thug Samuel Sturnham had been released early 'on licence' after serving half of a four-month sentence for his fourth drink-driving conviction. He was fitted with an electronic tag but ignored the curfew and went on a drinking binge. After downing twenty-one pints, he picked a fight with a customer in a pub and Mr Noble tried to break it up. Sturnham punched Mr Noble so hard, his jaw was broken and he suffered a skull fracture as he fell. Mr Noble died later in hospital. Sturnham, was jailed indefinitely for the manslaughter of Mr Noble in January 2007. Two years later (I did not realise that indefinitely was that short a time) he was told that he would be up for parole. Due to an administrative error by the Ministry of Justice, his case was delayed for six months. At the hearing the Parole Board turned him down because he still posed a grave risk to the public. Sturnham claimed that he suffered 'anxiety and distress' while waiting the six months to argue for his freedom. A High Court judge in London sparked fury as he granted Sturnham £300 compensation because the delay breached his human rights.

Emma Boon, of the Taxpayers' Alliance, said: 'Taxpayers want to see their money spent on frontline services, not fighting ludicrous human rights claims from dangerous criminals. While prisoners should obviously be treated with dignity and respect, human rights laws shouldn't open the door to a flood of dubious claims.' [*Daily Express* 16th March 2011]

Oh Dear, The Prison's Not Clean

You may think that you have heard it all, but did you know that prisons are not very clean places? Well, criminal Nathan Cassidy doesn't think so. He was arrested having broken into an elderly couple's home while they were sleeping and stole a handbag containing £105. Did he check to see if the occupants had cleaned before his arrival? He has fourteen previous convictions for twenty-nine crimes. He committed the burglary while on a suspended sentence for robbery and handling stolen goods. In court he avoided being sent to jail by convincing Judge Gareth Hawkesworth that he would not be able to cope with life behind bars because he is obsessed with cleanliness. So he was allowed to walk free from court as he would find jail 'too traumatic' because of his obsessive compulsive disorder.

The defendants lawyer told the court that: 'Because of psychological problems, including obsessive compulsive disorder in relation to cleanliness, custody would have a very traumatic effect on him more so than it would on the average prisoner.'

I think Cassidy is ideal for prison. Once inside he can get a cleaning job and the whole place would soon be spick and span. Oh, and there would be justice served at the same time. [*Daily Mail* 16th May 2011]

Is It Too Hot or Cold?

The prison compensation culture helped inmates in one prison who complained of being too hot or cold in their cells, pocket more than £160,000 from the taxpayer. The convicts are given ice cream and lollipops in summer and extra blankets and flasks of soup in winter. It is said that claims at a category B men's jail in London comprised 65% of 146 new compensation bids made to the Ministry of Justice in 2009. Inmates received £161,736 out of a total of £334,319 paid out in claims in prisons across the country.

Neil Atkinson, of the National Victims' Association, said: 'Less than 2% of the entire criminal justice budget is spent on the victims of crime and once again we have a clear demonstration of the way in which society has allowed the interest's of criminals to be placed above those of their victims. Victims of crime will be appalled to discover that taxpayers' money is being spent in this way.'

Emma Boon, of the TaxPayers' Alliance said: 'Prisoners are already detained at great expense to law-abiding taxpayers. It is a disgrace that criminals are able to claim so much, especially when budgets are stretched. Obviously, prisoners must be kept in humane conditions but we don't want this compensation culture to grow any further. The public wants money to be spent on things like guards and security. The minimum and maximum temperatures are sensible limits but we don't want inmates to be mollycoddled with ice cream and lollies.' [*Daily Express* 23rd March 2011]

Nice Prison -V- Nasty Prison

All countries have criminals and prisons, even beautiful and sparsely populated Norway has the full spectrum of jails, including maximum-security facilities. They also have a new and unique establishment, Bastoy Prison. The only way to get to Bastoy is to take a small prison ferry from the port of Horten, some two hours south of Oslo. Bastoy does not look like a prison because there are no high razor-wire fences, no concrete cellblocks and no watchtowers. Instead, the small island looks more like a tranquil Scandinavian holiday resort.

It is designated the final stop for a small group of male inmates nearing the end of their sentences. The crimes they committed range from murder to drug dealing. Whilst on the island, the inmates live in four-bedroom wooden cottages providing each with his own space. The cottages overlook pine forests, fields of wheat and inviting beaches. Another difference with this prison is that from the moment they arrive inmates are taught how to cook, clean and look after themselves. There are inspections to ensure that they clean their rooms and make their beds. Whilst at Bastoy, inmates undertake a number of work tasks from forestry to looking after animals and even providing crewmembers for the prison ferry.

The thirty prison officers at Bastoy work closely with the inmates to develop trust and it is customary for prison officers and inmates to call each other by their first names. In addition, the prison tries to help inmates deal with problems like drugs, violence and reconnecting with their families. While prison staff believe they work in the best prison in the world, the jury is still out on whether time at Bastoy is an answer for inmates to put a life of crime behind them for good.

Contrast that with Miami-Dade County prison, Florida, USA, which is claimed to be one of the US's most violent jails. The journalist Louis Theroux visited the prison and describes it as a bit like walking through a zoo, with cages housing up to twenty-four men. There is no privacy in the cells where even the toilets and showers are open to the other convicts. There's a TV, but that's on the other side of the bars, and exercise time in the 'yard' is limited to about two hours a week. The inmates have become unmanageable so prison officers don't spend time in the cells, but 'look in' from outside when they walk the passage inspecting once or twice an hour.

Theroux questions whether it's because of the nature and temperament of the inmates, or because of the conditions in the cells, or a mixture of both. One thing is certain and that it is a seriously aggressive culture and the only way to survive is to fight. From the fighting there evolves a pecking order in the cells with the most aggressive taking control. It would appear that when convicts fight the jailers do not get involved but pick up the pieces afterwards. The outcome of some fights left convicts battered, bruised and with broken bones. Some had been stabbed. In this environment there is no work, no training, no education, just violence. A handful of trusted convicts do work outside of the cells doing jobs such as cleaning. One of the more disturbing aspects of the jail is a practice called 'gunning', which is when an inmate masturbates in front of a female guard. It appears that they try to take advantage of the visual stimulus of a woman being present, but it's also seen as a victory over the prison officer.

In a separate part of the prison is a section for young offenders. When sentenced they are offered the opportunity to be rehabilitated by the jail's 'boot camp' programme. This is an alternative to a general custodial sentence for those who have been found guilty and are under twenty-one at the time of sentencing. One individual was sentenced to ten years in prison but if he opted for 'boot camp' and completed the six month programme, he would then be released. He failed and was sent to complete the ten years behind bars. The focus is on discipline and hard physical tasks. It can perhaps best be described as US Marine Corps basic induction training but for a much longer period. There is some evidence that those running the centre provide a 'father figure' influence to which the youngsters respond. Almost all of those on the programme are in for violent crimes such as attempted murder, car-jacking and armed robbery but not those convicted of murder. The objective is to guide them away from a life of crime and not to return to the prison and enter the 'zoo'.

Theroux describes a typical young offender through a fourteen year-old who has been attracted into a gangster lifestyle and had pleaded guilty to car-jacking. He had been raised by a single mother and it appears that some of his problems stemmed from not having a father figure around. We are told that this is a common theme with the young convicts.

The contrast between Norway and the USA is immeasurable and much can be accounted for in the cultural differences of the two countries. Both have criminal elements but it's the volume of violent crime that probably sets them apart. The worrying thing is that the UK will not evolve to the Norwegian model but has already aligned itself with the US situation. The evidence shows that in the UK, the prison population has become gang orientated and violence is much more predominant. Only strong government action can stop the slide into the 'cess pit' and I don't see that happening any time soon. [*The Sun* 21st May 2011]

The Clink

Among all the negatives about UK convicts and prisons there is one small positive. Chef Al Crisci opened a new gourmet restaurant serving food of the highest quality. The restaurant, called the Clink, seats up to eighty-five people and has an open plan kitchen which can be viewed from the restaurant, offering the guests the opportunity to watch food preparation. The interesting point is that its location is right in the middle of a Category B prison and all the chefs and waiters are serving prisoners. The tables and chairs have all been designed and constructed by prisoners and their poetry is displayed on the glass windows around the restaurant. The income generated goes towards the running and operating costs of the restaurant which is supplemented by donations. The Clink was officially opened on 11th May 2009, having been devised by Chef Alberto Crisci MBE.

Mr Crisci said: 'The objective is to train prisoners to a high level by signing them up to cooking and food service diplomas. We also engage with employers who are willing to offer them a job when they are released. If they need accommodation, then we have contacts who can help. All this in a restaurant paid for by private donations and run by a charity, at no cost to the taxpayer.'

The Clink was the subject of a BBC TV programme, The Prison Restaurant and shows a positive side of rehabilitation. We saw a well set out and well run restaurant. One offender who was working in the kitchen was offered a job at a top hotel for further training upon his release. On the down side we did see some convicts who, having been given an opportunity to improve their lot, fall to the wayside and were removed from the restaurant. That will not detract from the aim of reducing the re-offending rates of ex-offenders by training and placing graduates upon their release into the hospitality industry.

The Clink has employed three ex-offenders over the last year. All who have served time at High Down; Dean Masters was a serving offender for six years and now works for the Clink as a Head Chef and Head Waiter training and assessing offenders. Kane Sterling, released in November 2010, is also a Head Waiter training and assessing prisoners as well as co-ordinating all the booking administration. Government ministers need to go and see what can be done but they will expect a free lunch!

5

A Broken Society

Crime – A Badge of Honour

The problem today is that going to court and being found guilty of a criminal offence use to be a cause for concern and an embarrassing blemish on a person's character. However, for a growing number of people today they are just not bothered. In fact for many it is a badge of honour. This is, of course, a disturbing trend and means that there is a situation where authority and the criminal justice system means little or nothing to a growing swathe of our society. Indeed for many families it's a day out, kids in the youth court in the morning, adults in court in the afternoon. Some offenders could give the court as their contact address as they seem to spend more time at court than at home.

The Demise

How can you win when those in positions of power and authority pontificate with claims such as 'Society at its best for twenty years'? That claim was made by Jack Straw when he was the Lord Chancellor, the man in charge of our Criminal Justice System. In a newspaper article he explained that:

'British society is not broken and the recent spate of horrific murders should not cause an over reaction from judges, politicians and the public. Our society is in a much better state of repair than it was fifteen to twenty years ago...Yes, the most base elements of human nature have recently been on display, but these must be seen as what they are, the despicable actions of deeply disturbed individuals, not, as some would like to point out, a manifestation of a broken society.' [*Daily Telegraph* March 2008]

If you don't believe in aliens from other planets, then I think there is a good chance that you will have to change your views right now, because Mr Straw must be from another planet. He is certainly not from this one. As the man who, at the time, was the head of our Criminal Justice System, he does not seem to have one single idea, or even knowledge of, what is going on in the real world. However, reality was just round the corner when Judge Coldridge, who has spent eight years presiding over cases of divorce, children in care and family break up, spoke out that family breakdown is a cancer behind every evil affecting the country.

This is a man whose judgements span the spectrum of our society. He is a man who tells us that the threat of family breakdown today is as big as terrorism, street crime or drugs, but that it is far more serious in that it will be more destructive than any economic problems caused by international markets. Very much on the doom side, he says that it is too late to help families just by bringing back tax breaks for marriage. He says that there must be more effort to educate parents and children on how to keep families together. He has called for higher spending on family courts, more court time for family cases and modernisation of laws on divorce and family break up. This is a very interesting situation from a man in a position of authority and who really knows what he is talking about.

He spells out the facts and blames youth crime, child abuse, drug addiction and binge drinking on the meltdown of relations between parents and children. He says that the problem is on a scale the depth and breadth of which few could have imagined, even a decade ago. He made it plain that: 'It is a never ending carnival of human misery, a ceaseless river of human distress.'

However, he was not saying every broken family produces dysfunctional children but he was saying that almost every dysfunctional child is a product of a broken family. Now this is from a judge who is in charge of family courts across South West England and so he will have a great deal of experience of these types of cases.

He tells us that: 'Families are the cells which make up the body of society. If the cells are unhealthy and undernourished, or at worst, cancerous and growing haphazardly out of control, in the end the body succumbs.'

He then continues: 'In some of the more heavily populated areas, family life is, quite frankly, in meltdown or completely unrecognisable and is on an epidemic scale. In some areas of the country family life in the old sense no longer exists.'

He put his finger on the pulse when he identifies that: 'A large number of families now consist of children being brought up by mothers who have children by a number of different fathers, none of whom take any part in their lives or support their upbringing. These are not isolated or one off cases, they are part of the stock in trade of the family courts.' [*Daily Mail* April 2008]

He is quite rightly complimentary when stating that many single parents often do a fantastic job, but a great many do not and they are on the increase and that is the problem.

Throughout history there have been what were termed 'street urchins' who, having absolutely nothing, had to beg and steal to survive. Today there are feral children who do not know their fathers and are often abandoned by mothers who don't care or who are unable to control their offspring. They are left free to run wild and commit crimes, often in gangs. For them it is a question of survival but also evidence that our 'do-gooder' society has failed them and the general public who are the victims. The UK has become a nanny state where there are demands by those who contribute least and expect the most and get it!

The fact is that there has been a rise in robberies with the majority of mugging and robbery victims being school children. They are victims of a 'have and want' society and were probably attacked for their mobile telephones, training shoes or lunch money. In an interview on television a gang of black youths did not consider that forced oral sex was a crime of rape. Their view was that if a girl met with one of the gang members, the others could have sex without consent and it was not a crime. Other youths consider that stabbing somebody as part of a gang initiation to gain respect is not a crime. It's said to be 'cool' to carry a knife or gun. Others see designer shoes, clothes and mobile phones as must haves. Having no money is not a problem, you just rob somebody. If they object then you stick them with a blade.

There is a rise in child sex exploitation involving home grown gangs as well as those from former Eastern European countries. Recent cases have involved a racial element but, either way, they are peddling their vile trade in the UK. What does that say about our criminal law and indeed the members of society who use the services on offer?

* * *

I stood in a French supermarket when a very young boy shouted to demand something. When his mother refused to let him have it, he threw himself on the floor screaming and throwing his arms and legs about. It's a scene that you see in every UK supermarket, every day. The difference is in the outcome. The noise from the boy brought his father (yes mother and father is still fashionable in France) from an aisle where he had been obtaining products. He could see that the mother was attempting to talk to the boy but having no luck. The father got hold of the boy, pulled him up and gave him a quick but not hard, wack on the bottom. The impact was instantaneous. The boy stopped screaming and walked along holding his fathers hand. That continued throughout the whole time they were in the supermarket and whilst at the checkout.

In the UK the child remains screaming and having a tantrum for a long time, seeking to gain attention and whatever it was they wanted. In most cases the mother just gives in to the little horror. It's then a matter of another tantrum when he/she wants something else. This activity is multiplied throughout the supermarket as parents try to reason with their offspring, often more than one child performing at the same time. Members of the do-gooder and PC brigade are lurking and on patrol, ready to rush forward if a parent raises their voice, handles the child or makes a serious threat, like 'no you can't have it'. If action is required the police and Social Services then swing into action at such a pace that members of the SAS would be left breathless.

At this rate, the only weapon left for parents dealing with extremely difficult children will be a nasty look, but they should not be observed doing it. For it seems that shouting at your offspring could follow smacking in falling foul of political correctness clowns. Parents are now worried that they are letting their children down when they raise their voices to tell them off and fear they could be accused of losing their cool.

* * *

A European Commission report showed a 77% increase in murders, robberies, assaults and sexual offences in the UK since New Labour came to power. The total number of violent offences recorded compared to population is higher than any other country in Europe, as well as America, Canada, Australia and South Africa. [*Daily Telegraph* 2nd July 2009]

Government ministers can squirm and produce spin by the bucket load but the fact is that under Mr Blair and Mr Brown, the UK really developed a broken society and today's problems are down to them. They failed the country. At the time of writing, things do not look a great deal better under the leadership of Mr Cameron and Mr Clegg particularly the LibDem soft/liberal approach to crime.

You cannot compare the UK with other countries in Europe, particularly Scandinavia, because the UK has evolved to be in a class of its own with the resulting broken society and following the US model. Greed and crime permeates at the top of our society with MP's expenses, the activities of the financial institutions in the city as well as those at the bottom end, so the answers have to be radical to be effective. The problem is that there seems to be nobody in any government prepared to really get to grips with the problem. Those in power or waiting to get into power are all talk and no, or little action. If they are not do-gooders, then they are drawn into a vision of a do-gooder society, where crime pays. We saw it with New Labour and I am sure we will see it with the ConLib coalition government.

Church Minister JP

In the retiring room I checked the list to see who I was sitting with and in which court. I noted the names, one lady I had sat with many times and one with whom I had never sat. The lady who I knew pointed out our colleague and added that she was a church minister. Now 'book' and 'cover' sprang to mind as I had a vision of a winger who would have sympathy for the worst of offenders and that the answer lay in a nice cup of tea, a chocolate biscuit and a chat about not being naughty. As it turned out, she was one of the most impressive magistrates that I have sat with in court. The vast majority of magistrates, myself included, sit and listen to tales of woe, but never go down to grass roots to see the reality. This lady church minister, who I shall call Nicky, brought through her work/life reality to what it's like on the other side. She also brought home the real failings of the social welfare system from first hand experience. To coin a phrase, 'she's been there, seen it and got the T shirt'; the latter is now well faded.

Most churches have a mixed congregation but Nicky's catered for many of those who have very real life problems, in fact often it is a matter life and death. There are those with serious drug and drink problems, those who are chronic gamblers as well as many with mental health problems. There were even a few who were paedophiles. It is very clear that she works in a world that most of us do not really want to know about, the world of a real 'underclass'. When I first sat with Nicky and she explained that she was a church minister, I confess that the first thought that flashed through my mind was that there would be a sermon to her colleagues, about having to be lenient with those who passed before us in the courts. How wrong I was, because her life experience in dealing with what are often called the 'underclass' was invaluable, particularly in understanding what makes those people tick. From her, mercy comes at a price and sob stories are not included.

Nicky not only runs a church in England but has extended her work to set up a centre in India which includes a children's home and school. It is in a remote region where help is gratefully received and where parents want a better life for their children. In England she has a group of Elders, who keep the church working when she is not in the country. Her time in England is spent dealing with current activities, boosting the Elders' morale and setting them on the right track. She says that most problems are not from those they are trying to help, but from those in authority, trying to stop them.

She is, in my opinion and that of many others, a real no nonsense person and does not pander to the whims of her 'congregation' but gives them proper help and deals with their personal issues as best she can with limited resources. The majority of magistrates, and I include myself in that category, have no real life knowledge of the world where the 'underclass' exist. You would think that somebody with such experience would be a valuable asset to the Probation Service, Social Services and other welfare organisations, but that is not the case. In fact with some of the organisations it is the opposite and they openly 'harass' her in undertaking positive good work. I am very much reminded of the saying, 'those who do, do, those who don't, pontificate'.

I am indebted to Nicky for giving up some of her valuable time to talk through some of her experiences that serve to expose our court dealings with the 'underclass' that does exist as well as others who use every trick possible to get away with criminal activity. I have transcribed her views and comments as accurately as possible and I would add that I fully support her views and opinions.

She begins by explaining that there are two fundamental problems, the government (New Labour in power at the time) and social workers. Added to that, there is the real problem of the people who have serious issues and who the church try to help. A few of the unfortunates have died and she keeps wondering if that is a plan of the government, to kill them off early, because of some of the systems that there are for dealing with people with alcohol problems and mental health problems.

Nicky explains: 'I had a guy die recently, a bit younger than me but they are all younger than me that die. Its not the old people that die, it's the young ones and the cause is cronic alcoholism, with mental health problems.'

She went on the explain how the system works: 'I had one individual who lived in a local authority flat. It was taken over by a gang of drug dealers because he has some mental health issues and he's never going to be able to make the right decision. It reached a point that he had enough of being surrounded by these violent drug addicts and so he walks into the office of the local authority and hands over his keys. He tells them: 'have your keys back, have your flat, I don't want it'. Nobody asks him why and nobody tells him, you are making yourself intentionally homeless, because nobody can be bothered. So he hands them over and then he is living rough.'

Nicky continued to explain: 'We now have this guy who is living rough in a derelict house. He has mental health problems and is a chronic alcoholic. I approached the council to see if we could get him out of that environment and get him housed. The response from the local authority was, no, he made himself intentionally homeless. So I went to another council because his mother lives in their area. I explained to the council person exactly what the issue was, what had happened. So because his mother lives in their area she had a look at the case and decided that they could house the guy.

So the first thing he has got to have is a social worker because he hasn't got one. OK fine, get him a social worker. Now at this point in time, this guy is getting benefit of £90 a week of which probably £85 is going on alcoholic drink. So we have a social worker and what does the social worker do? First thing he says is 'you are entitled to much more money than this' and gives him £210, I believe, and what does he do with that? He drinks it!

This guy is actually doing better with £90 a week than he is with £210 and anybody in their right mind… you don't need a shred of common sense to work out, that if you give this guy any more money, all he's going to do is use it to drink chemical cider.

So they give him £210 a week and then they find him a flat and get the mental health people involved, who know everything, don't they, about mental health. Now this guy has nothing in his life except alcohol and his mental condition means that, quite frankly, he shouldn't live on his own, because he is vulnerable to anybody who comes by and pretends to be his friend. Most of them are drug addicts because they can fund their habit off his benefit, but no, he's got freedom of choice, so he can live anywhere he chooses. So we now give him a support worker. The only thing in that guy's life that he actually does, that is not drink related and is not damaging, is that he comes to church if I go and get him. The first thing the mental health worker tells me is that the church is a load of rubbish and he should not go. But that's the only thing in this guy's life that has any positive input whatsoever.

So what do Social Services do? Stick him in a flat, give him a pile of money and let him buy drink. He is a chronic burden to the National Health Service and he will kill himself eventually because they have let him do it because he has got choices, and every agency that sought to help that man did nothing but make it worse.'

The problem was very clear to Nicky: 'The Social Services are handing out money to people who, quite frankly, do not know what to do with it and are a menace to themselves and society. I had five people, well one's dead, so there are only four left; all of them had £200 plus in their hands every week, with all their bills and rent and everything else taken care of because they are incapable of doing it. People that work don't have that much money in their hands to play with. So what do they do? They drink, they take drugs and they get abused by people who want their money and the authorities let them do it and they tell them, 'you don't have to live anywhere where someone can restrict what you can do, because you have freedom of choice.' But with all of those people, when they get involved with the church we try and get them doing other activities and their lives are actually better. But we have no power to do anything.'

Nicky explained: 'I've been visited by Social Services in a situation where I do not have the right to speak. If they find out I am a magistrate, oh they'll listen a little bit, but if I say I'm a church minister they say, what do you know? You don't know anything! But the truth is some people need something even if it's only coming out and having a coffee with a group of people who are not going to rip them off. They can if they want, help out with a bit of painting and decorating in the church. That's got to be better than drinking themselves to death or gambling it.

All these people with these mental health problems should not be living as they do and given vast amounts of money, £28,000/£29,000 a year and there's no responsibility. They should have to go somewhere every day and participate in something positive to get their benefits and it should be like a job. Basket weaving! I don't care what it is, it could be go and watch a film, it could be anything, but there is nothing in their lives except here's the money now go away because we don't want to deal with you. The system is set up like that. I'd abolish it all tomorrow.'

Nicky continued: 'I have one woman, she is fifty, she can't read, write, count or tell the time. She shouldn't live on her own because she's got a mental age of an eight year old. But no, she's got freedom of choice, so they stick her in a flat where she runs up bills, doesn't pay them and in truth doesn't know what's happening. Does she have a social worker? Well she did have, but they won't see her any more because she never keeps her appointments.

They write to her but she can't read! She never keeps appointments because she can't tell the time, so what's she going to do? I have five people that take turns to look after her, because Social Services say she doesn't keep appointments. That is the basis of why she can't have a social worker. As an example, you go into her flat and the gas boiler is falling off the wall. It's dangerous and nobody will do anything about it. The reason given is the she's never there but the real problem is that she should not be living on her own – but she's got rights. I just think this woman is actually a menace to herself, but no, she's got a choice.'

Nicky explains the problems facing those who offer practical help: 'I'm sure that social workers are not all stupid, but an awful lot of them that I've met are. I just want to scream and run away because you think, here we go, tick boxes. You've got to fit into their tick box and if you don't fit they will make you. Can't they use common sense? Does anybody ever get hauled up for what they've done wrong, because you never hear about a social worker getting fired. They never get fired, they close ranks and they do the most ridiculous things. I hate them, I hate working with them because they will deliberately oppose anything you say, especially as a church minister. To be honest I have a congregation of people where probably half of them need social workers, but they are better off without them. It's a disgrace.'

Nicky is also very concerned at the way she and other Christian organisations are treated by the authorities and explains: 'Now if I was a Muslim, they would not dare treat me in such a way but because I'm a Christian they can do what they like. There is definitely an anti-

Christian undertone in this country that's getting worse. There was a survey of four city councils to find out how much money they would have to find to provide extra workers if every church stopped doing the community work that they are doing. In each case it was identified that there would have to be about eight full time workers to cover what churches cover. I wasn't in the survey because my statistics would have thrown the figures out as I've got a large number of problem people. But how many churches are there like mine?'

Nicky is very clear where the problem lies: 'Most of our drug addicts and our alcoholics are made that way because the government choses to allow it to continue. They fund their habits with benefits. They give them money and all they have to do is get depressed and that is it. With depression, they can do anything they like. Brought before the courts they can't be curfewed because they are depressed. They can't be made do to any unpaid work because they are depressed. There's not a lot left after that so the court gives them a conditional discharge. It's wrong and there should be a separate system to deal with them.

You have a real mental health problem, okay fine, but it should still be punishment, but it should be a separate system. The government does not want to deal with the problem, because it's not going to win an election, and to deal with the issues is going to take longer than the term of the one government. You are going to have to establish some far reaching and contentious systems in place.'

Nicky would like to adopt a system similar to that in the USA: 'In America you are only signed off unemployed for something like three weeks and after that you have to go back to work, you are not allowed to sit about. They have intervention teams, so those who have got alcohol problems and end up in A&E are visited by someone and immediately they've got back up instead of our option of, oh we'll sign you off or whatever and pander to it. If you have a job your employer is not allowed to sack you for being an alcoholic. They have to actually work with you. If you have a relapse and end up back in

A&E, there is intervention to get you back to where you are supposed to be. In the UK we let it drift and do nothing.'

Nicky is concerned that the government (New Labour) allowed harmful products to be available to the vulnerable:'Chemical cider, white lightning, I would ban it tomorrow. It's created entirely in a laboratory and it's meant to create alcoholics. It's banned in Europe and you are not allowed to buy it. In the UK we sell it and give extra free. The government has banned the extra bit free but it's so cheap and you don't have to go to a pub to get it. There are people who drink nine litres a day, or that's what they admit to. In ten years time we will have a nation of people with cirrhosis of the liver and they are not going to know what to do with them. In fact the means of dealing with it are far beyond what most governments would get stuck into because it's going to get dirty and unpleasant. Extending the opening hours, I mean what's that for except making money by taxing it. It's scary!'

Nicky was very annoyed when discussing the subject of employment:'Remploy is another interesting one. Do you know about Remploy? They provide training and work for mentally disabled people, or partly physically disabled and people who we would in the past have been called simple.'

Quote from the Remploy website:'At Remploy we focus on ability, not disability. As a specialist employment services group we provide disabled people, people with a health condition and those who face complex barriers to gaining a job with the support they need to find sustainable employment. Remploy helped over 6,600 disabled people into sustainable employment with many of the UK's top employers... As part of Remploy's drive to significantly increase the opportunities available to disabled people to find sustainable employment we are opening a network of city centre branches. We have over sixty years experience of working with disabled people and we share this experience with employers who see the value of recruiting and retaining a skilled and diverse workforce.'

Nicky explains her concerns:'I actually consider them to be the equivalent of our church in the workplace. The church had a guy who worked for them who was a chronic gambler. He was £10,000 in debt from gambling on fruit machines. Well, he would not turn up for work but they could not go round to try to coax him back. I found out that he was behaving very badly and as he was part of our church, I went with him to go and talk to the boss. My aim was to get him back on the straight and narrow. The outcome was that he went back to work.

Listening to the Remploy boss who had done the job for years was really fascinating. He told me the system used to work because we were allowed to make it work. What they used to do was, when an individual did not turn up for work they would go round and talk the individual into going back to work. They are not allowed to do that any more. So the individual doesn't get up and he's probably not going to remember to go to work every day or if something else comes up and he doesn't feel like going or it's raining he will stay at home. The boss cannot go round and chivvy him along, because that's all it ever took. So Remploy have been losing money left right and centre and the government is looking to shut the workshops down because the rules have been changed to make it impossible for them to operate.'

Nicky continued: 'At the church we used to do the same thing. We have a Friday coffee meeting at lunch-time, we provide a bit of lunch and chat with people who pour out their heart or just talk. We go round to pick an individual up to take them to church. They may respond to say they were not coming and so we would counter it with a comment such as, oh come on, you know it's only an hour. Come on, get your coat on, I will take you and bring you back afterwards, it's only an hour and you can have some lunch. With a little bit of coaxing, they would come a long, thoroughly enjoy themselves and you know for that hour, hour and a half, they have not been gambling, drinking or taking drugs. They will not have not been ripped off by someone who is just taking advantage of them. The thing is, you've actually improved their life just a little bit, with something that was positive as opposed to negative.'

So what will the government do with all these people which is a growing population?

'Well, we tax to death those that do any work and pay benefit to those who don't and won't. So they are upping the taxes and putting more money on just about everything they can. Just from the small group of people I've got, if that is multiplied over the country that's going to be a very high figure. Then add the whole load of them that don't come to church and never have done and you have a very real problem. How many of these people are there that we are paying £30,000 a year to in benefits, but you know, we don't need to. We could fund the National Health Service on what we are paying to idiots who have created empires in the Social Services and other departments who have no intentions of changing it.'

'Is there a solution?' I ask.

'I think you have to start again and stop the benefit system as it is and start asking very sensible questions about what people need to live on. There is a big imbalance. As an example, if you take a little old lady of ninety living on her own, she is entitled to, I think the government guarantee £95 a week to live on. Well if she can live on £95 a week, so can my chronic alcoholic. But the government, through its agencies are saying, 'we are going to give you more money'. If you are going to give the alcoholic more money then surely the little old lady of 90 should have the same. She's not going to be a burden on the National Health Service to the extent the alcoholic is for the next god knows how many years, until he or she kills themselves.

That sort of imbalance is wrong, but people need to have personal responsibility. For example, if you get a house then you have to have responsibility to match it. So if I'm going to give you £200 a week then you have to do something in return. If you can't guarantee to pay your rent yourself, we'll pay it for you and that be deducted from their benifit. I mean, we give these people money so they can get people to help them clean their flat or do their washing, but are you going to do that if you are a chronic alcoholic? No, it's going on drink. They then say they can't manage anything, their flat is a complete tip and they become depressed. They just drink. The governments answer? Give them more money.

Now common sense tells me that you give the guy a voucher and let the shop/service provider claim the money. Give them vouchers and don't give them money. What are they going to do with a voucher if it's only accepted from the individual in person and it cannot be swapped for anything other than services? It would exclude the purchase of alcohol.'

Nicky explains further: 'I have no objections to someone who's got a serious disability having enough money to live on, and having more than just the minimum because they've no means of changing their life. I have a little lady I've known for years, she does a part time voluntary job at a prison. She's got cerebral palsy and is in a wheelchair. She doesn't smoke, doesn't drink, doesn't take drugs and doesn't cause problems to society. I have no problem with her having a car to get around in and money to live on. She is getting the same as some of my addicts and quite frankly it's taking us all for a ride. I would abolish it all and start from an entirely different system altogether and limit benefits. It would be, you can have this money for this long and after that there wont be any more. Bit like America really, you can get unemployment benefit for twelve weeks and that's that. We are not going to keep you forever.'

But what would the courts do, because all they are going to do then is go out and thieve?

'I would make punishments for crime unpleasant. Prison should be unpleasant enough to make criminals not want to go back again and that's where we go wrong, our punishments mean nothing. A lot of those people who are regular attendees at court, know the system and know what will be offered and they choose where they are going to go and what they are going to do. And what are you going to do to someone who won't do anything?

Having been given a punishment many criminals take the view that they do not turn up for community service. What happens is that they are eventually brought back to court. The court adds some more hours and still they do not do the work. In theory the court is supposed to send them to prison but the shrewd criminal, and there are a lot of them, suddenly discover they have got mental illness and so the court will have to write all the punishment off.'

Nicky focuses on the dependency system: 'I have people who would rather live on £50 a week or whatever they get now than they would go and look for a job because it's secure. They have the view that I know I'll get my £50, it doesn't matter what happens in my life, whether I get up, or whether I don't, I will get that. So they would rather live, slightly poor and not have the stress of going out and working. I call them married to the State and there's generations of them. I have one woman in my church where there are four generations who live like that. Her kid of fourteen thinks you get your money from the post office. I asked her why I did not get my money from the post office? She replied that it was because I didn't have a book. I asked where I could get a book but she didn't know. I explained that what actually happens is that I go out to work and the government immediately takes £100 out of my wages and gives it to your mother for you and I don't get any choice. This is a complete shock to this kid of fourteen. But when she leaves school, she's going to have a flat and everything paid for and you think, how have we ended up here, with four generations of people who have done very well out of it and will continue to do so.'

Nicky considers it to be a growing problem: 'To compound the problem they are coming from outside the country to do it as well. A friend of mine who works with people who support them told me that there was an immigrant, from Iraq or somewhere out that way who came into the country. They gave her a house, completely carpeted, washing machine, fridge, cooker, in fact everything she needed to live. Then she wanted a transfer and moved to another house but she didn't get all the things the second time and she was absolutely furious. She got this house exchange and it didn't have anything in it, and she wanted new carpets, washing machine, fridge, all the luxuries and a taxi to take her children to school. And she was absolutely disgusted because she wasn't going to get it. She also gets benefits.

There are hard working people who have waited on a list for years, who were born in this country and they don't get it, so why are we giving it to these people from outside? There are people telling people in other countries how to get what they want when they come here. But we have too many benefits and many of these people are only coming here for benefits.'

I asked Nicky if she had any personal experience of this situation: 'My brother lived in Italy and there was a town where a lot of Eastern European people were going. Now not all of them were criminals, but you know, there was a criminal element. Crime increased in a place where it was practically non-existant prior to these people arriving. A lady got murdered and the government acted and sent them all back to where they came from because they didn't want them. It was a case of go away and don't come back. You may think that such action must be against European law, but they did it and nobody kicked up a storm. In Britain, we let everybody in and pander to their demands.'

I asked if Nicky had any real concerns over people in her church: 'I had a paedophile in my church and I made sure that everyone in the church knew who and what he was. Well how else do I deal with the situation because I have people with kids attending? It was an interesting situation because I have had a number of paedophiles through the church, but only two stayed for any length of time and one of them was actually out on license and he was the one that caused me the most problem because I don't trust these people. I can't afford to trust them.

Now I don't have a church full of children and at the time I actually only had two children so I'm not in great danger. I don't have a big building so they can't go anywhere and I can stand in the pulpit and just about see where they are. This guy came, I knew he was a paedophile because I had somebody in the congregation who knew him and warned me. He came and confessed what he was and was quite open about it, but I detected from chatting to him that he didn't have the least intention of changing. This disturbed me because he was out on license so I informed various people that this guy is here, especially the woman with the kids.

He didn't stay at my church for very long, before he went off to another church. It was a much bigger place and I thought they've got a load of kids up there and I ought to phone the pastor and tell him about this. So when I found out that he was going there regularly, I phoned them up but I had terrible difficulty just getting to speak to the pastor. The PA was a very bossy lady and in the end I told her that it was serious and important and she had better put me through. When I got to speak to the pastor I couldn't believe the rank stupidity of the man. He said that he had told his Elders. This interested me because I thought I've got a church and I'm quite interested to know how someone else is going to deal with this criminal. I asked how he was handling it? In my church everyone knows so if you want to invite the guy to your house and you've got kids and grandkids coming round, well you know and you can take responsibility for your actions. There are no secrets.

He explained that he had told his Elders in a church of two or three hundred. On a Sunday all of the children are in a separate building. I asked what happens when this guy is in church, do they always have someone with him, seeing who he is talking to and what he is doing? He said no. I explained that he's in church and he doesn't have to go where the kids are. You need to know who he is talking to, who's inviting him round for dinner, who is being friendly and making friends with him? He replied that he had not thought about it.

That comes down to confidentiality because we are obeying all the rules, he had told a few key people but actually that can be completely ineffective. Unless you sit with that guy and you monitor every person he speaks to, and in a church people tend to be quite open and friendly and absorb people in, he can cultivate the people with kids. They are very good at it as they are often very personable people.

I was horrified, I thought you're an idiot, you haven't actually thought it through. All you've done is follow the guidelines but the guidelines are completely ineffective. There is only one way to deal with it and that's have it out in the open. No secrets. We'll accept you, you are welcome here, nobody is going to beat you up or condemn you, but we are all going to know who and what you are.'

Nicky fears for the Christian faith in the UK and explains: 'There's been a few laws passed which are of a concern to me because I just think, there's going to be real trouble. There was a law passed that means if as a Christian organisation, I want to advertise a job, I am not allowed to ask for a Christian candidate. Now I'm a Christian organisation we have Christian beliefs and that's the whole reason we are here, but I am not allowed to advertise for a Christian. So if a Muslim applies for the job and I don't give it to them because they are non-Christian, I am in deep trouble.

So I wrote to Tony Blair when he was in power because he sold us down the river behind our backs. I told him that the issue needed to be dealt with because if the law is passed, it's wrong. In any organisation there will be regulations and if you want to work for them you sign your contract and accept the rules. If you don't like them, don't join and if you break them then you can be sacked. But what we as Christians are being told is that if I advertise and say these are our rules, this is what I want, I'm not allowed to. I've got to consider people who actually are completely inappropriate by nature of the fact that they are not Christian. I've actually known a Christian organisation take a token Muslim to keep everybody happy. A lot of Christian organisations don't want to advertise for anyone because of the wording they have got to put in the job application, I think the best you can say is 'sympathetic to our interests'. I'm sorry that's not good enough for me, we're Christians and I don't care who knows it, and why shouldn't I be able to say that?

If you don't want to work in an organisation that is Christian and you don't agree with the Christian ideals, then go and find a job somewhere else. We are not persecuting anybody or being rotten to you but we are actually saying, this is what we believe, this is how we run things. Why shouldn't we be able to say that, but we're not, we're not allowed to say that. The outcome is that in a lot of Christian organisations you get a job by word of mouth. If a Muslim organisation advertised and somebody applied for a job who was a Christian, they would never get the job and that's a fact.'

Other issues that concern Nicky are: 'Marriage is a frightening one. Do you know that if two homosexuals come into my church and want to get married and I refuse to marry them, I could be put in prison. Now it's not going to happen in my church because I don't have a building that you are going to want your wedding photographs taken in, but it is a matter of time before it does happen. If someone comes into my church and they are a transsexual, I am not allowed to ask them anything about it. If it's a man dressed as a woman, I've got to let them use the womens' bathrooms otherwise I am in very real trouble and I could go to prison.

Again, there is this issue of what are we being made to do? What about our human rights and the right to freely practice our religion? Well, in the UK we are not allowed to. But I'll tell you that if we were a Muslim organisation and we refused to employ a homosexual or a transsexual no one would bat an eyelid.'

Nicky expanded on the issues: 'There was another EU rule which says that any religious organisation that is under 200 years old, or under 200 members will become illegal. That eliminates most of evangelical Christianity and sidelines them into being illegal. My church could become illegal overnight. The Evangelical Alliance has said that as a member we, as a body can get round it, but we are concerned as to where it's going to leave a lot of churches.

If you are a Christian charity it's very hard work to be able to work properly and freely without having to constantly ask yourself, have we phrased this right, are we going to get had up by someone, is someone going to apply and accuse us of being racist or prejudiced or something, purely because we are saying, we are Christian. As a Christian organisation, I won't apply for funding, because of the hoops they are going to make me jump through and what I have to do to get it. The truth is, my success with these terrifying people is down to the fact that I am a Christian and the only things they are going to stop are the things that work.

By way of an example, I challenged the guy who was a chronic gambler with £10,000 worth of debt. What are we going to do about your gambling? He wants to stop but hasn't got the mental capacity to do so. So we came to an arrangement which required him to give me his card and I controlled his money every week. In one year he paid off £10,000 of debt and also went on holiday. So now he had no problems, his life was straight in order and going smoothly. But do you know what? I'm not allowed to do that even though it's a private arrangement.

All these organisations that are supposed to help, don't, they are not interested in the guy. The social worker actually told me, you know you can't do that. I said well I'm doing it and its working and I'm not stopping. Obviously if the guy said he wanted his card back, I've got to give it to him, but before I give him his card we'll have a discussion. I'm now not allowed to do that but those are the things that work.

There are people in our church who actually run a house for offenders. Now they are a Christian organisation, and they get funded by the local council but when they get inspected and they see a Christian poster up, the response is that it has to be taken down or they will stop the funding. Christian organisations are really coming under fire at every angle because we have these stupid laws that say you are not allowed to say anything. If we were Muslim they wouldn't dare say anything to us because they are afraid. It is so very scary!'

Nicky also has strong views on morality: 'The morality of this country has deteriorated into nothing. One of my closest friends is an assistant head teacher at a high school and she told me that they are not allowed to tell people the difference between right and wrong any more, you can only talk about it so they can make a choice. That's the problem, nobody stands up and says, this is wrong, you shouldn't' do it. So people say it's my choice and it's only wrong if I get caught. So if you have something and you haven't got the power to keep it and I take it from you, then it becomes mine.

I'm tired of girls who have babies to get money and I don't think they should get extra money for extra babies. If you are on state benefit and you've got one baby, then OK but you shouldn't have any more. There are people who work who can't afford to have loads of children because they work. Those that do not work, give them free nursery places and take away their right to sit on the dole. That would take the pleasure out of having all these kids because there is no need for it.

You can sit on the dole at present until your child is sixteen and nobody is going to ask a single question. You don't train, you don't do anything and you get on this ladder at fourteen, fifteen, sixteen or seventeen and you stay on it for sixteen years. Then what are you going to be fit for, nothing. And if you have more kids and space them out you can stay on the dole until you are about forty and nobody is going to say anything.

What should happen is that if you're on benefit, you've got a child, here's your free nursery place, now look for work. They will respond with a claim that it won't be fair because the child is too young. Sorry, but this is not what it's about. They should have thought about that and there is a responsibility that goes with having a child and if you want a child and want to stay at home and not work then you have to deal with that yourself. We as a society don't have to take responsibility, the individual does and the government has taken that away.

If they say, I've got one kid and I'm broke and I can't afford it, I'll have another one, well we're not paying for the second one and you do not get more money. We'll give you another nursery place so you are going to have to work now. You want extra money for the second kid, you are going to have to get a job. That would immediately remove all the fun out of it because the fun is, I get housed, I get benefit.

We need to go right back to school, we need to start in school and we need to really focus on getting respect. When I was a kid, if I got into trouble at school my mother would tell me off too. Now, a kid gets told off in school, parents come down, complain and they never ever side with the teacher. The teachers have no authority and the kids and parents know that. We've lost respect and discipline and I don't know how we get it back. We have lost that completely, people are afraid of kids now, because they could say something and that could get you into a lot of trouble. It's easy to make an accusation and you see teachers who are on suspension because of accusations and they are often on suspension for years. This is all because kids have said something and said it on purpose and of course they are guilty until proven innocent.'

Nicky continues: 'When I visited a prison there was a lot of ground inside just lying there as waste. They used to grow all their own vegetables, but now they can't because they don't have enough staff. We are doing it backwards. I don't think people should be allowed to sit in a cell for twenty-three hours a day and do nothing. They should be working and it should be hard and unpleasant, something that you are going to remember and you are not going to want to go back and do again. But we don't have that, now we have negotiation and we have manipulation with criminals saying I don't like that punishment, so I'm going to select another one and we agree to it in court. We let probation select punishment for people. I'm not happy about that and sometimes I read those pre-sentence reports and I think what are we here for?

We are given a set of guidelines and a set of sentences, but then we are not allowed to follow them through, or we are given that impression. Suspended sentences are one thing that I find very interesting. Everyone is so reluctant to follow it through and I hate that because I think a suspended sentence is great. It is your final chance and if you fall down on it, lock them up straight away, don't flinch from it, I'm not sorry for you, I don't see anything to change my mind, you have been told.'

So society is broken and it is going to take a lot of mending. There are those who think that it cannot be mended and that the country will descend deeper into the abyss. It is a matter for the British people.

The Human Rights Act – A Criminal Charter

In my opinion and, seemingly that of a great number of people in the UK, one of the most controversial pieces of legislation in the UK at the present time is the European Convention on Human Rights. The reality is that human rights were born out of the Second World War with the whole objective of stopping an organisation, a system, a government or a country doing what had occurred in Nazi Germany. The Nazis had undertaken the systematic extermination of people on the basis of race, religion or culture and it openly occurred through the period leading up to and during the Second World War. The objective of the ECHR was a way to guarantee the citizens of Europe basic human rights and freedoms and was approved in the UK in the 1950s although it was only incorporated into our laws in October 2000. The new legislation enables people to use the convention in proceedings in the UK courts, as opposed to taking cases to the Court of Human Rights in Strasbourg as had been the case previously.

Much of the existing law in the UK already provided safeguards for human rights but whilst the aim of the convention was to provide the basic human rights and freedoms, it was stressed at the time that it should not be regarded as villain's charter and that the convention would not provide defendants with spurious defences. It is this which has become a bone of contention because vast and growing swaths of people think that the Human Rights Act [HRA] has in fact become a criminal charter.

The principle articles of the Act are:

Article 2: Right to Life; Article 3: Inhuman treatment; Article 4: Slavery; Article 5: Right to Liberty; Article 6: Right to a fair trial; Article 7: Retrospective crimes; Article 8: Right to privacy; Article 10: Freedom of Expression; Article 11: Freedom of Assembly; Article 12: Marriage and the family; Article 14: Discrimination.

Looking at the list it's very easy to see how it covers the broadest spectrum of every day life and how the criminal element will, and in my opinion do, use it to make their case. Take, for example, the prohibition of slavery and forced labour. There were cases raised where people had been given community punishments where they had to work in the community, undertaking unpaid work doing a whole range of tasks. The Human Rights Act was used to challenge this because they said it could be viewed as slavery and forced labour. Fortunately common sense came in here and it was made clear that it was a punishment and not in the spirit and sense that was dictated by the Act in the first place. So if the Act can identify a punishment then being in prison is a punishment and so the Human Rights Act should not apply to the banal requests being made by convicts.

Let me make one thing very clear: Human Rights legislation is excellent and most people would not decry it, however, what is decried is the abuse of the legislation and its misuse in the legal processes. For example, it was reported in May 2007 that a Government Agency had directed that gangs of teenage criminals should no longer be called gangs, because under the Human Rights Act it might offend them. They must now be called a group. The basis of this change came from the Youth Justice Board who carried out an investigation and produced a report. It stated that many young people interviewed for the study resented the way in which the term had become used to describe any group of young people involved in anti-social behaviour. They felt adults attached the label to them simply on the basis that they were young and met in a group, assuming that crime was their main purpose for meeting.

It was argued that juvenile gangs do exist in some urban areas, but most young people involved in group offending do not belong to gangs, even if others label them in this way. A group of 'yob's' committing a crime is, in my opinion, the same as a gang activity. The Youth Justice Board wants to get a grip with the reality of what their groups or gangs are doing and identify actions to stop such activities. How about helping the victims of the gangs or so called groups?

Another politically correct focus today is that it's every woman's right to have children. OK, that's fine, no problem whatsoever. However, that right should not rely on the state benefits system such as we have at present. It encourages women to have children, because more children means more money. The outcome has been a growing number of cases where the mother, particularly teenage ones, can't cope which impacts on the child and eventually on society with the results being seen in court. It is in the minds of most people that having a child is a great responsibility and there should be basic considerations; loving parents, a good clean home, good home cooked food, sufficient funds to raise a child (it costs a lot of money to bring up a child.) However, for many women, good mothering skills which in the past were handed down from mother to daughter, are no longer there. A lot of criticism is leveled at single parents but many do a fantastic job and for many it's not by choice that they are alone and they go to work to fund and support their child. Good on them, it's the others that need sorting out.

I was told of a class of about twenty-five schoolgirls who were attending a careers discussion which focussed on what their plans were when they left school. Six or seven wanted to go onto further education or take up employment in a particular line of business. The remainder? It was a case of have a child as soon as possible. Didn't matter who the father was, anybody would do. Then get allocated a flat which would be furnished and they would live on social welfare benefits. The next part of the plan was more sex and more kids which would get them into a house and even more social money. The outcome of this is a growing section of the population who slob about, have sex with no precautions and have a number of children, all by different fathers. They do as they please and do not have one ounce of responsibility for their actions. They demand that all of this is paid for by the welfare state and that is a blatant misuse of the Human Rights Act.

It is not just the lower end of the social spectrum that plays the system. In January 2007 Cherie Blair, wife of the former UK Prime Minister, accused Sir Richard Wilson, Britain's top Civil Servant, of violating her human rights as he tried to control her desire for freebies. She apparently told him that she was entitled to cut price designer clothes under the Human Rights Act. Then there was another incident where Sir Richard Wilson was faced with repeated demands for money from Mrs Blair to spend on the refurbishment of Downing Street during his tenure, which was 1998 to 2002. On one occasion she allegedly told a guest being given a tour of number 10, 'Look at the state of the carpets, he makes us live with.'

In response, Wilson reportedly told the guest later, 'She's always trying it on, she needs to understand the public purse cannot be used for these things unless it is justified.'

When he criticised her she reportedly told him he was infringing her rights under Article 1 of the European Convention on Human Rights, on the individual's right to do as they like with their own property. The problem is, of course, that she was using her position as the Prime Minister's wife to undertake all these activities. Of course it was not her property but that of the state and indirectly, ours, the taxpayer that is. [Daily Mail, 22nd January 2007]

Do you need more evidence of abuse of the HRA? The case of Wayne Bishop is a good example. He was convicted of burglary and sentenced to eight months in jail after admitting burglary and dangerous driving. He was let out after only one month. The reason was that the Appeal Court ruled that the rights of his five children were more important than those of his victims or the interests of justice. Ah, that's nice. We are told that Bishop was the sole carer of his children, aged between six and thirteen, for five nights a week. It appears that his nocturnal criminal activities did not cause him any concern about the welfare of his children. Nobody seemed interested in who was looking after them whilst he was out committing crimes. His lawyer used Article 8 of the Human Rights Act, the right to a family life, and the judges accepted that argument. After being released, Bishop then boasted of how he had managed to make a mockery of justice and told the *Daily Mail*: 'I'm a lucky boy and I'm on top of the world.'

Now to get sent to prison in the current climate you have got to have a long track record of criminal activity or have committed a very serious offence. If you have a family and you are responsible for them then you do not go out thieving. If you do then you should have to accept the consequences. At the Appeal Court, Mr Justice Maddison and Mr Justice Sweeney agreed that imprisoning Bishop was not in the 'best interests' of his children, and ordered the sentence to be suspended instead.

Bishop told the *Daily Mail*: 'People need to understand my situation. They should leave me alone to live with my children in peace.' [*Daily Mail* 27th May 2011]

We then learn that the nice Mr Bishop had been called to his son's school in October 2008 to discuss why he repeatedly wore a bracelet in defiance of school rules. Upon hearing that the head teacher confiscated the jewellery from his five-year-old son, he went berserk.

Arriving at the school Bishop blocked the school drive with his car and told the headteacher: 'I'm going to do you over.'

He added: 'I'm not sticking to the rules. My son's not sticking to the rules.'

Bishop repeated the threats several times before heading into a corridor, still swearing, where a number of children were standing. During the twenty-five minute incident, Bishop again refused to move his car, saying: 'The feds won't be able to get in.'

Bishop left the headteacher fearing for her own and her pupils' safety after threatening to smash up 'every car in the car park'.

Bishop has convictions for nine offences including two for using threatening words or behaviour. He has been sentenced to prison on four occasions. When asked about the school incident, he said his behaviour had been 'out of character'. [*Daily Mail* 30th May 2011]

What a nice caring family man Mr Bishop is. He is a real role model to his children showing them how to make a mockery of the justice system. He now has an ace in that he can continue with his criminal activities and not face jail. The nice cuddly appeal judges have made it clear that the family comes before justice.

The Cost of the HRA

Did you know that membership of the European Court of Human Rights has already cost UK taxpayers more than £42billion and a sharp rise in compensation claims is now costing Britain £7billion a year. The Act, a legacy of Tony Blair's government, was introduced in Britain allowing individuals to bring cases in British courts under European laws and that fuelled a mass of compensation claims for so called breaches of human rights.

Do the words 'criminal charter' ring any bells!

Research by Lee Rotherham, a policy analyst for the TaxPayers' Alliance, revealed in December 2010 how the Convention has been used to shape British laws and has reached into almost every walk of life, from how our prisons are run to how we police our streets. It even affects how our soldiers fight wars. Dr Rotherham said: 'Fifty years on from the days of Stalin and Hitler, the Strasbourg court is no longer needed to protect us from a knock on the door at 3am, or being deported with a handcart. It carries an increasingly political agenda that is running roughshod over our laws and our courts, at major costs to the taxpayer and to business. This had left Britain facing more claims in British courts, where compensation is higher, and more appeals to Strasbourg.'

The law abiding taxpayer is forking out for cases such as the controversial ruling of a transsexual serving time for manslaughter and attempted rape being allowed to move to a woman's prison even though he committed the offences while a man. The court has also prevented the UK deporting foreigners found guilty of serious offences such as Learco Chindamo, who killed London headmaster Philip Lawrence in 1995. There are the Islamic terror suspects who are successfully fighting deportation orders and stopping the removal of genocide suspects to face trial in Rwanda. Then you pay for employees like Muslim hairdresser Bushra Noah to sue their employers over a dress code that did not allow her to wear a headscarf. How about the suspension of an honour set up by the Queen because it discriminated against non-Christians. To quote the old phrase, the lunatics really are running the asylum!

For those who don't know, Strasbourg is in France which, like the UK, is a signatory to the European Court of Human Rights. France, like the UK, has a problem with people who come from other countries and commit crimes. But unlike the UK, France deals with the issues, as does Italy. France's President, Nicolas Sarkozy, recognised the problem and decided that the Roma communities based illegally on the outskirts of major cities like Paris and Lyon had to go back to Bulgaria or Romania. They have been called magnets for prostitutes, aggressive beggars and criminals, the evidence being that when they move into an area, the crime rate escalates from almost nil to being out of control. When the police went to one camp following thefts in the area a police officer was shot. The French decided enough was enough and so the Roma were told to return to their home country as the France did not want them. The people who were in the illegal camps were taken to airports and biometric records were created of all those receiving the cash payment offered by the French government. They were then flown back to their homes in Bulgaria or

Romania. The empty camps were then dismantled by the police. Deportations took place most weeks, with men, women and children escorted to airports, before being placed on flights and being told not to return. No need to say how the problem would have been dealt with in the UK!

Then in 2010, judges were given powers to revoke French citizenship. What this means is that foreign born people who have been granted citizenship can be stripped of their status and passport and deported for certain crimes. This includes violent crimes against the police and other officials, repeated acts of theft, aggressive begging or for illegally occupying land. This is a country dealing with a very real problem. The UK should adopt the same stance because if people given passports abuse the country and its laws, then they should go back to where they came from, whatever the consequences. Although the European Convention on Human Rights applies to the whole of Europe, it is the British who go to extremes with its application and seemingly appease every challenge made where the HRA is quoted. I have been told by other Europeans that all the illegals flee to Britain and avoid other EU countries, because they just quote the Human Rights Act and 'the golden goose lays its golden eggs'. As somebody said to me: 'the rest of Europe dumps all of its 'unwanted' in the UK.'

A clear example of the UK failing was portrayed in a newspaper where the headlines read, 'A gang of Romanian gypsies jetted into Britain to plunder £800,000 in UK benefits – then flew back to spend the money at home'. They spent their ill-gotten gains in Romania to transform their home town from a dusty dump to a prosperous community full of posh new houses, BMWs and Land Rovers. They used forged Home Office residency documents and fake job references to obtain National Insurance numbers, which they then used to claim tax credits, income support, child benefits and housing handouts. They claimed they had children, producing bogus birth certificates and photos. But the kids either did not exist or were suspected trafficking victims. A British builder supplied the forged job references. Some lived in Britain while others made flying visits using low-cost airline Wizz Air. In fact one individual received £29,000 in benefits 'while still living in Romania'. Judge Gregory Stone jailed the ringleader for four years eight months. His wife got two years after claiming she had six kids to illegally receive £81,000 in benefits. Others admitted various counts of theft, fraud or laundering and received sentences of between six months and two years four months. A builder from Liverpool got nine months for providing references. How many others are doing the same thing? [*Sun* 18th May 2011]

As Dr Rotherham quite rightly says: Australia, New Zealand, Canada and the United States all get by very well without joining up to continental human rights courts. Britain can do the same. He suggests either replacing the Human Rights Act with a British Bill of Rights, withdrawing from the Convention or agreeing some opt-outs. He considers that it is hard to see how any member state or member of the Commission could argue that the UK would be in breach of its obligations, whichever option it took.

European Court of Human Rights

Britain has the worst crime rate in Europe because of Human Rights in that we have imported the very worst people the world has to offer and given them everything. We have terrorists, criminals, thieves, rapists and paedophiles from all over the world being assisted in every way because the UK is the only place that accepts the do-gooders understanding of Human Rights. It is no wonder that all the crooks, burglars and criminals head straight for the UK.Criminals arrive and we welcome them and give them help, benefits and homes, yet we cannot give those same benefits to the British people or our armed forces. The UK is now a broken society where the criminals are protected and the innocent abused and ignored.

The problem is in the European Court of Human Rights because that is where the judges sit and make decisions, decisions that directly affect hundreds of millions of lives. They are a failure because not many of them have any judicial experience and some struggle to understand the English language. Among the judges is one from San Marino, a tiny European enclave with a population of 30,000, the same size as some of our market towns. We are told that the panel also includes judges from Albania, Armenia, Macedonia and Azerbaijan. Those from Liechtenstein, San Marino, Monaco and Andorra have the same amount of say as Britain, France and Germany despite their combined populations being smaller than a London borough. They are also appointed by their home nation for political rather than for their legal expertise. The former English Lord Chief Justice, Lord Woolf, found that some judges did not understand either English or French, the two languages in which the court conducts its business, and that, as a result, they do not 'contribute' to its rulings. It will be no a surprise to learn that many of the judges spent their careers teaching law in universities rather than practising it in the courtroom. [*Daily Mail* 3rd February 2011]

The so called judges have blocked the deportation from Britain of countless foreign criminals and awarded thousands of pounds in compensation to alleged Islamic terrorists. Article 3 of the European Convention for Human Rights provides protection against torture, inhuman or degrading treatment. This is the clause that allows foreign terror suspects to fight deportation on the grounds that they would be tortured in their home countries if they returned. A string of terrorists have taken advantage of the clause and Britain has argued that the courts should be allowed to take into account the risks posed to its citizens. But the unelected judges ruled in the 1996 Chahal judgment that the only factor of importance was the protection of the human rights of terror suspects. What we are being told is that they can kill and injure hundreds in the UK so long as they are protected. [*Daily Mail* February 2011]

It will be of no surprise to learn that more than 200 foreign prisoners, including killers, cheated deportation last year by claiming they have a human right to a 'family life' in Britain. Tory MP Dominic Raab, who obtained the figures, said:

'It is one thing to argue against deporting an individual into the arms of a torturing state. But it makes a mockery of British justice to allow hundreds of criminals and suspected terrorists to claim family ties to defeat a deportation order. This is a novel expansion of human rights by the UK courts, and an escalating threat to our border controls.'

Currently, the law says offenders jailed for twelve months or more should be deported on completing their sentence but there is an exemption if removing them would breach their human rights. MPs fear judges are now going even further in interpreting Article 8. In some cases, criminals who are single with no children have won appeals to stay because their parents live in the UK. A Commission to consider overhauling the legislation is doomed for failure as Lord Lester, a QC who campaigned for thirty years for EU rights conventions to be incorporated in British law, will sit on the body as will Labour peer and human rights lawyer Baroness Kennedy. No hope there then! [*Daily Mail* 12th March 2011]

The Policy Exchange report written by Michael Pinto-Duschinsky, a human rights and constitutional expert, calls for the UK to review how well the court in Strasbourg performs over the next two years. If it fails to show any progress in its efficiency or in the competence of its judges, the UK should consider pulling out. That would mean that Britain's own Supreme Court would then become the final arena for cases brought by Britons under the European Convention of Human Rights, which would continue to be part of British law. Mr Pinto-Duschinsky states:

'Contrary to what has been stated by some opponents of such a reform, there is strong evidence to suggest that the UK's membership of the EU and Council of Europe does not require continued adherence to the judgments of the European Court of Human Rights should the UK opt for such a withdrawal.'

That sounds good. Why do have to wait for two years? Mr Cameron as the Prime Minister you have the answer to what the vast majority of the British people demand, so get to it! [*Daily Express* 7th February 2011]

6

Violent Crime

A Violent Society

Violent crime is only a very small proportion of overall crime in the UK but it is the type of crime that people fear the most. They are the crimes that attract dramatic headlines and photographs in the media and portray a violent society. Getting violent crime under control is crucial but do not ask or expect any government to do it, because they are not interested. Governments of different colours have had years to get to grips with the problem, but the reality is that they have not and it is getting worse. From my own personal experiences as a magistrate, the number of violent crimes has increased over the years and the punishments for such offences, have became more lenient to non-existent. Another major element is that ten or fifteen years ago the violence would involve a 'punch up' with people being battered and bruised. Now they are shot, stabbed or attacked with some other lethal weapon and often the victim was just in the wrong place at the wrong time.

Torture and Murder

In 1993, I was a Civil Servant awaiting delivery of office furniture for my additional staff. The truck arrived having made the journey from Liverpool. I showed the two men where the desks were required and set about making them coffee. One of the two was a typical Liverpudlian and he did the talking. The other said very little. During conversation I raised the subject of the tragedy that befell the area of Bootle (Liverpool) where a toddler, Jamie Bulger, was taken from a shopping centre by two ten-year-old boys then tortured to death. I was told that the quiet one of the two men was in fact Jamie Bulger's uncle. No wonder he had little to say.

It was an everyday situation when Jamie Bulger walked away from his mother for only a second, but it allowed Jon Venables to take his hand and lead him out of the mall with his friend Robert Thompson. They took Jamie on a walk for over two and a half miles. Along the way they stopped every now and again to torture the little boy who was crying constantly for his mummy. Finally they stopped at a railway track where they brutally kicked him, threw stones at him, rubbed paint in his eyes, pushed batteries up his anus and cut his fingers off with scissors. Other mutilations were inflicted but not reported in the press.

Remember, a three year old cannot possibly defend themselves against a ten year old, let alone two of them. What these two boys did was so horrendous that Jamie's mother was forbidden to identify his body. They then left his small beaten body on railway tracks so a train could run him over to hide the desecration they had created. There can be no doubt that the two boys would have understood at the time that what they did was seriously wrong, hence their attempt in trying to make it look like an accident. It is also a fact that children of ten know and understand right from wrong, unless their mental abilities dictate otherwise. Venables and Thompson became sadistic killers and Jamie was the innocent victim.

Later the following day, Jamie's body was found by the railway line at Walton, a couple of miles from the shopping centre. The hunt began for the killer. Initially, the predictable fear was that the little boy had been abducted by a murderous paedophile. Merseyside police examined the CCTV footage taken from the shopping centre's security cameras and to their horror, the pictures, although not very clear, revealed that it was not a predatory adult who had taken Jamie, but two young boys. The next question was whether these two youngsters could have been Jamie's killers or had they surrendered him to a paedophile and then decided to stay quiet through fear of the consequences?

The inquiry was led by Det Supt Albert Kirby, one of the Merseyside force's most experienced officers. He called a news conference to announce that two boys had been arrested at their homes within a few hundred yards of the murder scene. There were questions about the true innocence of children and how the adult world measured up to its responsibilities. These questions came to the surface at the boys' criminal trial at Preston in November 1993. A series of witnesses spoke of seeing two boys escorting a toddler along the route from Bootle to Walton. Their anguish was nearly unbearable. One or two broke down in tears as they lived with the thought that they might have intervened, particularly one who became suspicious about the way Venables and Thompson were treating the little boy who they insisted was their 'brother'.

The decision was made to place the two defendants before an adult criminal court rather than a juvenile hearing. It meant that, although during the trial they were known only as Boy A and Boy B, they were exposed to the full weight of criminal trial. This included a packed press bench and public benches crowded with the Bulger family and their friends and neighbours.

The mood on Merseyside had been witnessed long before the trial and at their first appearance on remand in Bootle Magistrates' Court, the huge crowd outside roared its anger and contempt as the van carrying the two boys was driven away. Several people attempted to attack the vehicle. The media followed the story in detail and I pick up the key events from the end of the trial when the judge, Mr Justice Morland, ruled that the two boys could be identified by name and so linked them forever to one of the most horrific murders of modern times.

The judge set a tariff of eight years detention for the two boys before they could be considered for release on licence. Lord Taylor later recommended ten years, but the then Home Secretary Michael Howard set the minimum as fifteen years. This was after representations from the boys' lawyers and an opposing representation from the Bulger family. By the late 1990s, the boys' lawyers were taking their case to the European Commission of Human Rights (ECHR). The ECHR challenged the position of the British Government, later re-inforced by the Court of Human Rights. It required that the Home Secretary should not set the minimum term of punishment. This meant that a new tariff had to be set by Lord Woolf.

This was the beginning of the injustice because he determined that the youths qualified for parole. He said: 'It was not in the public interest for them to spend time in the 'corrosive atmosphere' of a young offender institution, to which they would have been moved when they reached nineteen.'

Then a report stated that the killers of James Bulger were to be released which meant that Jon Venables and Robert Thompson, both eighteen years of age, would be granted parole and given new identities to protect them from vigilantes.

David Blunkett, the Home Secretary said: 'There had been a very thorough consideration of their cases by the Parole Board and it was satisfied there was no unacceptable risk to the public. Thompson and Venables are not free. They will remain on licence for the rest of their lives and are liable to be recalled to custody at any time if there is any evidence that they present a risk to the public.'

Mr Blunkett added: 'The murder of James Bulger was a terrible event for his family and the nation. But no public interest would be served by pursuing the perpetrators.'

Under the terms of their licence, the youths will not be allowed to contact, or attempt to contact, any member of the Bulger family or each other. They are also forbidden to enter the county of Merseyside without the prior written consent of their probation officers. Court injunctions forbid the media from disclosing their new names or publishing contemporary photographs for fear of endangering their lives.

Lady Justice Butler-Sloss, the President of the High Court's Family Division, awarded the two boys (now men) anonymity for the rest of their lives when they left custody with new identities. They would also leave custody early only serving just over half of their sentence. When the injunctions were granted, Dame Elizabeth Butler-Sloss said:

'There was a real possibility of serious physical harm and possible death from vengeful members of the public or the Bulger family.'

For the next few years the youths lived under a status officially described as 'supervised independent living', effectively watched over by a small probation team twenty-four hours a day.

Denise Fergus, Jamie's mother, said: 'Thompson and Venables may think they have got off lightly and can hide. But I know different. I know that no matter where they go, someone out there is waiting.'

Ralph Bulger, his father, said: 'I feel angry, frustrated and completely let down by the system.'

You would have to be a very strange person not to agree with the family. The two boys disgustingly and violently took Jamie's life and, in return, they each get a new life. How much money has all this cost the taxpayer and how much more is it going to cost?

The parole hearings were held before a tribunal under the chairmanship of a High Court judge and included a consultant psychiatrist and an experienced independent lay member. They heard representations from lawyers acting for the youths, who were questioned 'rigorously' by the panel about their attitude to their crime and their expectations for the future. The panel considered psychiatric reports from the trial and assessments of the youths' current circumstances. It also reviewed their school records and considered any further offending that might have taken place during their detention.

Dominic Lloyd, a solicitor acting for Thompson, said: '…his hearing had not been 'a tea and biscuits affair'. It was a rigorous, strenuous, hands-on examination of the crime and the individuals. He has accepted responsibility for his part. He has shown great and real remorse over a long period of time in a genuine way.'

Former Home Secretary, Michael Howard, described the murder of Merseyside two-year-old James Bulger as a 'uniquely and unparalleled evil and barbarous act'.

Mr Howard defended his much-criticised setting of a minimum fifteen-year sentence for Jamie's two schoolboy killers. He said: 'If that act had been committed by an adult, I would have set a tariff of at least twenty-five years… So I made a very substantial allowance for the fact the offenders were young. If they remain in custody for fifteen years, they will be released when they're twenty-five…They will have virtually the whole of their adult lives in front of them. This was not a privilege they allowed James Bulger to have.'

Of Lord Woolfe's decision, Mr Howard said: 'It may well be that the Parole Board had no alternative, but I think Lord Woolf was wrong to decide that eight years was sufficient time for Thompson and Venables to spend in custody.'

A European Court of Human Rights judgment quoted Susan Bailey, of Prestwich Hospital, who described Venables' journey to admitting his part in the murder. She said:

'That in 1997 Venables, then fifteen, had 'worked through the essential stages of coming to terms with the murder'.

Dr Bailey added: 'He had moved through the normal sequence of psychological reactions: denial-disbelief, avoidance, sense of loss, experience of grief, ownership for his part in the murder (emerging from the process of re-enactment spanning a period of two difficult years) shame and remorse, which was ongoing and would remain forever.'

The work of Dr Bailey and others was carried out in the secure unit where Venables had been detained since his arrest. Thompson had the same intensive treatment at the separate secure unit where he was held. Eve Jones, one of the psychiatrists who worked with him, explained some of the difficulty in another report cited by the European court.

Dr Jones said: 'winning Thompson's trust had been a long drawn out process . . . partly due to his fear of retaliation and media interest and partly due to his innate fear and dislike of psychiatrists'.

Like Venables, Thompson came to admit what he had done and has exhibited remorse. The pair have never discussed the murder with each other. The reason being that they have not seen each other since the day a jury found them guilty of murder at Preston Crown Court in November 1993. They have led similar lives as residents of secure units where they had to follow rules. On weekdays they were woken at 7am, had lessons from 9.15am to 3.15pm and were locked in their rooms in the evening. Their lights were switched off at 10pm. Over time, both Thompson and Venables developed good relationships with staff at their respective establishments. Most other inmates who passed through were unaware of their identities. It is claimed that newspaper stories about Thompson being involved in violent incidents have been found to be untrue.

Although they did not do well in their primary school, they both developed educationally. They passed GCSEs and have sat A-levels. We are told that Venables has shown an aptitude for computer work and Thompson has revealed an artistic side to his character. His paintings hang in the foyer of the unit where he was held. He has designed and made a wedding dress and created a coffee table for his mother who visited her son regularly.

Thompson was visited by Sir David Ramsbotham, the former Chief Inspector of Prisons, who was impressed by his artwork and intellect. Venables turned his bedroom into a shrine to Manchester United and as part of the preparation for his release, he was recently taken with his father to watch the team play at Old Trafford. The thinking behind such outings being to get him used to being among large crowds and to try to reduce his fear of being recognised and attacked. Those who have worked with Venables have reached similar conclusions. One said: 'He has come to terms in a wholly realistic way with the sheer awfulness of what he did.'

Thompson chose to attend Shakespeare productions at Stratford-upon-Avon for his outings. A source who knows him well said: 'Bobby Thompson is a credit to the system he is in. He gives the overriding impression of a young man who is mature, sensible and considerate beyond his years.'

Dame Elizabeth Butler-Sloss, granted an injunction preventing the publication of material identifying Jon Venables and Robert Thompson and referred to 'the almost unique circumstances of this case'. Butler-Sloss concentrated on the common law right of confidence, and Articles 2 and 3 of the European Convention on Human Rights, dealing with the rights to life and freedom from torture. [*Daily Telegraph* 30th June 2001]

Now this is where I have a very real problem. These two knowingly tortured this small boy to death. They get a good education and follow their chosen vocation whilst the authorities gush all over them. We have a committee who now deem them fit to return to society. After only eight years they get out with a new identity, a new life and loads of cash to start this new life. The public cannot know their new identities or where they are living because of freedom from torture. What did they go into custody for in the first place? A private education!

I also have a very real concern about all of this in that there is an element of society who have come to 'like the boys' and now say that they are good, educated with some personal skills and able to be released. Because of their situation they have new identities, a new home and a new life, all at the taxpayers' expense. You will never know if the person living next door to you or in your street is one of them? Nobody I have ever spoken to is happy about that and can you blame them. These boys were not worth one penny that has been spent on them let alone the millions of pounds they will have cost society. They should never, ever have been released. In my opinion, those who advocated their limited time in custody and move back into the free world, must have some acceptance of the crime they committed. It is that which is of the most concern because society now seems to consider that the most heinous of crimes, is just part of growing up.

Another lasting legacy of releasing such people is the fear that innocent individuals can be drawn into the debacle. Alarm spread following the distribution of leaflets alleging that 'the notorious child killer Robert Thompson', was living under an assumed identity in New Zealand. The leaflets, claiming to be from a British group called James Bulger's Memorial Group of Concerned Citizens, asked: 'Are You Living Next to a Monstrous Murderer?'

It identified a man by his first name and stated that he was being harboured by British relatives. However, New Zealand police have investigated and say they are satisfied the man is not Thompson and they have dismissed the pamphlets, which were circulated last June, as 'scaremongering'. When the killers were released under new identities reports alleged that Thompson would be sent to New Zealand. [*Daily Telegraph* 21st Feb 2011]

Having already spent a small fortune on child killer Jon Venables, more has to be spent to give him a new secret name. It means that he will have to learn another fake background and be given a new set of documents, including a passport and birth certificate. He will not be able to return to the town where he was living when he is released from his latest prison sentence. It is understood that a serious security breach has revealed details of his current identity. Apparently when Venables, who is now twenty-eight, was jailed again last year for internet child sex abuse crimes, he had told some people who he really was. A Home Office source said:

'...the new security breach is considered so serious that a new identity is the only answer, because we believe so many people will have learned who he is and it would be impossible to protect him.'

Venables is to appear before the Parole Board where a panel will consider freeing him from his latest jail sentence. After all this time and money, leopard and spots springs to mind. Many say it is just a matter of time before there is another victim.

Sadistic Violence

In August 2009, two brothers aged ten and twelve pleaded guilty to carrying out a pre-planned attack of extreme, sadistic violence. They robbed, sexually abused and intentionally caused grievous bodily harm to two boys aged nine and eleven years. The attack lasted almost two hours during which two innocent boys endured unimaginable violence. They were throttled with a cable and barbed wire, punched and kicked in the head and battered with branches, bricks and rocks. They were forced to eat nettles and swallow glass, crawl across a stream and commit humiliating sex acts. Plastic sheeting was put over them and set alight and an old sink was smashed onto the elder boy's head. The younger boy was forced to urinate into the other boy's mouth. He was then told to kill himself and he pretended to ram a stick down his throat. It was the same stick that had been driven into his arm and a lit cigarette pushed into the wound as well as burning his ears and eyelids. The thugs filmed their actions on a mobile phone.

Once the thugs had departed the scene, the younger boy knelt by the others side and was told that he was blind from the blood and couldn't move. He told him to go and leave him to die there. The younger boy set off to get help. He was barefoot and bleeding but managed to drag himself back to the village. The elder boy was found a short time later at the foot of a steep ravine. He was unconscious, naked from the waist down and half-submerged in water. He had been left for dead after the sink had been smashed down on his head.

The court was told that the thugs had lived with their parents and five elder brothers in a semi-detached house. They grew up in a violent and abusive household with an alcoholic father and a mother who smoked cannabis grown by the father on his allotment. They were beaten, allowed to watch graphic horror and pornographic DVDs and had their meals laced with drugs when their mother wanted a 'quiet night in'. At one point, the thug's parents were claiming as much as £400 a week in benefits, which was being spent on drugs and alcohol. A sign outside the house read: 'Beware of the Kids'. It was only during the case that the full extent of the failures by the authorities became apparent. It transpired that the brothers' former neighbours had complained dozens of times to the police and Social Services about their behaviour and violence, but nothing had been done because the children were under the age of criminal responsibility. The court heard they had been on the child protection register and that one of them was on bail to appear before a youth court on two charges of actual bodily harm and one of burglary at the time of the attack. They watched their older brother stab and mug an elderly woman. During the hearing the defendants were seen to grin occasionally at their social workers and solicitors. They didn't react at all to anything said. They showed no remorse for any of their actions. As one would expect, their parents were not present.

It was found that the assault was the culmination of months of relentlessly ascending violence perpetrated by the two boys under the noses of police and Social Service officials. All of it was carried out with no regard for right and wrong. They had no fear of retribution as they regarded themselves above the law, because as far as they were concerned there was no law. They carried broken bottles and threatened to 'glass' anyone who informed on them. They would deliberately push boys in front of moving cars and wait to watch the impact. They would set fire to girls' hair and knock elderly women off their bicycles. Once they slaughtered a group of ducklings in a park.

The Crown Prosecution Service accepted their guilty pleas to lesser charges so as to save the victims from having to relive their ordeal giving evidence in court. It was said that the brothers would still face the same maximum term of life imprisonment. The torturers were given an indeterminate sentence but ordered that they serve a minimum of five years before they could even be considered for release. It appears that the police told the families that it was unlikely they could be released for at least ten to fifteen years. The do-gooders will, no doubt, ensure that they are released at the earliest opportunity, to be yet another misuse of the Human Rights Act.

Appalling blunders which led to the two boys being free to attack have been spelled out in a 'devastating' report. However, they will never be revealed to the public or even the judge who oversaw the torture trial. Now that is criminal and must be a cover up of the highest order.

We are told that the executive summary of the 'serious case review' into the handling of the two brothers while in the care of the Council discloses that the attack was entirely 'preventable'. It says social workers missed thirty-one chances over fourteen years to intervene with them and their family. But just one person has been disciplined. So it appears that what must be criminal actions by a social services department are to remain unpunished. [*Daily Mail* 21st February 2011]

Sounds so very familiar!

Haringey Horror

In February 2000, the story of Victoria Climbie became national headlines. Victoria, aged eight, was tortured to death by her great-aunt, Marie Therese Kouao, and the woman's boyfriend, Carl Manning. Victoria was born in November 1991 in the Ivory Coast and her parents wanting her to escape the poverty of Africa, entrusted her to her great aunt who brought her to Europe.

Kouao initially went to Paris but was pursued by French authorities over benefit payments and so she and Victoria left France and went to London. When they arrived in England, Victoria's name was given as Anna because of the new identity on the false passport used to get her into Europe. Nice to see our immigration authorities exercising due diligence and failing to spot the false passport of what would have been an illegal immigrant. They stayed at a hostel in north London and Kouao got a job as a hospital cleaner. Kouao and Victoria, who spoke no English, were on a bus when they meet Carl Manning, the driver. A relationship developed between Kouao and Manning and within days they moved into his home in Tottenham, north London. Soon after Victoria was suffering abuse from Manning and that abuse would escalate to her torture and death.

It was on the 14th July 1999 when Victoria was taken for her first visit to the Central Middlesex Hospital. The doctor accepted Kouao's story that Victoria has inflicted the wounds on herself by scratching at scabies sores. At this time, the daughter of her childminder suspected that Victoria had non-accidental injuries and made her views known. The child protection authorities were alerted as a precaution. Haringey social worker, Lisa Arthurworrey, and PC Karen Jones were assigned to the case and they cancelled a home visit scheduled for 4th August after hearing about the scabies. Now call me old fashioned, but can it be right that in our so called modern society that a child with scabies and wounds does not raise issues of poor child care. We have a police officer, a social worker and a doctor who fail to take any form of action. Is it normal for children to have scabies and wounds?

We are told that Manning forced Victoria to sleep in a bin liner in the bath every night. Then Kouao told social workers that Manning had sexually assaulted Victoria but then withdrew the accusation the next day. PC Jones who was tasked to investigate, did so but in the form of a letter which remained unanswered. Because there was no response she did not take any further action.

On the 24th July 1999, Victoria was taken to North Middlesex Hospital's casualty department with scalding to her head and face. Following examination, doctors immediately suspected that the injuries had been deliberately inflicted and the authorities were notified. When Lisa Arthurworrey and PC Jones investigated, Kouao told them that she poured hot water over Victoria to try and stop her scratching her scalp. She said that Victoria caused other injuries with utensils and her explanation for the injuries were accepted.

Victoria was discharged from the hospital and collected by Kouao. Again, old fashioned me raises the issue that a child attends hospital having been scalded and Kouao admits to poring hot water over the child and that's OK?

It was on the 24th February 2000 that Victoria was rushed to North Middlesex Hospital suffering from a combination of malnutrition and hypothermia. She was then transferred to an intensive care ward at St Mary's Hospital in west London where the following day she died.

Dr Nathaniel Carey, the Home Office pathologist who examined her body, found 128 separate injuries and scars, many of them cigarette burns, and described them as: 'the worst case of child abuse I've encountered'.

Social workers, doctors and police all had contact with her while she was being abused. Lisa Arthurworrey was Victoria's social worker and one of a number from Haringey Council blamed for failing her. Following the death of Victoria she felt she was made a scapegoat and described child protection in Haringey as being chaotic, with workers in conflict. She described meetings with her boss, Carole Baptiste, and stated:

'Ms Baptiste used most of the time to talk about her experiences as a black woman and her relationship with God.'

Carole Baptiste refused to attend the subsequent Public Inquiry as a witness. She became the first person ever to be prosecuted and fined for failing to give evidence at an inquiry. When she did eventually cooperate, she put the blame on Lisa Arthurworrey, Victoria's social worker, however, she did condescend to admit that she had not read Victoria's file properly. Oh that's OK then. I thought she had failed as a manager.

Consultant paediatrician, Dr Mary Schwartz, saw Victoria at the Central Middlesex Hospital where she decided her cuts were due to the skin disease scabies. So Victoria was allowed to return home to her abusers. Two weeks later, Victoria again attended hospital however, this time she was taken to the North Middlesex where she was examined by Consultant Dr Mary Rossiter. She felt Victoria was being abused but confused colleagues by writing 'able to discharge' on her notes. So Victoria was again sent home to her abusers. It is also interesting to note that Victoria was taken to different hospitals probably in an attempt to cover up other visits.

Police officers also failed Victoria and it was said that child protection work in the police had a low status and that those involved were nicknamed 'the cardigan squad' or 'the baby sitters'. It seems that PC Karen Jones failed to inspect Victoria's home for fear of catching scabies off the furniture.

Carl Manning and Marie Therese Kouao were charged with the murder of Victoria Climbie. The prosecution also made it clear that the blame lay not only with Kouao and Manning but the authorities responsible for child protection who had been incompetent. Manning denied murder but pleaded guilty to child cruelty and manslaughter. Kouao denied all charges. On the 12th January 2001, Manning and Kouao were found guilty of murder. In sentencing both of them to life imprisonment, Judge Richard Hawkins said:

'What Anna (Victoria) endured was truly unimaginable. She died at both your hands, a lonely drawn out death.'

Another outcome of the case was for Lisa Arthurworrey to be dismissed by Haringey Council on the grounds of gross misconduct following disciplinary proceedings. What of the gross misconduct failings by all those in the line management chain up to the top of Haringey Council. Well it wasn't their fault was it, never is!

* * *

For many it was no surprise that in 2008, Haringey was in the news again. The very thing that Lord Laming had promised would never happen again, did.

A newspaper article set the scene: 'When the infant known in court only as Baby P was brought home from hospital days after his birth in March 2006, it was as a bubbly, blue-eyed boy with the first signs of curly blond hair. He was, according to those who came into contact with him, a lively child with a ready smile. After seventeen months enduring abuse of an almost unimaginable cruelty, the boy had been reduced to a nervous wreck, his hair shaved to the scalp and his body covered in bruises and scabs. Physical injuries included eight broken ribs, a broken back and the missing top of a finger, while the emotional damage was almost incalculable. Despite it all, Baby P was said to have still attempted a smile.

The jury was told that details of the intervening months, leading to the baby's death last August, would "fill [them] with revulsion". But even this could not prepare jurors, one of whom could not hold back tears, for one of the worst cases of sadistic brutality and sordid child neglect to come before a British court.' [*The Times* on November 12th, 2008]

The mother, Tracey Connelly, who aged twenty-seven, had been taught at a boarding school where she gained GCSEs. When Baby P was born, there was concern that she was suffering from post-natal depression. However, it was when the baby was two months old that she was diagnosed as suffering from chronic depression and began to receive counselling. We are told that she had drink and drug problems. She rarely cleaned the filthy house which smelt of urine and when officers visited the house they ended up covered in flea bites. Investigations revealed that she shared the house with the boy's grandmother, obviously a good role model. The mother appeared to be more devoted to her dogs, a German shepherd, a Staffordshire bull terrier and a rottweiler. It also housed a violent boyfriend, Steven Barker aged thirty-three, and a second man, Jason Owen with his fifteen-year-old girlfriend. Barker was subsequently tried and convicted of the rape of a two-year old girl.

It will be of little surprise that Connelly never had a full-time job but spent hours searching the internet for pornography. She had parted from the boy's natural father after having had affairs with two other men. Clearly this is all acceptable behavior in our modern society and a reasonable environment in which to bring up a baby. Well the do-gooder authorities clearly thought so. We are told that while the mother dabbled with the computer, her boyfriend tortured the boy. He beat him, swung him around by the neck or legs and pinched him. He forced him to follow commands where at the click of a finger he would have to sit with his head bent between his legs; twenty minutes later a second click would be the signal that he could sit upright again. Other tortures endured included placing the baby on a stool and spinning it around until he fell off. Jason Owen also subjected the boy to similar torture.

The police became involved October 2006 following concerns being raised by a GP who noticed marks on the boy. The mother, when questioned, made up a story and insisted that his skin 'bruised easily'.

When the police went into the house they found dead mice and chicks lying around. These were for a snake that the boyfriend kept in his bedroom. We are told that the man was also said to enjoy torturing animals and would skin frogs alive before breaking their legs.

It was two months later in December, when the GP sent them to the Whittington Hospital, North London, after inspecting a head injury. The mother told staff that the child was 'a head-banger' fond of 'rough and tumble play'. She claimed that fingermarks were merely the result of when he was caught after being lovingly held and thrown into the air. At the subsequent trial, Detective Superintendent Caroline Bates told the court that after bruises were discovered on the boy, the police did not want the child returned to the mother, but they were overruled by Social Services. A month later, in January 2007, with no decision made on any charge against the mother, the boy was allowed back home. What was missed was that the boy grew too old for milk and jars of baby food he had to scavenge for bits of broken biscuits from older children. It was to be revealed that he was even seen eating dirt in the garden.

The boy was taken to St Ann's hospital, Haringey where he was examined by a consultant paediatrician, Dr Sabah al-Zayyat, who noted that the boy appeared 'cranky' and 'miserable' but did not find any indication that he had fractured ribs or a broken back. In fact he had eight fractured ribs and a broken back, injuries that would have left him in terrible pain and unable to move his legs. At the trial Pathologist professor Rupert Risden described the injury of the broken back: 'This is the sort of thing that might occur in a road traffic accident.'

At the trial two medical experts told the court that they believed those injuries would have been evident to an examining doctor.

On August 3rd, 2007, an ambulance was called to the house. Its crew found the boy already stiff and blue in his cot. He was taken to North Middlesex hospital where he was pronounced dead. The subsequent postmortem examination revealed the boy had a broken back, eight fractured ribs, missing fingernails and toenails, multiple bruises and an injury to the inside of his mouth. He had also swallowed one of his own teeth. The court heard that his back had been broken, by slamming him down over a bent knee, or a bannister, which would have left him paralysed.

The boyfriend, Barker, and Owen were found guilty at the Old Bailey of causing or allowing the death of a seventeen-month old baby. The mother of the boy had pleaded guilty to causing or allowing his death at the beginning of the trial in September. On the orders of the Judge, Stephen Kramer QC, the jury found the mother, boyfriend and Owen not guilty of murdering the baby.

To give some indication as to the severity of the trauma endured by the jury, the judge excused members of the jury from serving for ten years, telling them: 'You have heard evidence of a harrowing nature and you have seen things which in the course of your everyday life you would not be expected to see.'

I know I have old fashioned views, but it is not right in our so called modern society that a child can be born into this sort of situation and continue to live in that environment. It is as if we have not moved on from the Victorian poverty era. A defenceless child suffers injury after injury including missing finger nails, part of a finger missing, countless bruises, open wounds and eventually a broken back. What does it take to remove a child from such obvious abuse? The Social Services who are supposed to protect vulnerable individuals did nothing. It is astounding to believe that no action was taken against the mother prior to his death.

This situation alone is appalling and if the home environment described is acceptable, then everybody from the Prime Minister to the most junior social worker has lost the plot. If all the signs that were available to the numerous people and agencies involved did not set alarm bells ringing, then is this the sort of home that many children in the UK are brought up in and we only hear about them when they have been tortured to death and the truth is revealed in a trial?

The problem is that with the implications of the Human Rights Act, the liberal do-gooders and the politically correct put terror into the people on the front line. This creates a situation where nobody wants, or is able, to stand up and take real responsibility. So it is the Human Rights agenda that has to bear the brunt of the blame for the current situation. It is all the responsibility of the local authorities' politically correct senior (social care) management who in turn, employ politically correct managers below them. The staff who go out and do the job will in turn have to follow politically correct procedures and fear making alternative decisions, having been trained by the looney left 'thought police'.

Martin Narey, chief executive of Barnardo's, made a statement which may have not been delivered at the most appropriate time, but it was very relevant. He said: '...had the boy lived to become a teenager, he might have turned into a 'feral, parasitic yob''.

The objective of Mr Narey's use of words was to focus attention on the need to tackle causes of such abuse. From the information we have about the Baby P case, his words are probably true and it needs a dynamic reaction to try and get action before it happens again, not the

260

namby pamby pandering that is the current trend because it does not work. The fear is how many other young children must suffer before we return to reality?

On 27th May 2011, the media portrayed Sharon Shoesmith, the former head of Haringey Social Services, as ultimately responsible for the Baby Peter case as she walked from the Court of Appeal. She had won her case against her sacking over the Baby P scandal. The ruling leaves her free to claim a potential payout of possibly millions. Judges ruled that her dismissal from her £133,000 a year post was 'procedurally unfair' because she was not allowed the chance to defend herself.

It is understood that there was a damning Ofsted report, which had identified 'insufficient strategic leadership and management oversight' in her department. This led to a situation that allowed baby Peter Connelly to die with over fifty injuries. Miss Shoesmith was the manager in charge of the department responsible for the safety of the child. She failed in that role and it is presumed that the action taken to remove her from the position of authority was done on the basis of gross misconduct.

Faced with the damning Ofstead report, Ed Balls, the then Labour Education Secretary ordered Miss Shoesmith's sacking in December 2008.

James Eadie QC, for the Government, said: 'Mr Balls had to take urgent action following the "ghastly findings" of the Ofsted report. It uncovered "dangerous" failings in Miss Shoesmith's department which were threatening local and national confidence in effective child protection.'

But the Appeal Court judges decided that Mr Balls had not given Miss Shoesmith 'the opportunity to put her case'. They said: 'She was denied the elementary fairness the law requires.'

In my opinion the ruling is wrong and in fact with a failing of this magnitude perhaps a gross negligence manslaughter prosecution should have been considered. Certainly there should be no compensation or re-instatement. But baby Peter was a victim and as I have said many times, victims have no rights.

Haringey – You are Not Alone

Abid Ikram and Sumaira Parveen were jailed in 2007 following the death of sixteen-month-old Talha Ikram, in Ealing, west London. The baby died in September 2006. He had suffered a broken leg, had cigarettes stubbed out on his skin, three broken ribs and had his leg sliced open so the tendons could be seen. A pathologist said the little boy's injuries resembled those of someone who had been in a car crash.

* * *

Then Joanne Mallinder, aged thirty-seven was found guilty of killing her baby boy after Social Services returned the child to her. She had suffered thirteen miscarriages and a stillbirth before giving birth to baby son Jack. The baby was rushed to hospital on February 13th 2006 after he stopped breathing. Police were called in after doctors at Great Ormond Street Hospital in London discovered three-month-old Jack had severe brain damage. He was also found to have six fractures to his arms and legs which were injuries consistent with shaken baby syndrome. He eventually died from his injuries thirteen months later. Basildon Crown Court heard how Mallinder and her partner, Gareth Cox thirty-two, were set to have little Jack adopted, but changed their minds when he was born. He was put into temporary foster care until they made preparations for him at home. Less than two months after he was given back to the couple, ambulance crews were called to their flat where paramedics discovered the baby's heart had stopped and he was not breathing. Jack's dad, Mr Cox, said he gave the baby mouth-to-mouth and chest compressions until ambulance crews arrived and took him to Basildon Hospital. He was later transferred to Great

Ormond Street. The baby's mother was charged. However, the charge was upgraded to one of murder when Jack died. Mallinder was cleared of murder but convicted of manslaughter. Mr Cox told the jury that Joanne had fallen pregnant accidentally after suffering thirteen miscarriages and a Christmas Day stillbirth as well as post-natal depression. The court heard Jack remained in hospital for two weeks as he only weighed 4lbs 10ozs when he was born and then Social Services put him into foster care for two weeks.

At court, Judge Philip Clegg said: 'This was a distressing case, extremely distressing.'

Sentencing was adjourned to Luton Crown Court for the preparation of psychiatric and pre-sentence reports. After the case Thurrock Council's head of children's services said lessons had been learned from Jack's death. Rob McCulloch-Graham, corporate director of children, education and families, said the events surrounding Jack's death had been reviewed by an independent social work expert. He said: 'There have been lessons learned. These have been put into action in Thurrock and other boroughs have been informed as well.'

* * *

In January 2009, paramedics were called to the home of Miss Harris and her partner to attend to a twenty-one month old baby called Bobby. The police were informed that Bobby Harris had received several injuries. He died from the injuries less than an hour later in hospital and Miss Harris and her partner were arrested. A post mortem examination found the child had suffered multiple injuries. The couple lived in a three-bed semi on a council estate in Bexleyheath, South-East London, with her nine-year-old son. Bexley Council stated that Bobby was not on the 'at risk' register and that officials had had no dealings with the family. They had moved into the house a few months previously and it was not known if they were on an 'at risk' register anywhere else. A near neighbour said her son was friends with Miss Harris's eldest son. It is claimed that she seemed to be a good mother and was always checking on both the kids. She was not seen to ill treat them in any way. Another neighbour considered that they seemed like a normal family that doted on their children. They had only been in the house a few months and kept themselves to themselves.

A Metropolitan Police spokesman said: 'A post mortem held at Great Ormond Street Hospital revealed the cause of death to be multiple injuries'.

* * *

In another case, in another place, James Howson aged twenty-five was told he must spend a minimum of twenty-two years in prison after being found guilty of murdering his sixteen-month-old daughter, Amy. The baby girl's spine was snapped in two. Her mother, Tina Hunt, was given a twelve-month suspended sentence after admitting cruelty. The court heard that health visitors went to the house but were shunned by Howson, who went to extreme measures to make sure all visitors were vetted.

* * *

A ten-month-old baby died in December 2007 after a number of referrals to Social Services, including indications that he and an older sibling were at risk of harm from their eighteen-year-old mother and sixteen-year-old father. Craig Goddard pleaded guilty to murdering his three-month-old son, Alfie. The mother, Lindsay Harris, admitted the offence of Perverting the Course of Justice after the baby died of head injuries.

* * *

In another case, thirteen month old Alex Sutherland was allowed to live with his mother even though she admitted drinking up to six bottles of wine a day. Health and social workers had closed the file on the youngster claiming the risk of harm to him was 'low'. The social and health workers missed seventeen chances to save him after they were repeatedly contacted over concerns that the mother was abandoning the boy to go drinking. The warnings were of 'chronic neglect' of the baby who was malnourished and underweight. The outcome was that the police broke into the family home to find the baby in his pushchair by a lit gas fire. He had charring to his body from the fire, was covered in faeces and had unexplained injuries on his body. It was described as a 'scene of unimaginable horror'. Whilst the cause of death has never been established, the mother was jailed for twenty-seven months after she admitted neglect. A report by Manchester Safeguarding Children's Board into the baby's death condemned social and health workers for a catalogue of failures saying his case was 'poorly managed throughout' and his neglect was 'both predictable and preventable.'

[*Daily Mail* 2nd February 2011]

This is very small selection of such cases but it is a tragic reminder of the evil that prevails in our broken society. In these cases torture and murder seem to be acceptable to the do-gooders who place human rights and political correctness before the basic rights of the victims, who in these cases are children. The harsh reality is that there will be many other cases and what is being done to stop further acts? I will hazard a guess that nothing has or will be done if it infringes on the perceived rights of perpetrators.

7

Society Crime

Parental Control?

The prosecutor representing the local authority put forward the case against the woman in the dock. She was a single mother and was being prosecuted for not ensuring that her two daughters aged almost fifteen and almost fourteen attended school. She was one of many attending court that day for the same offence. It is of course a legal requirement for all children to be schooled until the age of sixteen. She had been co-operative with the local authority staff and had in fact been active in getting the girls to attend school. But as the responsible adult she was held to account if they failed to attend and remain in school.

The defendant told us that as a single parent she had to work and in fact had two jobs. This meant that she relied on her daughters attending school. She had, over a period of time, received numerous warnings about their non attendance and had meetings with the school management to try and resolve the situation. She had taken both girls to the school and watched then enter the building. They just walked through the corridors and out of another door and out of school. She had confronted them but they took no notice of her. She then took them to school and deposited them into their classrooms. As soon as they could, they just walked out of the school. She had lost pay due to having to take time off because of their actions.

We heard that the two girls were very upset at seeing their mother in court but they did not want to go to school. It was boring and they learned nothing. They hated it. It was explained to them that their mother could be fined and even go to prison. Nothing seemed to make any difference, school was not on their agenda. So we, as the bench, were faced with having to take a course of action. We could fine the defendant and there may have been an option of a short prison sentence. None of these options were going to get the two girls into school. The defendant had cooperated with the authorities and taken action to get the girls to school, but all had been ineffective.

We took the view in this case that a full discharge was appropriate. The defendant was grateful and even the local authority people in court understood our reasoning and accepted the verdict. We hoped that they could resolve the situation and that the girls would return to school.

However, the other cases of failing to attend school were not the same. We heard of intimidation and threats of violence as well as total non cooperation from parents. In court it was not what we wanted to hear and the outcome was that a number of fines were handed out. It was interesting to note that some schools were not sorry to see children not attending because when they were there, they were disruptive. The problem is that the disruptive children often come from disruptive homes and the situation perpetuates itself so the schools will then have children who follow the pattern. That situation is made much worse because there is no discipline either in the home or at school. The outcome is more people in court.

Violence in Schools

The Association of Teachers and Lecturers (ATL) surveyed more than 1,000 teachers in March 2010. From the evidence gained it showed that 89% of staff had dealt with low level disruption such as talking and not paying attention, but over 50% had reported verbal attacks, and nearly 40% intimidation. Some 83% of staff had reported physical aggression such as pushing and shoving, while 48% had reported the use of fists and 42% the use of legs. The survey found that over a quarter of school and college staff have had to deal with physical violence from a student, and just over a third of teachers had been confronted by an aggressive parent or guardian.

In fact, a report in the *Guardian* newspaper said that physical attacks are far more common in primary schools than secondary schools, with teachers reportedly being threatened, pushed, scratched, punched, bitten, kicked and spat at. Teachers said the failure of many parents to act as 'good role models' was leading to deteriorating behaviour in lessons. In some cases, staff said mothers and fathers became abusive after staff attempted to discipline their children. [*Guardian* 29th March 2010]

ATL general secretary Mary Bousted said she had found, from her time as a teacher, that she had never got to meet the parents she had wanted to meet the most. She said: 'They were simply absent from their children's lives. We must say that there are certain standards we need you to adhere to to bring up your children.'

Staff in state schools reported higher levels of disrespect, verbal abuse, physical attacks and intimidation than those in private schools.

The then Schools Minister, Vernon Coaker, is reported as saying that: 'Good behaviour and an atmosphere of respect should be the norm in all schools. We have given head teachers clear legal powers to enforce discipline which means they can get tough on poor behaviour without fear of being taken to court, including using reasonable force to control or restrain pupils.'

One head of department at a state secondary school said: 'I have been physically assaulted twice – both times violent behaviour was aimed at another student but in their rage they hit me – and sexually assaulted twice. I feel that we get no support from government – they have no idea of the reality of inner city schools.'

Another senior teacher from a state primary said: 'I have had a threat to my life from a parent because I told a child to complete their homework during part of their 'golden time'. It was threatened that they and their family would kill me when I came to or from school.'

A female secondary school teacher said: 'I have been trapped in an office by a father and older brother of a student who were angry that he'd had his gold trainers confiscated until the end of the day. Two weeks ago I had a parent come in looking for me. He didn't actually find me, but he threatened several senior staff and rampaged around the school. Police were called.'[*Guardian* 29th March 2010]

In December 2009, fourteen children aged five or under were being suspended from primary schools in England every day for violence against teachers or pupils. Thirty of the children sent home were aged only three. There were 830 four-year-olds disciplined for violence and 1,750 five-year-olds. Ten children aged four and twenty aged five, were suspended for 'sexual misconduct'. Twenty, five-year-olds received fixed period exclusions for bullying and there was a slight increase in the number of suspensions among pupils aged under eleven for incidents of racist abuse, from 340 to 390. [*Guardian* 31st December 2009]

Scotland Yard revealed in June 2009 that there had been nearly 900 rapes or serious sex attacks in schools. The figures were the first of their kind produced and they show that sixty-five victims were raped in secondary and primary schools in London in the past five years. A further 826 were the target of other sexual assaults. In 2008 the number of alleged rapes rose 60% on the previous year to thirty-two. The statistics suggest the vast majority of victims were schoolchildren under the age of sixteen and as many as one in three were under eleven.

Disclosing the figures, Commander Mark Simmons, head of the Met's violent crime directorate, said the force was urgently trying to assess the cause of the problem, which mainly involved attacks on girls. He said: 'Sexual assaults and rapes are always serious offences. When you start talking about young people, and particularly young people in what should be a place of safety, then that becomes even more serious. But we need to be wary of making parents hugely concerned by the headline numbers. We are talking about just under 200 in the last year across the whole of London schools.'

The senior detective in charge of investigating the school sex attacks said that, in some cases, police did not press charges against boys accused of having sex with girls under thirteen for fear of 'criminalising' them. The issue is that in some cases it was consensual sex even though both may be under the legal age. [*The Sunday Times* 28th June, 2009]

More information came from a Freedom of Information request about the number of times police were called to schools. Only twenty-five of thirty-nine police forces in England responded and they showed 7,311 recorded incidents where officers were called into schools. But the real number of incidents could be higher because they only relate to recorded crime and fourteen police forces either refused to respond or did not do so fully. [*Guardian* 23rd December 2008]

Then in 2009 it was announced that schools would get stronger powers to ask for the imposition of parenting orders, which could mean families being forced to attend classes to learn how to control their offspring. If they still failed to keep children in line, they would face a £1,000 fine and a jail sentence if they did not pay.

Mr Balls who was at the time responsible for Education said: 'Every parent has a responsibility to back our teachers and make sure the rules are enforced. We all have to play our part to make sure that happens. And that doesn't just mean 95% of parents, but all parents – including the very few who aren't taking their responsibilities seriously. Schools already have Home-School Agreements which set out the school's rules and should make clear to parents what is expected of them and their children. But heads tell me that not all parents are willing to cooperate. And when pupils and parents break the agreement, it's hard to enforce it.' [*Daily Telegraph* 28th June 2009]

The then Home Secretary, Alan Johnson, told the *News of the World* that parents sometimes needed structured help and support from professionals to deal with difficult youngsters. He said:

'I want to make sure that more consideration is given to the parents' role when a teenager gets into problems and is being considered for an Asbo. Parenting orders are not punishments – they are a way of giving adults the skills they need to help them fulfil their responsibilities. If a teenager is in danger of going off the rails, then one of the best ways to deal with it is to give parents more support at an early stage.'

Life in the front line as a teacher can be very serious. Take the case of a teacher who was attacked by a twelve-year-old pupil and has had to take ill-health retirement as a result. At fifty-one years of age he had taught the school for eight years. After a violent attack he was left with post traumatic stress disorder (PTSD). During the incident in a school corridor, a pupil jumped on his back and then attempted to strangle him while he lay unconscious on the ground. The teacher was on his way to seek help from another senior teacher to discipline the student, who had been causing problems in a colleague's class. Only a week earlier the same student had attacked a security guard at the library across the road from the school. Despite the headteacher knowing about the incident, the pupil's violent past was never made known to staff. Following the school attack, the pupil was prosecuted and pleaded guilty to actual bodily harm (ABH). A union backed compensation claim resulted in Mr Adams receiving a £275,000 payout.

Then in November 2010, the new ConLib government announced a magic formula to sort out the schools. Former soldiers are to be drafted in to help restore discipline in classrooms in a radical shake-up of the schools system. Education Secretary Michael Gove said:

'I can't think of anything better than getting people who know all about self-discipline, teamwork and a sense of pride into our schools to complement the huge numbers of great teachers we have there.'

Under a 'Troops to Teachers' programme the government would pay tuition fees for anyone leaving the military to take a teaching qualification. Depending on their qualifications, it is said they could be fast-tracked as teachers within six weeks.

To improve discipline, Mr Gove plans to give teachers stronger powers to search students for pornography, tobacco, and fireworks as well as phones and cameras if they believe they are going to be used to cause harm. They will be given greater powers to restrain violent pupils, put them in detention as well as excluding them. Schools would be backed in introducing uniforms and traditional prefect and house systems as part of the reforms.

There is also to be protection for teachers against malicious allegations and laws will give them anonymity against claims until they are charged with an offence. The appeal system for exclusions will be toughened up. A new network of teaching schools will be modelled on teaching hospitals and graduates will be expected to have a 2.2 degree to enter teacher training. 'Teach First' will be expanded to attract more top graduates for subjects where there is a shortage of teachers. Hundreds more schools will be encouraged to become academies, freeing them of town hall controls. Academies will get more powers and parents and charities will be helped to set up 'free schools'. [*Daily Express* 25th November, 2010]

Violence in Hospitals

The individual who stood before us really did not want to be wasting his time standing in the dock. He looked bored and uninterested. I had to tell him to speak up when addressing the court. He gave his personal details and pleaded guilty to common assault against a member of staff at the local hospital. The prosecutor read out the details of the prosecution case which said that the defendant was on a night out and got very drunk. He was involved in a fight, was injured and losing blood. The police were called and they had trouble in controlling him as he turned his violence on to them. The ambulance arrived and the medics set about the task of emergency aid prior to taking him to hospital. Whilst the police held him secure, the medics applied treatment. In the process of the treatment he got an arm free and punched one of the medics in the face. A second ambulance was called and the medics provided assistance to both the other medic and the injured medic. When the defendant was able to travel he still remained aggressive and the medics would only take the man if the police were present. The defendant arrived at hospital screaming abuse and attempting to punch everybody who came close enough. The medic also entered the hospital for treatment. A doctor and a number of nurses, male and female, attended the defendant who remained aggressive and abusive. A male nurse attempted to examine the wound but was struck with a blow by a clenched fist that sent him backwards onto the ground. The situation had become very serious and there was a risk of harm to others including other patients. Calming measures were taken and eventually the defendant was treated and left to sleep off his drunken state. Photographs of the ambulance medic and the male nurse were submitted and were not a pretty sight. A glance at the defendant in the dock still showed that he had no interest in and no concern for his actions.

The defendant's solicitor began to paint the dramatic picture of the thug's life. He drank to excess, was aggressive and fought, but it was the result of his past. He didn't like people in uniforms or of authority and when he got drunk he saw them as a threat. His girlfriend had kicked him out because of his violent behaviour, he could not keep a job because he didn't like people telling him what to do. Getting drunk was the only option he had found to drown his sorrows. We were told that he had pleaded guilty at the earliest opportunity. That was not correct because he had earlier pleaded not guilty to a charge of Actual Bodily Harm, but pleaded guilty when the CPS downgraded the charge to Common Assault. That moved the offence from possible prison to a fine. The NHS and the CPS persuaded the injured staff members to accept a prosecution on the lesser charge. We listened to the remaining speech but found no mitigation or remorse. Our deliberations were straightforward and we gave the maximum penalty possible at the time and awarded compensation to the injured parties. We all left that case disillusioned with a system that, in our opinion, had, yet again, failed the victims.

Figures obtained under the Freedom of Information act by MP Mike Penning, a member of the Health Select Committee, revealed that by the middle of 2007, only one in 1000 assaults on nurses and other NHS staff resulted in a prosecution. The offences ranged from physical violence and sexual assault to verbal and racial abuse and attacks by dogs on staff, including health visitors or midwives when attending patients homes. What he found was that from a reported 5,762 assaults since 2002, only five prosecutions were brought. Either the offences were not passed to the police for investigation or a case could not be bought because of lack of evidence or witnesses.

A story that caught my eye because of the headlines: 'Violence 'part of the job' for nurses.'

It was a case in October 1998 when deputy ward manager, Steven Charles, was threatened by a knife-wielding patient at a hospital. He was told in court by a magistrate that violence was part of the job. The court heard how the hospital patient waved a six-inch blade at him and told him he would kill him. The confrontation ended peacefully and Mr Charles was uninjured. The patient was given an eighteen-month conditional discharge and ordered to pay £70 costs. However, chairman of the bench, Christopher Hoarer, refused to pay compensation to the nurse. He said: 'We are not ordering compensation because to a certain extent the risk goes with the parish.'

It is always difficult to comment on the actions of another magistrate because of not being present and hearing all of the facts. It did however draw much comment and one quote from an unidentified source stated: 'Magistrate Christopher Hoarer told a male nurse this week that he should not expect compensation for being threatened with a knife, as enduring such brutalities go with the job. Oh dear! This will just confirm the already wide-spread public opinion that being an out-of-touch pompous oaf inevitably goes with the job of being a magistrate. This is a very tragic reflection on the role of a magistrate and it is certainly not one that magistrates in general would want to adopt.'

At the time, the Royal College of Nursing made a statement on this point and said that violence should not be part of any nurse's job and no nurse should have to go to work in fear. The Royal College of Nursing (RCN) said the issue of compensation was of minor importance, it was the magistrate's attitude that was shocking. The RCN and the *Nursing Times* carried out a survey of 1,000 nurses; 47% of those polled had been slapped, punched or spat at in the past year; 88% needed medical attention; almost 85% were verbally abused. A spokeswoman for the Department of Health admitted no one should be subjected to violence at work, least of all the people providing treatment and care.

The Health and Safety at Work Act provides a legal framework that no one is expected to go to work and accept violence against them as part of the job. The exception is where violence is a foreseeable part of the job such as a police offer. In that situation they are trained and equipped to deal with it. A nurse is not and management in hospitals and other welfare services have to manage the safety of the staff and other patients. This means that all employees placed in a vulnerable situation must have personal safety training to help them recognise the signs of potential violators, and enable them to employ tactics to avoid violent encounters. If it means employing security personnel in hospital accident and emergency departments, or engaging police officers in emergency units then so be it, but do not expect nurses to have to put themselves at risk to carry out their job of caring for patients.

Although nurses are often in the front line, it is unacceptable to expect them to wear body armour, as was suggested in a TV programme. The possibility of violence against staff has to be addressed before it gets to this stage. However, the growing fear of knife crime in Britain is forcing hospital trusts and local authorities to supply body armour to frontline workers, including A&E staff and hospital porters. The Oxfordshire-based Body Armour Company received about 10,000 orders for protective vests with frontline NHS staff accounting for most of them.

Corporate Crime

I absolutely love the publication *Private Eye* and their delving into the 'goings on' in large businesses; the NHS and local authorities etc. It usually involves failings in management, large amounts of money becoming unaccounted for, large pay offs to senior staff following their personal failings and all manner of dodgy dealings. For the most part when in court, I dealt with the bottom end of society and the *Eye* puts the top end into perspective. Actions, albeit untested in court, by scores of individuals and corporations, could well see the real need for a prison development scheme. I know it's in an article and we must not believe all that we read, but the *Eye* is somewhat different. They print the truth and are prepared to go to court to defend what they say. So the issue is that I have sent people to prison for lesser crimes than many we read about.

A story that caught my attention is about the £6billion Vodafone tax bill. Yes, six billion pounds. Now everybody knows Vodafone, it's visible on every high street, sometimes with two shops. Its services are used by millions of people so they bring in the money. Why can't they pay their taxes? The following are extracts from *Private Eye's* ongoing investigation: 'The *Eye's* revelations of Vodafone's multi-billion-pound tax dodging, cheerily approved by HM Revenue & Customs boss Dave Hartnett, prompted protests across the country last week.

Pointing out the resemblance between the amount of tax avoided by Vodafone and planned cuts to the welfare budget, demonstrators managed to shut down scores of Vodafone stores from Portsmouth to

Edinburgh (despite the efforts of police, whose numbers such large scale tax avoidance will help to decimate).

Vodafone and its chums at HMRC quickly got their heads together to agree a 'line': the figure of £6billion the *Eye* put on the tax dodged was an 'urban myth'. HMRC press secretary, Paul Franklin, even commented on a *Daily Mail* website that the deal that saw Vodafone pay just £800m (with time to pay on another *£450m)* was reached 'following a rigorous examination of the facts and an intensive process of negotiation that tested the arguments of both parties. As a result it was agreed that Vodafone's liability was £1.25billion and at no point was a liability greater than that established.'

In issue 1270, the *Eye* told us that under tax self-assessment laws no liability is established until a negotiation is complete and investigators were always after several times this amount before their more customer friendly boss Hartnett stepped in and gave away billions of pounds of taxpayers' cash.'

• *Tax dodging: Don't pay as you go . . .'* [*Private Eye* No: 1275]

It appears that the issue over tax began following some sort of bad deal which if correct is some sort of management failing. Because of that, the wheeling and dealing began. Another edition of *Private Eye* reported the story which highlighted the issues:

'When Vodaphone bought German engineering company, Mannesmann, a decade ago for €180billion, it desperately wanted to use the mother of all tax avoidance schemes so the taxpayers would subsidise what turned out to be a massively over-priced mistake.

An epic legal battle began, with Vodafone resisting the taxman's efforts to get all the information on the deal and arguing through the courts that the British laws striking out the tax benefits of its deal were neutered by European law granting, they claimed, the freedom to establish anywhere in the EU (including its dodgiest tax havens) without facing a tax bill... Vodafone Investments Luxembourg Sarl's accounts show that, up to March 2009, €15.5billion income was stuffed into the company, suggesting it is now heading to the €18billion mark and resulting in €5billion in lost tax and interest so far.

But, armed with strong advice from eminent legal counsel, tax inspectors were confident they could win the cash back... But they reckoned without HM Revenue & Customs' 'permanent secretary for tax', Dave Hartnett, and his customer-friendly approach to big multinationals. Despite HMRC's victories, Hartnett moved the case from his specialists and lawyers to a more amenable group to negotiate with Vodafone's head of tax, John Connors, who until 2007 was a senior official at HMRC working closely with Hartnett on handling big business... The fruits of these talks, conducted without consulting HMRC's litigators and specialists in the tax law concerned on the chance of success in the courts, was a bill for Vodafone of £800million, with another £450million payable over five years and remarkably an agreement that the arrangement can carry on into the future with a promise of no challenge from HMRC. The *Eye* understands that the settlement also swept up several other Vodafone tax avoidance schemes...' [*Private Eye* No: 1270]

So it seems that 'who you know' and 'job's for boys' appears to play a part in the operation on both sides of the fence. If only they could do major take over deals with as much panache, but they probably had to bargain hard against professionals as against 'pals' in trusted positions of power. So it seems that while the UK is attempting to salvage itself from going down the toilet by grabbing money from the hard pressed public, we can all sleep peacefully knowing that a 'good deal' has been done. Oh the deal! the *Eye* reported on that:

'Tax inspectors had been asking Vodafone to cough up more than £5billion and the company had set aside £2.2billion to pay for the case. But when the deal was sealed the bill conveniently dropped to... £1.25billion. Tax officials are known to be furious with the derisory settlement and its implications for scores of similar disputes. The deal certainly fits with Vodafone's avowed approach to tax: 'The maximisation of shareholder value will generally involve the minimisation of taxation [*Private Eye* No: 1268]

Then we hear...

'After Vodafone cut its notorious sweetheart deal with HM Revenue & Customs, saving it several billions in tax, it agreed to hand over a much smaller amount than HMRC wanted but still asked for (and was given) time to pay. Thus the British mobile phone *giant* will hand over just £0.8billion and have a further five years to pay a remaining £0.45billion. Other taxpayers might think this a bit rich given a study by Bloomberg last week. It revealed that Vodafone, having sold shares in companies in China and France, is now sitting on a cash pile of £9billion!' [*Private Eye* No: 1277]

Courts are being closed, police force numbers being reduced and no more new prisons are being built but the government lets a company get away with not paying their tax. The give away is £3.75billion. Where I ask, are all the criminals?

Tax avoidance is illegal and a crime. Allegations must be investigated and appropriate action taken, otherwise reasonable protest spawns into direct action which is what was witnessed on the 5th December 2010. The Arcadia Group which includes Miss Selfridge, Dorothy Perkins and Topshop were being targeted to highlight schemes which activists say have cost the Exchequer billions of pounds in revenue. Some members of the public were very rightly angry and hundreds of protesters descended on a variety of shops and other businesses in nineteen major towns and cities including Boots, Vodaphone, HSBC and Barclays.

One of the protestors said: 'If people like Philip Green paid their taxes we would not have to make public spending cuts.'

Another protester said: 'The tax gap is an estimated £120billion, £25billion of this down to tax avoidance by extremely wealthy individuals and big businesses.'

Tax avoidance has been estimated by the TUC to have cost the country £25billion in revenue, including £13billion attributed to individuals.

It was billionaire retailer Sir Philip Green, head of The Arcadia

Group who was appointed as an adviser to the government on efficiency in the public sector earlier this year. He produced a report which described 'staggering' wastage in Whitehall spending. However, he states that his tax affairs were not 'relevant' to his suitability to lead a government spending review. [*Daily Mail* 6th December 2010]

I offer no apology when I say that I found many senior civil servants to be incompetent or not playing by the rules. It's a job for life and it's all chums together. I must emphasise that my personal 'hands on' experience is generally limited to the particular organisation that I was with and indeed one small part within it. I thought that senior civil servants were/are supposed to be non-political and answerable to the public, but that does not always appear to be the case. Still you will not need me to state the obvious, as we have been bombarded through the media over the years, with the failures from a wide range of government departments. The tragedy is that we have come to expect failure and so it has become a real and accepted part of our daily lives, and it is costing literally billions of pounds. Not to worry, there is plenty more cash to be got from the working public.

Civil Service Crime

This story involves, in my opinion, a criminal activity within the civil service, an activity that was accepted by the upper echelons of the organisation. Perhaps the most alarming aspect is where a government department has inspectors who have considerable powers to take enforcement action against wrongdoers, including prosecutions. Whilst there have been and are today, many excellent civil servants at operational level, the bad ones seem to be those who are noticed.

It was during my fifteen years as a civil servant that I witnessed serious internal criminal activity that involved senior civil service management in a cover up. This was made worse because, as a magistrate, I actually believed in justice. I had to, because how could

I go to court and, if necessary, send somebody to prison if I could not determine right from wrong and the seriousness of a given situation based upon clear evidence. However, those principals do not apply to the civil service, as they appear to be above the law.

I managed a team of inspectors, empowered by a warrant with considerable powers. The bottom line is that the integrity of an inspector needs to be beyond doubt and unfortunately that was not always the case. The actions of one such inspector followed his being recruited into the civil service. There was allegedly some discrepancy about whether he should actually have been allowed into the civil service. This came to light when one of my inspectors was told by a unit manager that, when the individual who I shall call Inspector X, attended his recruitment interview he scored below the level of acceptability. He was only recruited because the organisation desperately needed inspectors. So from the very beginning there was doubt on the credibility of the particular individual. The inspector openly told people that he had undertaken a particular type of skilled work, when in fact he had never ever done so. Well that may not be a crime in its own right. Embellishing one's attributes may be considered to be acceptable, however, for a warrant carrying civil servant with considerable powers including prosecution, having impeccable credentials and integrity is paramount, or it should be.

I began to have concerns that things were not right when I received adverse comments about the individual from a number of people who I knew to be very reliable sources in industry. But, I did not have sound evidence as none of the people who spoke to me were prepared to make their knowledge officially known. However, some evidence did bubble to the surface when I received a telephone call from a senior administrator who was based in London. She experienced first hand the bullying tactics of the individual. She asked me about the validity of Inspector X's qualifications. I had to say that I had never seen them and could not comment if they were genuine. However, I was able to say that it was alleged that there was some doubt about his professional competence. She then told me that during an internal office move, she found a certificate of competence with the individuals name on it. Now, in the course of her work she dealt with a lot of competence certificates and was considered to be an expert on them. In this case it was a certificate that she had never seen the like of before and was not issued by a recognised organisation. When she described it to me I agreed with her assumption with the comment that it was a cause for concern. The certificate was issued to Inspector X and it indicated that it was for a professional qualification that he did not have.

She continued to say that she challenged Inspector X when he was in the office and her words were: 'he snatched it off me and told me to keep my nose out and my mouth shut, it was none of my business'. He then confronted her again in the office kitchen where he was aggressive and threatening to her. Of course this was unseen and unheard by any witnesses. She was very concerned by his actions and asked what she should do. I asked if she had copied the certificate before he took it back but unfortunately she had not. All I could do was advise that there was a formal complaints process but we both knew that with this individual there would be no action. In fact she would be the villain in the eyes of management. In addition, she would become a greater target for his aggressive bullying. Her salvation came when he was moved to another office and she had little contact with him. I did raise the matter with my line manager at the time and asked if the matter could be looked into. However, it went no further as nobody wanted to 'rock the boat!'

So here we have an individual who was telling people he had obtained a number of professional qualifications, when in fact evidence appeared to show that he had not. He was aggressive to those inside the organisation as well as the public he dealt with. His peers in the organisation knew the situation but senior management refused to do anything about it. In fact this came to a head when he was promoted. He was one of the junior members of the group and reasonably new to the civil service, but he was promoted. During the promotion process, it became known to members of our group that he had given examples in his promotion application of things that he claimed to have done before joining the civil service. We knew he could not substantiate the claims. I made this known to my line manager and offered evidence that they could follow up. People both inside and outside the organisation were already asking, what power he had over senior management. They considered that complaints would be taken seriously and investigated, especially about a civil servant. The saying 'one bad apple in the barrel...' In this case it appears to be 'bad apples' promoting a 'bad apple'!

Following a fatal incident, I was the case manager and had appointed a member of my team as the investigating officer. It was a normal procedure. It was a very difficult case in that the company was at the forefront of its industry and had set many high standards for health and safety. As the investigation progressed, I was asked at a meeting with the managing director of the company, if we were proposing to prosecute. I explained that it was the organisation's policy that, following a death, the company involved would be prosecuted. He asked me what the charges or the likely charges would be. I thought that they would probably be management failings, but he would have to wait for the official investigation report to be produced. At that point he indicated to me very clearly that if that was the basis of our prosecution, then the company would plead guilty. So I was now looking at a guilty plea from the company to be heard in the Magistrates' Court. It would be a matter for the court to decide whether it was suitable for hearing in the Crown Court. Our case at this point was based on failure to have adequate risk assessments and other issues that were of a management nature.

As soon as management made the decision to prosecute our solicitor's office became involved. Over the years we had had numerous solicitors appointed to the case but the one who started the process got it wrong and we had to live with that. We were told by the solicitor's office that we were going to have to have an expert witness and they nominated Inspector X. As the investigating team we were not best impressed and, I was overruled because that's the way they wanted to go and they had taken control of the case. Inspector X had not been involved with the case at this stage, but he was now brought in and given a copy of the prosecution case and evidence. This was the case we were going to prosecute on and he was asked to give his opinion based on that. He insisted that he had a copy of the whole bundle. It was explained to him that there were fundamental flaws regarding our organisation and the equipment, we couldn't use that as evidence. He decided otherwise and produced a statement that opened up the case beyond that for which we had substantial evidence.

Inspector X prepared his statement and submitted it to the solicitor who issued it to the company. We were not consulted or given sight of the document. The first we knew was when the managing director of the company telephoned me. He told me that because of the contents of the statement neither the company nor their insurance company could accept the claim that they caused the death. We then entered into three years of legal process to go to trial. Inspector X stated that they (the company) caused the death. There was not one shred of evidence and we knew that on that basis, the case would be thrown out of court. E-mails were sent to Inspector X trying to get him to focus on the case and the evidence, as opposed to going into the world of fantasy. That was not resolved so we continued to plod on.

At this time the case was being directed by the solicitor's office and I was, at one point, actually excluded from the what was going on, even though it was my case. We eventually brought our unit manager into the melee because, in true civil service style when it all went wrong, they would hand it back and say it was not their problem. Now my role as case manager with that responsibility, found that there were things going on where Inspector X was talking to the solicitor's office. The problem was that neither I nor the investigating officer were informed. To this very day we don't know what those discussions were about. I do know that industry were aware of what was happening and our organisation looked very foolish.

The managing director of the defendant company telephoned me. He had the expert statements. He challenged me about the qualifications of Inspector X. I could not discuss the case but identified that if he had evidence he would be able raise the matter in court. To follow protocol I raised the matter with my line manager and my instructions were just to let the case run. I went back to the company and just said that we can't comment, all the information of the prosecution case had been made available and the organisation would proceed to court. Privately I hoped that justice would prevail and that the company would provide the evidence and that Inspector X would fail in court. I then received another telephone call from the managing director of the company who told me that he was trying to get an expert witness but they were unable to get one. The reason was that the people they were approaching had also been approached by Inspector X or had been warned by others that if they acted for the defendants against the organisation then he would be in a good position to, 'deal with them afterwards'. I told the managing director that he needed to make an official complaint. But he decided with the court case looming, not to take any action at that time.

I was living with this knowledge for a couple of days but decided that I had to approach our personnel department. I knew it would be me under threat, but I gave details anyway. The information was sent to the deputy director general at the time. The incident was investigated but the managing director would not give the names of those threatened. The industry knew that Inspector X was untouchable and could damage their businesses (yes he told them he would damage their businesses). I gave a statement as did my investigating officer to the internal investigators. We took it seriously and it went to line management who also took it seriously. But it was like trying to push water back up a waterfall. Internally, nobody ever came back to us either in writing or verbally to say what the outcome was. We were eventually to find out that it was a complete cover up.

We knew that the defendants were requesting information relating to the case that they knew we must have had (called undisclosed information). However, the solicitor's office were denying them access. They then requested copies of Inspector X's competences in the form of log books and competence certification. As an expert, he was obliged to make them available to the court. These log books and certification could prove his competence or not as the case may be. He refused to disclose them. Yes, it was a point blank refusal. You may ask why? The defendants knew why and it was because he had made a false statement. He claimed to have qualifications that he did not have. Two days before we were going to trial the investigating officer came to me and said that we had a problem. The situation was that nobody could locate Inspector X, our expert. The solicitor's office had been trying to locate him as they required him to make his professional documents available to the defendants.

Inspector X eventually made a telephone call to the solicitor's office. A lawyer told us that it was a very strange call. He would not tell them where he was. He then said that he would not make his documents available even if the court directed him to do so. So our expert witness, put on a pedestal by the solicitor's office and management, had just disappeared and nobody knew where he was. Even his team members didn't know where he was. Now, you would think that alarm bells would be ringing, but no.

The Friday before the trial on the Monday, we were loading all of the case material into a car ready to travel on the Sunday. I received a telephone call from one of our well respected inspectors in London. He was very concerned and explained that he had been telephoned by two people unconnected with the case or each other. They had been visited by Inspector X who demanded that they write letters or produce documents to state that the inspector had obtained qualifications that he did not actually have. My colleague advised them, quite rightly, that if they did do that they would be perjuring themselves and could be prosecuted. Thankfully, even though the individuals (heads of businesses) were threatened by Inspector X, they would not cooperate. I went and relayed the information to my line manager at the time and told him exactly what was going on. I was told to just carry on as he was unable to do anything.

It was very eleventh hour when a call from the solicitor's office stated that the organisation was going to make an offer to the company that the allegation that they were responsible would be removed. So we reverted to the situation of some three years previous when I was first approached by the managing director stating that they wanted to plead guilty.

In effect, Inspector X's statements were removed from the case. I did query why we had had a change of heart but of course that met with the usual silence. However, my colleague in London told me that somebody in the solicitor's office told him that they pulled the case to defend Inspector X. In other words had we gone to trial, the other side had substantial evidence, including a high profile witness, that would have shown him not to be competent in his job and, certainly as an expert witness. When we were at court on the Monday morning Inspector X arrived and to my knowledge he did not bring his professional qualification documentation with him. No surprise there then!

The judge, who knew nothing of the goings-on, actually made comment in court that he was going to sentence on the basis of a Magistrates' Court trial but, he gave them quite heavy costs because the case had gone on for so long. The company was fined and had to pay costs of £40,000 however, had the case gone to court three years previously the company would not have been exposed to the very high costs. In addition they had considerable legal defence team fees.

It resulted in an official complaint to the Director General of the organisation by the company involved. Following the complaint there was a fudged internal investigation. I, among others, was interviewed because of the seriousness of the complaint and I advised other inspectors to tape record the interview for their own protection. My interview was tape recorded at my request as I did not trust our management to record fully the information I gave. As it transpired neither did my collegues and they, like me, used a double tape recording machine. We provided the tapes and one went to the organisation and we kept a copy of our own statement. The specific issue is that the company had made serious allegations against Inspector X. It was in relation to his qualifications, experience and training. He had put the information in his expert witness statement and they alleged that is was not true. The company provided substantial evidence. But it soon became obvious that there was a cover up. The last I heard was that the company took their case to the parliamentary Ombudsman with the help of their MP. I have not heard of any progress but I doubt they will get justice.

8

Society Reborn

Nothing New!

The problems we encounter in the UK today are seemingly not new as Plato observed in the 4th Century BC.

'What is happening to our young people? They disrespect their elders, they disobey their parents, they ignore the law, they riot in the streets inflamed with wild notions and their morals are decaying. What is to become of them?'

The point is that things are supposed to get better, not worse, so we have not progressed much since that time. The very real problem is that there are the do-gooders who look through rose coloured spectacles and live in a dream world. They have opened the door and told people that they can do as they please thus removing societies foundations of respect, responsibility and honesty. They then have the audacity to pontificate and tell us that everything is good. Those same do-gooders ignore the activities of the thugs, yobs, thieves, parasites, rapists and killers etc who, despite what we are told officially, are an escalating problem. I am increasingly of a mind that those who pontificate actually get some sort of perverse pleasure out of others being murdered, stabbed, shot, raped, assaulted etc. There are alternative options that will cost money but the benefits far outweigh the cost society is paying with its blood, real blood, and tears. I will tell you a story...

Sort, Sharp, Shock

I was part of a small group of magistrates and legal advisors visiting a prison. It was a part of our training and development programme, after all, if we were sending people to prison, it was essential that we had at least seen the inside of one. On this occasion it was a bonus because we got to see a young offenders institution that was sited inside an adult prison. Once over the fact that the young offenders section had high walls to stop them getting out, the inside was not that bad. There was an abundance of rooms for the inmates as well as a communal area with a pool table, large television and access to a large gym. There were workshops where inmates could be taught a variety of skills, many of which would have been useful to them once they were released. On the day we visited we did note that there were not many attendees in the workshops and most of the youngsters just hung about talking and not doing anything useful or constructive.

'Oh, we have a fairly relaxed regime here,' explained one of the governors who was showing us around.

I did manage to ask if the inmates did any work and educational training.

'Oh yes, our clients can attend educational lessons if they want to.'

'Do they do any work,' I ventured.

'Oh no, we can't make them work,' was the reply.

'So they can just hang about all day, if they want to?' I asked.

There was a pregnant pause.

'As I said, we can't make our clients do anything if they don't want to.'

I was about to point out that they were convicts not clients, but in the interest of not being flung out, held back on my comment.

Somebody asked what the food was like.

'Oh, we have a treat for you,' said our mentor. 'When we have lunch it will be the same food as our clients, in fact it will be prepared by them.'

I turned to one of our legal advisors and whispered, 'I like porridge.' She laughed. He heard and gave me a look of death.

We moved on to continue our tour and have coffee and biscuits. I noticed that I had the eye of one of the prison officers who was accompanying us. He reminded me of Mr Mackay the prison officer in the Ronnie Barker television programme *Porridge*. You may remember Mr Mackay's approach to prison officership. It involved strutting back and forth in front of the prisoners, taking great delight in yelling at them with phrases such as:

'There's going to be a new regime here, based not on lenience and laxity but on discipline, hard work and blind, unquestioning obedience. Feet will not touch the floor. Lives will be made a misery. I am back, and I am in charge here.'

Our Mr Mackay did not have the accent, but otherwise he was a clone. He came over and asked what we thought about the prison. I said that I thought it was very lax with not enough drive to get the inmates motivated and working. I swear his eyes sparkled. He explained that at one time the youth offending wing carried out short, sharp, shock sentences. These were sentences which were based on a military regime of long days doing drill, cleaning, learning to look after oneself, education to name but a few. It was designed to be hard with strict discipline and little or no luxuries. Our Mr Mackay said that often the new arrivals were cocky and deemed uncontrollable, but we soon sorted that out. Not everybody benefited from the regime and no doubt there were failures, but then that was the case with all punishment options. They did not tolerate bullying by the inmates. In fact by the end of the day all they wanted to do was sleep and he assured us that overall the system worked. I noted that some of my colleagues were not impressed with short, sharp, shock as an option.

Perhaps they thought that slobbing about all day and plotting crimes to do once outside was better. I was not going to ask.

Magistrates get to see a broad spectrum of society, particularly at the start of criminal careers and see the effects of a broad range of so called anti crime measures. Short, sharp, shock does have its place.

However, I did find another magistrate who agreed and stated: 'As a magistrate of twenty-eight years I have seen many types of intervention used in trying to reduce crime rates and re-offending. Some are much better than others and all require resources which are available to varying degrees, but the one which did make an impact was the short, sharp, shock...'. [M. Holwill www.civitas.org.uk]

We sat for lunch but were pleased to see that the prison staff sat with us and had the same food. However, I did wonder if anything unpleasant had been done to it, but it was most enjoyable and there was not a sighting of porridge. Our Mr Mackay was not done with those willing to listen and he produced a small collection of letters which were from former inmates who had endured the military style regime. He said they were just a small selection but one we focused on was indicative of them all.

The letter began with the reason for his incarceration and the impact that crime was having on his life. He had not bothered much with education so good jobs were not available. His long-term girlfriend had finished with him and so he felt crime was the only option. No job, nobody to tell him what to do, a life of nothing. Then he received a short, sharp, shock prison sentence. From the moment of arrival, it was strict discipline and everything at the double. Military drill (square bashing) and physical training. Boots to be highly polished. Clothes to be cleaned and ironed, personal hygiene attended to, more drill. Rooms to be cleaned spotless, inspections, outside areas to be swept, more drill, more physical training. Education classes (even for short sentences) more drill, more physical training, more cleaning and more inspections. Meals were plain and simple and there was no television, pool tables, gym or music. It was basic and raw and at the end of the day it was lights out, silence and sleep. He did his time and returned home.

He was, in his words, a new person and managed through the help of friends to get a job. He got back with his girlfriend and was to be married. He was studying at night school. His final comments were to thank all the staff and in particular our Mr Mackay who had provided many words of wisdom. It was a short, sharp, shock and it worked. I read a few of the other letters and whilst not so well written or in so much detail, they gave the same response. I looked at our Mr Mackay and put the case that clearly from the small sample of evidence, strict discipline and everything at the double, combined with education and training, even for a short period, albeit not in every case, it worked. He agreed and said there was a lot of other information that provided proof. I asked why it was stopped. He said that pressure groups (do-gooders) who attack anything that is constructive in the penal system put pressure on the government and they stopped it. He said that in his long experience in the prison service anything that impacted on a prisoners' soft life and that worked, was abandoned.

I then explained that I am an advocate of National Service but that it needed to be a selective system with options. There is no value in just shipping all young people off to a military style camp for two years. He fully agreed and said that with a time frame of two years and a properly planned and run regime, there would be a dramatic change in the face of Britain in a short time. My Mr Mackay had an ally in me but we doubted if it would ever come to pass as it had been proven over the years, that governments do not want real change as they seem content to allow crime to flourish.

National Service to Cure Yobs

So what was National Service or otherwise known as conscription? Well it covered the years 1945 to 1963, when 2.5 million young men were compelled to do their time with 6,000 being called up every fortnight. Women were not required to undertake conscription. The reason for National Service was that in the immediate post war period, Britain had a number of obligations and only a limited number of men still in military service. There was Germany to be occupied with 100,000 troops as well as Austria. In the Middle East there was Palestine to be policed, Aden to be protected, the Suez Canal Zone to be controlled as well as Cyprus, Singapore, Hong Kong and a chain of lesser military bases. In October 1950, the service period was extended to two years. After basic training that included square bashing (drill) physical training, weapons and field-craft skills, the new recruits would be posted to join regiments at home or abroad in war zones like Korea and Malaya. However, national service draft was supplying more men than the services could absorb. It was draining resources to train them, and taking fit and able young men out of the economy. In those days there was plenty of work.

So the decision was made and National Service ended on 31st December 1960, but those who had deferred service for reasons such as university studies or on compassionate or hardship grounds still had to complete their National Service after this date. The last National Serviceman was discharged on 13th May 1963. Whilst most detested having to do the two years service it gave many a start in life.

Prime Minister, David Cameron, suggested a compulsory period of up to four months' voluntary work for all school-leavers. However, he then talked of a new form of national youth service that all young people would have to do. However, whichever scheme he adopted it would be voluntary and that defeats the object. The good people will get involved but those who are causing the real problems in society and need guidance and help, are never ever going to volunteer for such a scheme. Even if it is compulsory the yobs would not turn up and so who would be responsible for there attendance. I am all for supporting the 'good' people and helping them get on, and their are already many good organisations providing development, but they need to be adequately funded. However, it is the untouchables that must be targeted.

Leo McKinstry produced an interesting article and I have quoted it in part because it portrays valuable arguments for National Service:

'Journalist Andrew Marr is a long-serving BBC political editor... Marr makes a sterling defence of National Service... Having pointed out that in London in 1954 there were just four crimes involving firearms, he argues that the official requirement for all young men to serve two years in the military meant that large numbers of potential criminals were taken off the streets. More importantly, he claims, National Service 'provided discipline and the habit of obeying and issuing orders'. Marr writes that 'two generations of boys were marched off for short haircuts and taught to polish their shoes by fathers who had been in the services'... ultra-liberalism has failed disastrously when it comes to inculcating feelings of patriotism or respect for others. Too many young people, particularly those from difficult backgrounds, know all about their rights but little about their duties. Their lives are without purpose or guidance. Sullen, inward-looking and resentful, they use drugs, crime, promiscuous sex or alcohol to fill the vacuum. Even when they break the law they are told by lawyers, social workers, or the courts that they are victims of society so they escape any meaningful punishment and continue to wallow in nihilism... National Service, which this newspaper [Daily Express] has long campaigned for, is a way of breaking that cycle. It might sound authoritarian but then obedience to authority is precisely what wayward youngsters most lack. Thanks to enfeebled social workers, soft teachers or fractured families, aggressive teenagers have found that they can get away with anything. A spell spent helping others or serving the nation would rob them of some of this arrogance... There were few tears at its ending, yet in the decades since its abolition we know instinctively that something has gone badly wrong in the way young people are reared in Britain. The drug problem, high teenage pregnancy figures, the explosion in binge drinking, widespread violent crime, the mood of near-anarchy that prevails in the inner-cities, and the distrust between ethnic groups are all signs of this... The abolition of compulsory military recruitment has also coincided with a dramatic fall in the rigour of punishments for young offenders.' [*Daily Express* 11th June 2007]

Mr McKinstry provides a vision of a broken society that needs drastic action so that it can be put back together and I fully agree.

Terence Blacker in his article under the heading, 'The merits of bringing back National Service' stated:

'A well-organised, compassionate form of National Service, one that was neither grindingly military nor squeakily goody-goody, but which offered people of seventeen and eighteen a choice of practical, active options, would broaden the horizons for some and offer an escape route for others. It might come as a shock for the bloody-minded or over-indulged but it would also offer a parachute into adulthood, a chance to meet people from different backgrounds, a taste of work but without pressure to succeed'. [*The Independent* 11th July 2006]

Mr Blacker's option is fine for many young people but not for the parasites, yobs, thugs and feral youths who are an increasing part of our society and are creating real long term problems for the country.

A New National Service

What is the new National Service? The vision is not one of calling up every male once they reach a particular age and they would not be part of the conventional military, but they would come under military laws. We already have armed forces who can recruit suitable personnel. Most importantly, the new National Service should include females. There are many former service men and women who, for whatever reason, are no longer able to continue with a military life. Rather than put them on the scrap heap and waste their talent, they could provide the ideal resource to run such centres. National Service would not be required for those who had proper employment or were in full time education, training or university. Those who had been employed but had been made unemployed through no fault of their own, (company going broke etc) would not initially be expected to be conscripted unless, they became long term unemployed, dropped out of university or were not active in seeking a job.

The system would need to be very selective:

Category 1. There are those who, because of circumstance have 'lost their way', are unemployed, have a very poor education, no discipline, no ambition. They could be victims of drink and drugs and in need of guidance and training.

Category 2. There are those who, because of circumstance have really 'gone off the rails'. They will be unemployed and probably unemployable, have very poor to no education, no discipline, no ambition. They could be involved with drugs, gang violence or other crimes and will generally have a criminal record.

All Categories would serve for two years and receive graduated pay as they evolved within the system. All would be assessed medically for fitness. Because of the nature of the service, people would not be automatically ruled out on medical grounds and females who had children who met the criteria of 1 and 2 would have to do service but it could be of a more local nature.

At the start of initial training all conscripts would be provided with a uniform in line with current military training. All personal belongings, including jewellery of all descriptions, would be removed and securely stored. Hair would be cut. The days would start at 5am and continue until 9pm. Lights out would be at 10pm. A uniform would be the only clothing allowed and the programme would include military style drill, physical training, sport, personal hygiene, cleaning of rooms and facilities. There would be inspections of people, accommodation and work tasks to generally maintain the property. There would be a balanced diet. Medical staff would oversee any medical issues such as those suffering from drug abuse. Nobody would use weapons of any description so it would not be a military force but would be under military discipline and rules. Those who wanted to move to the armed forces could apply the same as any member of the public and if accepted be transferred.

Initially there would be no television, radio, personal music systems, mobile phones, 'goodies' from a tuck shop or a social centre. However, personal items such a toiletries would be available for purchase. The establishment would be 'no smoking' and there would be no alcohol, drugs or sex. Bullying would not be tolerated and, if it occurred, dealt with. As the initial phase continued each individual would be assessed for education and training possibilities.

With Category 1, those who were assessed to be suitable and adaptable would move to the next phase and spend more time in education and undertake a range of proper training courses. Good performance would allow more access to television, music, 'goodies' and a more normal life. As time progressed more goodies and leave would be available and those assessed as suitable, could then apply to be sent on overseas or UK based aid projects. Anybody in Category 1 who does not perform or becomes a problem could be moved to Category 2.

Category 2 would be those who are deemed to be a problem and would be sent to separate centres. The initial induction would be expected to last longer and have more problems, as it would be anticipated that there would be a lack of cooperation. This would require some of the toughest of instructors such as former commandos, paras and special-forces forming the core structure. It would be a carrot and stick approach with a focus on the carrot. Those who adapt could then move onto education and training and even Category 1 where it could be possible for them to apply to be sent on overseas or UK based aid projects.

There are going to be females with young children who could not undertake National Service as described above. However, they would not be allowed to use the fact that they have children as a way to avoid some sort of service. Those who, as has been done for years, manipulate the system to provide a good life for themselves would have to serve for the two year period. They would undertake training and children would be looked after in a crèche provided at a centre. The basics of caring for children could form part of the training. They could even learn how to wash nappies, remember Mrs H. All categorys would work on areas of land devoted to growing vegetables that they can use, and even be taught how to cook. This would not be run by social workers managed by do-gooders but by professional people with appropriate skills.

People with disabilities and people with genuine illnesses would not be expected to be called but they would all be assessed by specialist doctors who could determine their physical and mental abilities and capabilities. It may be that they are able to attend a centre where they can get training and even work placements. The organisation Remploy set the standards and without the do-gooders interventions provide the foundation for work activities.

The problem of absconders would also need to be addressed. Those who do not want to participate will either not attend in the first place or depart soon after arriving and will have to be dealt with. Those that can be found easily will be and without doubt, the majority who abscond will commit a crime and end up in police custody or in court. They can, following any court punishment, be transferred for their National Service. Those seeking benefits would be identifiable and 'no service' equals 'no benefits' and the individual can be reported.

If an individual absconds or commits an offence whilst on National Service and is jailed (the centres would have their own cell blocks) then their time served stops. It only continues once they return into the centre to continue with their service. The process would be one of getting the individual to complete their service, be a good citizen and avoid breaking the law. Without any doubt there will be a considerable number for whom National Service will not work and they may not move on much from the induction phase. They will in due course be destined to spend much of their lives behind bars. The up side is that many who under the current system are lost, would in the new system, be saved and contribute to society.

Yes that is a very simplistic description of what in reality would be a life line for many people. No matter what the government says there are not the jobs available and that is a major issue. However, for two years the 'wasted youth' would be off the streets, learning about respect, discipline and receiving a basic level of education. So jobs could be made available to them that are currently filled by foreign workers because of a lack of skilled home-grown recruits who currently scrounge and sponge off the state.

There Are the Good

Now it's not all bad news and whilst young people often get bad publicity, and in many cases they deserve it, there are young people who are good members of society. The key issue is keeping them away from the influences of the undesirables and that is not always easy. Much excellent work is done by youth organisations and one such example was achieved in a TV programme that caught the imagination. It involved fifteen youths from Croydon who learned just how hard it was to be a WWII paratrooper. The carrot for those who were successful was a parachute jump into Arnhem in the Netherlands from a World War Two aircraft.

Now, I do not like TV reality shows as they generally bring out the very worst in people. They bring people down to the lowest levels, focus on those with problems or they are about has been so called 'celebrities' clutching at straws and with a 'look at me' attitude, in a vain attempt to become greedy, be noticed and talked about and do nothing for society.

However, this programme was different. The volunteers came from Croydon which was chosen because the town is twinned with the town of Arnhem in the Netherlands. They were selected from more than 100 teenagers who applied to take part in the course and were led by a squad of former paratroopers, who specialise in working with young people. For five days the candidates were based in a Second World War-style army camp, where they underwent basic fitness and battle training. They had the same kit as their 1944 counterparts, similar rations, but no mobile phones and no modern luxuries. The aim of those who passed the training was to parachute from an original Dakota DC-3 aircraft over Arnhem on the 66th anniversary of the Second World War battle, during a huge memorial service.

It was a mixed group and some found the physical training pretty hard which does reflect on today's softer society. There was plenty of mud, the infamous log race, the carrying of heavy weapons and the grueling assault course. Roughing it and eating field rations, added to the reality of the training. They then faced up to a re-enactment battle with masses of noise and action. There were complaints about the food, long days, tiredness and uncomfortable clothing but they were encouraged to work as a team and so they got on with it. One lad had to leave the course through an ankle injury and three were sent home for sniffing aerosols. Injury is a fact of life but for the others to waste the opportunity of a lifetime was tragic.

Having endured the hardship they then began parachute training. The first part was to learn how to land which is important because if you get it wrong, bones break. Two of the girls had trouble getting to grips with the landing process which requires legs to be slightly bent, feet and knees together and a roll to one side once on the ground. The group then spent some time at the British military parachute school at Brize Norton. There, under the watchfull eyes of the instructors, they jumped out of a mock-up fuselage, and from the ten metre high system that requires the volunteers to jump out attached to rigging, where they are lowered to the ground to do a proper landing. Apart from the two girls they all did very well. They then travelled to the Netherlands for an intensive week of parachute training.

Before being allowed to jump out of the Dakota they had to do a jump from a smaller plane. Weather caused delays, but ground training could continue. Then at the end of a windy day the weather changed and they could do the obligatory first jump. However, the instructors had to make a decision as to whether the two girls had progressed enough to allow them to proceed. One passed and unfortunately the other had to return home. Those remaining made a successful descent and were now ready for the big day.

At 1,500 feet over Arnhem aboard a Second World War C-47 Dakota and in front of a large audience of veterans, families and general public attending the ceremonies; the ten youngsters departed the aircraft in a professional way to land safely as a group. They then had chance to meet the veterans and swap stories as well as placing flowers on the graves in the Airborne Cemetery in Oosterbeek. I know it was television, but it was a success and gave a very small group of young people an insight into what is possible and hopefully a step on the ladder.

I have made my views known about reality shows but 'Michel Roux's Service' on BBC2 was worthy of much praise. Michel was on a personal mission to train eight young people from all walks of life for front-of-house futures with a difference, none of whom had previously considered this as a career. With help from Fred Sirieix they began to train and transform the young people into great waiters. The series showed that it was not just about good service but it required discipline, working as a team and self confidence. It really meant developing essential life skills. They were thrown in at the deep end and provided service at a number of very high profile hotels and restaurants. They were not without fault and tantrums but with Michel's calm leadership they evolved. Only one fell by the wayside and was sent packing. The prize was that two trainees would be selected for scholarships in the business however, Michel had a hard task in the selection process and in the end awarded three trainees with work scholarships. Then following the six-month scholarships each would complete three week-long placements at leading venues. Good fortune did not stop there as one trainee was offered a job by Fred Sirieix to work at his hotel. Another went on a management trainee course and one who was destined to be one of the winners but was not committed to front-of-house as a career began work in bar service. If this was adopted by other oganisations it would provide a beacon of light and a future to young people.

Vision and Reality

There have always been protests and there always will be. Some like the 'Save our Forest' campaign are successful and get government policy changed. However, other protests have taken to the streets and many have ended being quite violent and vicious. The problem being that what began as a large peaceful protest march is taken over by the anarchists and a full-blown riot ensues drawing the masses into it and wreaking havoc. One incident occurred in London when Parliament Square was cordoned off and the police struggled to contain the student unrest. The police were subjected to physical violence from wood, metal, bottles of urine, snooker balls, fireworks, bricks, steel barriers, paint-bombs and smoke canisters. Fires were created from piles of placards and rubbish skips. The thin blue line had to use batons to hold the marauding hordes back, while mounted officers advanced into the crowds to disperse them. Anarchists deliberately tried to injure the police horses by throwing metal bolts, steel poles and sticks to rain blows down upon the animals. Fortunately none of the horses, all wearing protective plastic eye shields, leg armour and nose guards, was seriously hurt.

Then a mob of some 300 rioters spotted the Rolls-Royce carrying Prince Charles and the Duchess, who were being chauffeured to the Royal Variety performance. They attacked the car which was rocked, kicked, spattered with paint and had a passenger window smashed. The chanting 'Off with their heads!' could clearly be heard on television coverage. It appears that a thug managed to shove the stick through a gap in the rear window and poke the Duchess in the ribs. The very real issue is that if a rioter could jab the Duchess with a stick he could have stabbed her with a sharp object or shot her. Royal protection officers, including the one in the royal limousine, were seconds from drawing their guns when the driver managed to get away. Then we heard of what was described in the media as 'a rabble of masked and hooded vermin' who turned a student demonstration into anarchy when they defiled a statue of Winston Churchill by urinating on it. They ripped flags from the Cenotaph, the nation's sacred memorial to those who died in the name of liberty. They then lit fires and sprayed slogans on the ground close to the Houses of Parliament. One educated and wealthy offender at the Cenotaph claimed that he did not know what Cenotaph was! If the so-called educated act in this way what hope is there for the uneducated. [*Daily Mail* 10th December 2010]

For those who don't know, the Cenotaph is a memorial to those killed in the service of the country. It began with the First World War [1914 – 1918] and the horror of the events are dramatically portrayed in *The Soldier's War* by Richard Van Emden through a letter from Pte John Scollen, 27th Northumberland Fusiliers (4th Tyneside Irish) prior to going 'over the top' to attack the German trenches.

'My Dear Wife and Children

It is with regret I write these last words of farewell to you. We are about to make a charge against these awful Germans. If it is God's Holy will that I should fall, I will have done my duty to my King and country and I hope justly in the sight of God. It is hard to part from you but keep a good heart, dear Tina, and do not grieve for me, for God and His Blessed Mother will watch over you and my bonny little children and I have not the least doubt but that my country will help you. For the sake of one of its soldiers that has done his duty. Well, Dear Wife Tina, you have been a good wife and mother and looked after my canny bairns and I am sure they will be a credit to both of us.

My Joe, Jack, Tina and Aggie not forgetting my bonny twins Nora and Hugh and my last flower baby whom I have only had the great pleasure of seeing once since he came into the world, God bless them. I will try and get to do my duty whilst on this perilous undertaking and if I fall, then you will know that I died in God's Holy Grace. Tell all of my friends and yours also that I bid them farewell now. My Dear Wife and children, I have not anything more to say, only I wish you all God's Holy Grace and blessing so goodbye goodbye and think of me in your prayers. I know these are hard words to receive but God's will be done.

From your faithful soldier, Husband and father John Scollen. B Coy. 27th. S.B.N.F.

Goodbye, my loved ones, don't cry.'

Like millions of others, Private John Scollen did not return, he was killed shortly after writing the letter. I am beginning to believe that he and the millions of men and women who died in two World Wars died in vain.

Ok, there is a mountain of doom and gloom but there does remain some hope for the future. For example, scouting in the UK is experiencing its biggest growth surge since 1972. Figures released show that in 2010 there were 16,568 new youth and adult members in the UK. This is a 3.35% rise in membership since the last figures gathered in 2009 taking the total membership in UK Scouting to 499,323. We are told that a large part of this growth is due to the fact that there are record numbers of teenagers joining which according to UK Scouting, is the fastest growing age group. The Combined Cadet Force, the Sea Cadet Corps, the Army Cadet Corps, the Air Training Corps are all very active. There are many other youth and young adult organisations all thriving but too many to mention. They are providing a valuable service to young people across society with challenges in topics such as adventure, education, acting, music, the arts and travel to name but a few. The critical aspect is that these good worthwhile organisations need to be supported and that includes money and that has to come from the government. All elected governments squander millions if not billions on overseas aid to countries that either do not need it or do not deserve it. Instead of giving cash to go in some dictator's bank account or an official's pocket: provide goods, equipment and workers to undertake projects in the UK as we have to find jobs for our increasing number of unemployed. Some of the money saved can be diverted to youth projects.

The focus of the book has, for the most part, been on those at the bottom end of society but it must not be forgotten that over at least the past fifteen or more years our Prime Ministers, some Members of Parliament, Industry Fat Cats, some leaders of Local Authorities, bankers, some heads of public services etc have not led by example. Their participation has shown either direct dishonesty or absolute financial greed to the severe detriment of everybody else. I have heard from many people over the years who say that in many cases the wrong people are in prison. Others have said that by 'their greed' or 'mismanagement' they set the UK on a course to become a bankrupt nation whilst they spent and grabbed for themselves the counties wealth. Yes there are a lot who should be in prison and we all have views on who that should be but the prisons were and are full!

As the UK struggles with its rising crime rate and its do-gooders battle to make crime pay, you may be interested to note that other countries have their own problems. For example in Malawi's financial capital Blantyre there is a clampdown on the serious crime of farting in public. To eliminate this heinous crime a Local Courts Bill had to be introduced. It states:

'Any person who violates the atmosphere in any place so as to make it noxious to the public to the health of persons in general dwelling or carrying on business in the neighbourhood or passing along a public way, shall be guilty of a misdemeanour.'

Now many think that there are more important issues to be dealt with and one local could not understand how the government hoped to enforce the new law and gave a more graphic response:

'We all fart in public and it will be difficult to tell who has done it.

Some do it silently. In some cases it is like teargas which goes like shhhh! Our legislators need to concentrate on discussing development projects… This will not work. We will keep on farting.' [ITN 10th February 2011]

As somebody pointed out to me, there are so many in the UK who seem to communicate from that end of the body, that if there was a similar ban here then nothing more would get said or done by the do-gooders. Interesting point!

The one thing that is certain is that the last government who held power for so many years did nothing to support victims of crime. They did nothing to reduce crime. The real outcome was a multitude of do-gooders who gush over those who commit crimes, and the more serious the crime, the more gushing there is. A more difficult change will be of people's attitudes where the most heinous of child torture, gives way to society's obsession of following and wallowing in the daily drudge of 'celebrity' publicity seeking activities and dramas of who is doing what and where and with whom.

In conclusion, I now fear that there will be no change under the ConLib government based upon what Mr Clarke the Justice Secretary, said during a 'phone in'. He infuriated victims after seeking to defend a proposal to halve rapists' prison sentences if they pleaded guilty. He repeatedly insisted that some rapes were not as 'serious' as others. He indicated that not all involved an 'unwilling woman' and when challenged over whether 'rape is rape', he replied: 'No, it is not.'

The Council of Circuit Judges, which represents 652 Crown Court judges, warned that under the proposals a rapist who would have otherwise received a five-year sentence might serve as little as fifteen months. The judges said: '…an offender who admits rape faces a starting point of five years, or sixty months, in custody. Under the new system, an early guilty plea would reduce this to thirty months and he would be released on licence after fifteen months.

They added: 'If the defendant had been in custody awaiting trial, the victim may see him on the streets only weeks after he appeared in court.'

Louise Casey, the Commissioner for Victims, said: 'A discount of 50% offends many victims, underplays the harm that may have been caused and can seem to be placing administrative efficiency over justice. I am concerned that the proposal to increase the maximum discount will not achieve its intention of getting more people to plead guilty, while alienating victims further and placing administration above justice.'

Ministers argue that encouraging an early guilty plea will spare victims the ordeal of giving evidence in court and increase the 6% conviction rate for rape. Giving evidence in court is unpleasant for all victims and sexual offences will be particularly so. It is said that the reason why rape has one of the lowest conviction rates for any crime at 6 % is because the victim cannot face seeing their attacker in court. So raise the sentence for rape and have a system put in place where a victim can give evidence to the court, without having to face the rapist whilst doing so. It is already being done with other offences and minors giving evidence to a court. More women will then come forward and as a result there should be more convictions. For those found guilty the judge can impose a sentence that fits the degree of seriousness of the crime based upon the evidence given in court.

Equally worrying was the revelation that the proposals could see 'soft justice' applying to burglars, robbers and other serious criminals. The reason is that it is part of the government's sentencing proposals with the aim of reducing prison places by thousands. Ministers also want a relaxing of the rules for prisoners handed indefinite jail terms to make it easier for them to be released. Only those who pose a 'very serious risk' will stay inside. [All national newspapers 18th May 2011]

There was a claim that courts will be encouraged to hand out tough community punishments instead of shorter jail terms so that 6,000 fewer prison places will be needed by 2015 than predicted. Let me be very clear, there are NO tough community punishments. From my experience and the word of others, community punishments are a soft option and often a joke. Added to which the number of convicts who do not even complete the sentences is increasing.

I have always advocated that prison terms are not of a sufficient length. In fact jail sentences have reduced so much that with all the discounts, it's hardly worth locking convicts up in the first place. The problem is that a convict gets a sentence of six years, pleads guilty and it's reduced by a third, so that is now four years. Because convicts only serve half the time that is further reduced to two years. So a crime that warrants six years is only actually worth two years. That cannot be right. In the same conditions, give convicts a 50% discount and they will end up serving only fifteen months. That is six years reduced to one year three months. That is not justice!

Custodial sentences must be modified. A small discount could be allowed for a timely guilty plea prior to going to court. There should be no discount for a change of plea to guilty once the case is being heard. If a convict gets a jail term of five years then they should serve five years. If they break the rules whilst in prison, then time is added on to their sentence and they are put on basics. It is very clear that the soft options do not work. The tough options may not be the answer but at least the murderers, terrorists, rapists and violent offenders will be locked up and causing nobody harm.

The next step would be to reject the extreme politically correct, the army of do-gooders, sort out the misuse of the Human Rights Act, deport all foreign convicts when they leave jail or where they continue to commit crimes. Finally, deal properly with victims. These would be positive steps forward for the country to be a place where crime does not pay.

Addendum
England Burns

I had completed the book and it was a case of sit back and await the publisher to publish and extol my views on crime and injustice in the UK. Over the years I had witnessed an increase in criminal offences and endured the pathetic punishment system that favoured those found guilty. In this way I had to a degree, observed the break down of society that had spawned the elements for mass criminal activity.

Then in August 2011, like millions of people, I watched the news unfold showing serious riots, looting and arson erupt in London and other cities around the UK. It was back to the computer to make a small last minute addition to the book. It is sad to say that I was not surprised or shocked by what I saw or heard. It is what I have predicted and expected would happen. It was just a matter of when. Nobody in authority can say they did not know it was going to happen or how bad it was going to be. The situation has been fermenting for a long time and is not a 'flash in the pan'.

I believe that this is just the beginning of a time when angry and violent people will roam the streets to do what they want, when they want and to whom they want. They have a total disregard for community, law, morality, respect or authority. As we have seen it can draw those on the fringe of trouble into the fray when the more professional looters, criminals and arsonist lead the way. I would describe it as a criminal cancer that has been developing over the years and, as I have portrayed in the book, criminal elements are in every part of society. They all have a total disregard for any authority or the law and feed on greed. The do-gooders have pandered to them leaving victims abandoned and ignored.

Television showed us dramatic images and it was not just young people who went on the streets of London and other cities to rob, loot and attack the police and public as well as burn down buildings. It is a fact that there were older people involved in the looting because the young do not own crime. The fires were much like the images we see of the wartime Blitz following a bombing raid. Fire crews braved the incidents and were attacked when they approached the fires. Police in riot gear appeared unable to control the unlawful activities because of the sheer numbers of aggressive people involved. It was disappointing to hear the BBC reporters referring to the criminal thugs as protesters. This was not a protest but a total break down of law and order. Then there was a reporter from an American news network dressed in steel helmet and armoured vest portraying to the world parts of London burning and looted.

This situation is not a result of the current governments cuts. Of course they will not help, particularly with cuts to youth workers funding but it all began a long time ago with Prime Minister Blair and his New Labour Party. I witnessed the changes in the courts and the changes in criminal activity and the move to pathetic punishments if indeed you could call them punishments. Mr. Blair and his cronies brought us a criminal charter in the form of the Human Rights Act, extreme political correctness that removed discipline and, the enhanced welfare benefits that made it better to scrounge than to work.

He allowed the opening of the UK boarders to a mass influx of asylum seekers, migrant workers, migrant non-workers and foreign criminals. There was little work or housing for them and where they did take up lower paid jobs, the indigenous layabouts stayed on benefits. Mr. Brown moved into power and he and his cronies virtually bankrupted the country whilst continuing to add to the foundations of what the Blair government had spawned. I would add that the opposition politicians whose past governments brought the country to its knees financially and morally should remain very quiet throughout all of the events that have and will happen. They created the conditions that led to what we have seen and were responsible for the beginning of a potential major catastrophe for England in particular.

We have heard many debates about the causes and oft quoted are breakdown of the family a total lack of parental control and the removal of discipline, both in the home and at school, stripped away by the do-gooders. There is no respect for law and order, the police or the courts. One very real problem is that there are far too many people in the country and the population is rapidly expanding. There is not enough employment now and there will not be in the future. Housing and services such as schools and hospitals as well as the vast sums of money required to support them are not going to be available.

Other causes include the very public lives and antics of so-called celebrities who flaunt their wealth and display often appalling behaviour. People are blitzed by adverts urging them to buy 'trendy and cool' products that are mostly beyond their pocket. They see the bankers who dragged the country into a pit of despair continue to take massive bonuses. They have seen politicians, their so called leaders fiddling their expense, milking the system for which many have received just a hint of punishment.

They see Council leaders and their dodgy dealings, big businesses not paying their proper share of tax. With that vision and with nothing to loose some people have decided that they want some of the rewards and will go to the extremes we have seen to get it. These were not people desperate for food or shelter, they were rioters and looters who were well-organised using Blackberrys and social networking sites to coordinate their illegal activities. They were aggressive, vindictive and bent on theft of goods and total destruction. It was chaos, with hundreds of innocent people at risk of harm, four of whom were murdered and many others actually harmed with homes and businesses destroyed.

I cringed when I saw the Home Secretary Theresa May on television telling us that: 'the way we police is by consent. British policing has always meant and always depended on the support of local communities and that's what we need now.' Well Mrs. May, tell that to a woman and small child who were taken by ambulance to hospital with burns and breathing difficulties after a shop below their flat was set ablaze. Tell that to the woman who had to jump from a window to escape a fire beneath her flat. Tell that to those who have been assaulted, to the families whose relatives have been killed and those who have lost homes and businesses. What the communities really want is law and order but it will be a case of what the do-gooders demand and that will be soft, fluffy and pandering. It will cost the country a small fortune, which it can ill afford.

The front line police officers followed government policy and were as usual, 'damned if they do and damned if they don't'. When they get tough and use tactics such kettleing and mounted officers to control a baying mob they are deeply criticised. When they have to modify the tactics and take a less aggressive approach they are wrong. It was very clear that the police were limited in numbers and, in the beginning, were clearly not in control. Added to which it was not just one area of disorder but it spread to many parts of London. The outcome was that public said that there were no police to protect them and looters carried away goods, buildings began to burn and fire fighters arriving at the scene of fires were, in some cases attacked. At one point Roy Ramm, a former Metropolitan police commander, had warned that the Met could lose control of the streets.

We know that the police will spend hours identifying many of the rioters and looters and arresting them to put them before the courts. The magistrates will no doubt have their hands tied whilst the do-gooders pontificate so that all will be forgiven. I doubt that this government will be any different to those we have endured in the past, as I doubt that they have the will to really deal with the problem.

The public is allowed to set up internet petitions on a Government website on any subject. Petitions which attract more than 100,000 supporters must be debated in the House of Commons. One of the first petitions that flooded and apparently overwhelmed the system was to demand a debate on the restoration of capital punishment in Britain. There will be no difficulty in reaching the 100,000 signatories as there has always been a majority in Britain in favour of the death penalty.

The final word on that subject goes to a YouGov poll which was undertaken for the Sun newspaper on 9 August 2011 which reveals that two out of three people in Britain want the death penalty reintroduced for child killers. The poll found 62 per cent believe those such as the Soham killer Ian Huntley, should face capital punishment. However, only 38 per cent of voters would back the death penalty for every type of murder. The poll found 65 per cent backed capital punishment for serial murderers, 63 per cent for terrorist killers and 53 per cent for killers of police officers. The figures were obtained after the new online petition to bring back capital punishment.

Politicians of all parties had better listen and understand that their cards are marked by the public they are letting down and who in their thousands, if not millions are sick of the do-gooders influence and the injustice that permeates a sick society today. Those who demand justice and a change in society overwhelmed all sort of media forum where the public can voice their opinion. But will they be heard and will anybody take? For that to happen, somebody needs to be listening.

Selected Bibliography

Bailey, Brian, *Hangmen of England*, W.H. Allen, 1989, ISBN: 0 491 03129 7

Bloggs, E.E.WPC. *Diary of an On-Call Girl – True stories from the front line*. Monday Books, 2007, ISBN 978-0-9552854-7-9

Copperfield, David, PC. *Wasting Police Time – The crazy World of the War on Crime*. Monday Books,2007. ISBN: 978–0–9552854–1–7

Mansfield, Michael, *Memoirs of a Radical lawyer*, 2009, Bloomsbury, ISBN: 978 0 7475 76549

Robertson, Geoffrey, The Justice Game, 1999, Vintage, ISBN: 9780099581918

Sources of Information

BBC News
The Daily Express
The Guardian
The Independent
Private Eye
News of the World
The Sun
The Magistrate
The Daily and Sunday Mail
The Daily and Sunday Telegraph
The Times
The TaxPayers' Alliance

The Crabb Enigma
Mike and Jacqui Welham

Matador – ISBN: 9781848763821
www.crabbenigma.com

EyeSpy Magazine
The Covert World of Espionage
No: 70 2010

There is no question the authors have a deep insight into the case, and clearly they have done a tremendous amount of research – made clear from earlier works such as Frogman Spy.

Is the Crabb Enigma worth reading? – Absolutely, and there is a brilliant photo section and snippets of information that we haven't seen before.

Nautical Magazine
January 2011

'All in all, this is a serious attempt to establish the truth, one which will have to wait for another 45 years or so. In the meantime, the reader has an opportunity to agree or disagree with the authors.'